NATURAL CAUSES

THE WILD LIFE OF A WILDLIFE FILMMAKER

STEPHEN MILLS

Chiselbury

Published by Chiselbury Publishing, a division of Woodstock Leasor Limited, 14 Devonia Road, London N1 8JH, United Kingdom

www.chiselbury.com

ISBN: 978-1-916556-30-0

Cover design by Indra Murugiah

To
Suzan, Millie, Liv, Turlough and Kate

CONTENTS

INTRODUCTION

I see this book as a sort of moral tale. The moral is that if you have a dream, a mission, a wish to change the world, you can do it. You can do it as long as you accept that the dream may shrink, the mission may creep a little and the change you make may be very small and that all those little bites out of your ambitions in no way render them pointless. The tale is mine. When I was young, I wanted to do something to save nature, to make others realise how much it mattered, to change the way people thought about it. I set out, ill-equipped and ignorant, as one tends to be when young, on a meandering path towards this goal and it would appear that I just kept going. I didn't save the world but I helped to save bits of it. I think my tale, about a fairly ordinary person with a big sense of fun and a big sense of the beauty of nature, proves that life is worth living, that having a purpose improves it and that such a life, however modest, will make a difference. Small steps, persistent small steps: that's all it takes to make a contribution. I was not alone. It turned out that lots of people, what has become my informal family of other naturalists, film-makers, writers and campaigners, also wanted to change the world. The golden years of wildlife broadcasting to which I was privileged to contribute, have been part of that. We have helped to place environmental issues and a concern for nature right at the centre of politics. This was almost unthinkable when I was a boy.

If reading my story encourages anyone – anyone who wants to do something but is intimidated by the unreachable achievements of those who have gone before, who is afraid that what little they can do will not matter – if it encourages them to keep taking small steps, never to stop and to try to find happiness in the things that matter, because that's where it lies, then I will feel my book has been worth writing. Above all, this book is for young people starting out, and especially those who care about the ineffably beautiful natural world. All you have to do is stay true to those feelings, follow the tiny golden thread of purpose and your life will have meaning.

FOREWORD: A BOOK OF HOPE

I am lucky to be alive. I don't always feel lucky. I am over seventy, overweight, overwrought and overdrawn. Nevertheless, I am lucky. I was lucky to be alive after a very angry mother lion tried to kill me in the forests of Gir. I was lucky to be alive after an even more incandescent mother rhino smashed headlong and furious into the camera case I was sitting on in Assam. I was lucky to be alive there too, after I was struck by lightning. And in Ireland when the little two-seater plane I was filming from ran out of fuel, and on Everest where I was ferried about by a frenzied Russian helicopter that later crashed killing everyone on board including some of my friends.

But what I actually mean is that I am lucky ever to have been born. I am the youngest of four brothers. The middle brothers are twins and when our mother was fomenting their genes and filling them with her own brand of brilliance in her tummy, she developed Pernicious Anaemia. This was a killer back in the 1940s. She was desperately ill and hospitalised for months. My father was warned to expect the worst and our oldest brother Terry, just two at the time, and a loquacious little genius, was not even allowed to see her, a trauma which robbed him of speech for more than a year. When cuddly Chris rolled sleepily out followed by David, as lean and eager as an eel, my parents were told there must be no more children. Another pregnancy would likely be fatal. You would surely need strong magic to go against such a doom-laden prediction. Or luck. Or perhaps I was an accident. If so, they never let on. Whatever the case, less than five years later, there I was.

Actually, perhaps it's my brothers who are lucky. My mother always told me, very cheerfully, that I was so ugly in the early months, maybe years...that, had I been her first born, she would definitely have stopped the ball rolling right there. She would have had no more children for fear of a repeat. She may have been joking. My mother and I seemed to find a lot of things funny together. She used to sit on in my room after putting me to bed laughing hilariously at my silly stories and imitations. Sometimes she laughed so much I wasn't quite sure we were on the same page but still, it was very gratifying. Not so for my father, however. He found it quite irksome. The odd thing was that, though she doted on him in every other way, she never, ever laughed at his jokes. "Your father" she would pronounce, in front of him "is just not funny." Mind you, he did have a very strange sense of humour. For instance: a troop of British tanks was rumbling through India when they came upon an elephant standing like a statue straight across the road from left to right. The tank commander hooted and shouted and eventually dismounted explaining to the elephant that his tanks were in a hurry and if he didn't move, he'd have to be flattened. He didn't move and the tanks regretfully rolled over him. About a mile further on they came upon another stony looking elephant, standing straight across the road from left to right. This time the tank commander was brusque. "Oi, you, out the way" he said. "We met one like you back up the road and we had to run him over." At this the elephant stirred, shed an enormous tear from his tiny eye and replied 'But that was my brother. We were only playing bookends."

When he was very young my father was obsessed with horses. He wanted to learn to ride. Not just ride, but trick riding. He wanted to learn to tent peg, which meant picking a peg from the ground on the end of a lance, at full gallop. The only place to learn this sort of palaver was the cavalry, so at the age of fifteen he faked his birth date and signed up with the North Somerset Yeomanry as a territorial. He was an athletic chap and he was soon able to tweak an imaginary enemy's specs off with his galloping stick. But there was one snag. There was a real enemy in the wings and as a territorial you were first in line for conscription. In late 1939 he was packed off to Palestine on his horse. The North Somerset Yeomanry fought in the British Army's very last official cavalry battle, in Syria, before common sense prevailed and horseback fighting was abandoned. Horseless, my father volunteered for the Commandos - a new cadre of cut throats, freed from uniforms and square bashing. In September 1942, somewhere in the Sinai Desert the troop carrier he was in drove over a landmine and was blown to smithereens. There were 37 lively, optimistic, young souls squeezed into that rattle trap. Of those 37 men, our father was the only survivor.

When I look at my clever, successful brothers, at the diaspora of their talented children, and my own – teachers, doctors, judges, artists, mothers and fathers - and the tumbling troop, 23 at the last count, of what would have been my parents' great grandchildren, I have one thought. All of us, all of our hopes and plans and poems and passions, would be nothing, would never have existed if, on that dry, dusty day in the desert, my father had been sitting in another seat.

1

THE GREAT ESCAPE

Lone Gunvald-Teilmann wanted to bring her horse to England. As far as I was concerned, anything Lone wanted was a fait accompli. Except it wasn't accompli because we were in Norway, we had no money and no appropriate transport and the horse was anyway in the possession of a racing stables in Oslo. Frøy, or Frøykongen, to give him his full noble name, was a Norwegian trotting horse. This meant he trotted, very fast. He didn't canter or gallop. He trotted. I can testify to this because much later I used to ride him through the country lanes of Oxfordshire. We had no money for a saddle so he would shake me on his back until I was a bag of bones, much to the delight of my more skilled equestrian friends. The memory still brings tears of laughter to their eyes even now, fifty years later. I did suborn him into cantering eventually. But he was clever. If he saw a large rabbit-hole looming ahead he never jumped. He turned. Very sharply. He would turn, I would continue, landing in a muddy heap. But then he would stop, come gingerly back, put his head down apologetically to give me a nudge and wait for me to clamber back up on his back. Frøy was adorable.

He was trained to trot very fast in front of a sulki, a little light racing chariot, and he was supposed to win money. On this basis

Lone, who'd been away filming with me, had lent him to a man who had promised to look after him and pay for his stabling in the hope of recouping his expenses from the winnings. Unfortunately, Frøy hadn't won very much and the man had not kept his share of the bargain. This was a fairly typical Lone transaction. Consequently, her horse was now being held hostage for unpaid bills. Before we could take him to England, or ride him or do anything with him, we had to spring him from prison.

Lone had already reconnoitred the stables and she reckoned that if we hit them swiftly and silently after midnight we could manoeuvre Frøy through the railings, down a lane and out onto the main Oslo highway. Provided, of course that Frøy kept his head and didn't spook his livery companions and provided thereafter we didn't become cannon fodder on the road or get caught by the Gestapo. For us in those days all police were Gestapo. First, however, we had to find somewhere where we could keep him.

It was the summer of 1972 and we were just completing the editing of our first television documentary. This had come about in a somewhat serendipitous fashion. Lone was a gifted photographer. She'd been to the prestigious Paris Film School, though without completing the course, and very recently, she'd landed her dream job, working for Per Høst, Norway's leading wildlife and anthropological film-maker. But Per had suddenly died, all his contracts of course were cancelled and Lone was suddenly out of work. We'd got the news the previous Christmas when we were actually staying at Per's house and Lone was stricken. So I, with the blithe ignorance of youth, had rolled over in bed after she told me and said, "don't worry, I'll write you a film script and we'll make it together." I knew absolutely nothing about writing for television. In fact, I knew pretty well nothing about anything except birds and Shakespeare, in that order. But being with Lone gave me completely misplaced confidence. Two days later we'd tiptoed into the offices of Norsk Rikskringkasting with our script, but how do you find someone to read it? You push Lone in front of you and tell her to ask people. That's what you do. Within an hour, we were sitting in a bright, modern little office talking to a surprisingly kind lady producer called Ada Haug. I've no idea what persuaded her to give us a chance – maybe Per's name, maybe Lone's portfolio of beautiful black and white photographs – but whatever it was, we had walked out with a commission to make a half hour documentary.

Lone was much older than me but despite all her mad adventures, a spell at the Oslo Music Conservatoire, being fluent in five languages and having photographs hanging in the National Museum in Oslo, she had never made a film before. And I was straight out of an English boarding school where the main focus, of the boys at least, had been on rugby, rowing, cricket and hockey – certainly not on film-making. What I had managed, mysteriously, was an Open Exhibition, later a Postmastership, to Merton College, Oxford to read English and this was to be our subject: the peculiar life of an ancient institution seen through the eyes of a modern-day student and his friends. So, my first blissful year at Oxford had passed in a whirl of excitement, fascinated by Lone and our project.

We were allowed to edit the film in the NRK cutting rooms but only after midnight when most of the proper film-makers were safely tucked up in bed. For the inept and inexperienced, in other words us, this was a long, long job. We shot on sixteen millimetre negative film and worked from a positive print that had to be physically cut up into the chosen pieces. These were hung in a clean tub from little hooks so they were ready to be reassembled in the correct order. The growing final cut was passed back and forth on motorised plates through a viewer and the music, background sounds and speech were re-recorded onto special sixteen millimetre sound tape which could be moved across sound heads on parallel plates so that each scene could be perfectly synchronized. It sounds tedious but I still remember the exhilaration we felt when the first car in our picture drove down the High Street in Oxford emitting just the right exhaust noise and how wonderful the students looked, pouring out of their exams, squares tossed aloft, champagne flowing and all to the tune of "Grumbling Old Men" by the Incredible String Band. The machine you used for editing was called a flatbed and if you were lucky, you had a Steenbeck which, being German, was the best. Years later I was to have my own studio with my own top-notch Steenbeck but even after forty-odd films, I never ceased to marvel at that magic moment when a flat piece of celluloid hummed miraculously to life.

To finance ourselves during the weeks of editing, we had both taken jobs washing floors at a military barracks in Oslo. There were a lot of floors and because most of the inmates were unwilling conscripts doing national service, there were a lot of lumps of sticky sweet goats' cheese stamped rebelliously into the linoleum. But we were to get an unexpected reward. Next to the barracks Lone spotted a tumbledown barn with potential. We tracked down the owner and he was quickly melted by Lone and, perhaps to a lesser extent, by her tale of her lost horse. For the next week, added to the snip snip of midnight scissors and the swish swish of mid-morning mops, came the whacking of nails into wood. I've only ever been adept at hitting my own fingers and thumbs but Lone managed to make even hammering look graceful and soon we had the use of a surprisingly solid makeshift loose-box with its own small paddock, not five miles from where Frøy was confined.

As the son of a former Commando, I'd like to tell you how the midnight raid on the stables was timed like clockwork; how I climbed over the roof in the pitch black with only the shine from my teeth to guide me so I could unhitch the latch from above while hanging by my feet from the guttering. All this is partly true, but in the meantime Lone had walked silently up to Frøy's stall, opened the door and by the time I was back on terra firma she was leading him quietly away. Clip-clopping him for four miles down the central reservation of the dual carriageway at 2 a.m. was, admittedly, a surreal experience. Looking back, I'm amazed no-one challenged us, I can only think that the world was more orderly in those days and that youngsters like us who moved harmlessly outside the margins were simply not noticed.

Frøy was not yet in England but at least he was firmly back in Lone's life and we began to think constructively. Lone had charmed another farmer. He had an old red barn about twenty kilometres south of Oslo, stacked to the rafters with loose wood, rusty trolleys, chicken huts and other agricultural waste. Tucked at the very back, there was a little bucket-shaped cart on which Lone had pinned her future. The farmer had said she could have the cart if we could extract it from the debris, so one day in late August we headed south. Apart from her Canon camera and, now, our Bolex cine camera, Lone had very few possessions. But she did have a car. Well, a car of sorts. If I had lined up a hundred cars for you to choose from you would have guessed which was Lone's immediately. It was a rather rusty, yellow 2CV van. One of the windows at the back had a hole in it. So did the petrol tank. This limited your range to however far you could travel on the twenty litres or so it accepted before the fuel began to leak. Although, since 2CVs were reputed to be able to run on bananas we never saw this as a problem. Under the crinkly paintwork of the bonnet could be read, very faintly, the name of the butcher who had long ago owned the van and proudly touted his Wienerschnitzels to the hungry folk of Oslo from its once pristine interior. His name and thus the car's, now and forever, was Barndorph B Bensen. Later, when we were commuting back and forth to England, we used to take the long road to Gottenberg in Barndorph. He never let us down. At least not entirely. I remember one spectacular winter journey when it began to snow more and more heavily. Other cars ground to a halt but Barndorph sailed lightly, if erratically over the crispy surface. But we had two problems. The first was that the windscreen wipers were very slow and each began to amass a growing ball of snow on the end. We dared not stop and after an hour Lone was having to sway widely from side to side to keep ahead of the snowballs that were rhythmically swinging in and out of picture. The other problem was that there was a hole in the floor and as the snow got deeper it acted like a carpenter's plane piling the snow up under my feet until my knees were nearly touching my chin. To keep us from getting swamped I had to ball up the snow in my bare hands and lob it out of the hole in the broken back window. I kept this up all the way to the boat. Here Barndorph finally called it a day and we had to push his comatose shell up the ramp onto the car deck. But by the next morning he'd perked up again so this doesn't really count as a failure.

When we arrived at the vast red barn, I was dismayed at the challenge facing us. I had earmarked that day to go birdwatching with my friend Viggo so I was already a bit testy. We hauled and shoved and panted and pushed, excavating a cart-size tunnel to enable extraction but then a nasty thing happened. Some sort of metal frame fell against Lone's hand and broke her finger. I felt horrible for being, well, horrible and now I expected dire retribution. Lone could make an awful fuss about little things and this was a big thing. A little finger but a big incident. But she cried a bit and then got straight back to work. Boy did she want that cart.

When we finally levered it out and hauled it into the open air, we stopped to examine our prize. It had two large wooden wheels – one on each side for people who don't know what carts are – both rimmed with iron. It had a bench seat and a charming click door in the back, a bit like Barndorph's but without the hole. And it had strong arms to which a horse could be attached, even a Norwegian trotting horse. Our spirits lifted. Especially mine as I didn't have a broken finger and didn't have to drive home. There was no doubt this was a cart with potential. This was a cart that could keep us company for weeks. This was a cart that could take us to England. But first we had to get it back to her mother's house in Oslo. Barndorph had no tow bar but he did have a fully opening back door, so we threaded the two prongs of the cart into the back of the car, where I sat, holding onto them for dear life as we bumped and churned our way the 20 kilometres back to the city. Somehow, the traffic police, who can be quite insistent over matters of legality in Norway, didn't spot us. But neither of us was thinking about that. We were thinking about our new, hard-won prize and what we were going to do with it. We were going to cross Norway by horse and cart and we were going to make a film about it.

2

THE COTO DONANA

Lone and I first met in early May 1971 in the Coto Donana. In those days the Coto was for me the most beautiful, the most romantic place on earth. It must have been my brother Terry who first drew my interest to this wild waterland in southern Spain. Terry was seven years older than me and by the time I was nine or ten he was already out the door, a rucksack on his back, a pair of stout boots on his feet, to hitch-hike his way through Europe and Greece, or the Middle-East, through Turkey and Afghanistan to Iran and back. He would return browned by exotic dust and sunshine, with arrowheads and daggers, pieces of porcelain and poisonous potions like ouzo and arak. He would sit on the kitchen table, swinging his legs and tell his stories. I loved those stories. I loved the ardency of his flow. I loved the way he was always the hero of his tales, how he threw the French gendarmes in the Seine, how he tackled the inappropriate advances made to his handsome companion at two am in a Turkish dosshouse, how he held a jellaba-clad pickpocket upside down to shake the stolen money out of his pocket. At the age of 16 he was already studying Greek, Latin and Ancient History at Oxford. He was immersed in Hittite culture and the legends and archaeology of ancient Greece. He told me after one trip how he'd been sleeping on a rock in the ruins of Mycenae and waking at dawn he'd watched a man and a cart that looked exactly as they would have looked three thousand years earlier, drifting silently down the main street in the mist. When he looked again, they had disappeared. Were they real, had he dreamed them or were they ghosts going on an endless round, visible only to the tiny number of people in the world who would know what they were? One day Terry bottled all this up and put it away. He decided he wanted to be a millionaire by the time he was thirty – a real millionaire with estates in Britain and France – and he joined a Merchant Bank. He explained to me that the people he was working with, though very clever, were only interested in the intricacies of money. So just as he had learned to do all those years ago as a heart-broken toddler, he stopped talking.

But back on the kitchen table he was still my old Terry and the stories I liked best were the ones about the wildlife he'd seen. One trip that grabbed my attention was with his schoolfriend Guy Watt in a rattly old van in which they bumped through the backwaters of Spain. Guy later spent seven years as a forester with his canoe in the Solomon Islands so he was a good judge of backwaters. When they reached the edge of the Coto Donana, they could hardly believe such a wilderness could still exist in southern Europe. Terry told me how the great Rio Guadalquivir left Sevilla, its oranges and its fiestas, and slowly fanned out into a maze of natural canals, or caños as they are called, that weaved and wound through a vast marshland. The main river flowed out into the Atlantic at Sanlucar de Barrameda. To the south lay the busy city of Cadiz but beyond the northern bank the marshes, or marismas as they were called, stretched on and on for hundreds of square kilometres. About 20 kilometres short of the sea the marismas slowly morphed into savannah type grassland punctured by freshwater lakes and dotted with stone pines. Beyond that rose a wide band of sand dunes that stretched 70 kilometres from south to north and rolled the last seven kilometres to the ocean.

There were little pine forests in the dune slacks and the edge of the marismas was marked by stands of ancient cork-oak trees. This was the place for me. What wonders might such an impenetrable, water-logged Eden contain?

Now there were books to be read. Firstly, by Abel Chapman, an English hunter who, one hundred and sixty years before, had punted his way through Donana with a flat boat and his shotguns. In his book "Unexplored Spain", he described how, on the 11th of February 1907, he had shot more than thirty teal with a single cartridge. While this sounded like superfluous slaughter, it raised exciting possibilities. If he could hit so many ducks with one shot, just think of the dense clouds of birds there must have been, and perhaps still were. Next was "Portrait of a Wilderness" by Guy Mountfort. This described a series of expeditions to the Coto during the 1950s by an extremely distinguished group of people led by Mountfort and including luminaries like Field Marshal Lord Alanbrooke and the pioneering photographer Eric Hosking. For years this was my favourite book. Here I learned that the marismas were indeed still packed with life, with rails and terns and ducks and spoonbills, herons and bitterns, otters and even mongooses. And most exciting of all, the Coto was one of the last strongholds of two of the rarest species in Europe: the Iberian lynx and the Spanish imperial eagle. Perhaps there were fewer than 50 pairs of either of these fast-vanishing creatures left anywhere.

So impressed had been Guy Mountfort's team, that they set about trying to preserve the area. The Coto had always been a hunting reserve for Spanish nobility. Large swathes were still owned by the Gonzales-Byas families and by the Marquess of Borghetto. But there were talks of draining the marshes and throwing up tourist developments so there was some urgency. It was partly through the offices of those well-connected people in Mountfort's party that the World Wildlife Fund was established in 1961, with a view, among other things, of buying as much of the Coto Donana as possible as a National Park. The first purchases were made in 1963 and in 1964 the

Donana Biological Station was set up in the old Medina-Sidonia Palacio at the heart of the reserve.

After Terry's stories and the books, I knew I would one day visit the Coto and that it would become important to me. This became something of an obsession. I badgered and explained and plotted and planned and so one day in late March 1967 I found myself on a Spanish train heading south with my best friend Toni Strubell. We were fourteen years old. Toni's parents lived in Madrid and, for the next ten years they must have dreaded my visits because they knew I was a bird of passage and that I would, within a day or so of arriving, be taking their beloved son with me. But though anxious and protective, they were always extremely kind and, in fact, supportive. Now, as we sat blissfully on the train, full of excitement, Toni clutched a hundred peseta note in his hand that we were to give to the foreman at Las Marismillas as soon as we arrived. This, his father had insisted, would assure us good treatment forthwith. For indeed we were on our way to the Coto Donana.

Toni's mother's family were Catalan, minor nobility of a lost cause and a lost line. His grandfather was a famous surgeon. The young Josep Trueta had earned his stripes in the 1930s treating war wounds during the Spanish Civil War. As a staunch anti Francoist he had been forced out of Spain but the British, with war sounding in their ears, grabbed him with open arms. For seventeen years he had been Professor of orthopedics at Oxford's Nuffield Hospital and he had cut and pasted many of Spain's aristocracy. It turned out that he knew the Marquess of Borghetto who still owned the southern half of the Coto, and its beautiful hunting lodge, the Palacio de Las Marismillas, the Palace of the "Yellow Marsh Flowers." The Professor had spoken to the Marquess and now the two urchins were welcome to camp for as long as they could in the heart of Donana.

Under Franco's rule much of Spain had remained in the 1930s. Forty kilometres outside Madrid, from Aranjuez all the way to Sevilla we hardly saw a tractor. The land, if it was tilled at all, was worked by donkey. But to our young eyes it seemed peaceful. We felt we could handle the slow surprises of life in this ancient countryside. Only the night in Sevilla posed any worry for us. There a young man offered me his sister. I would have liked a sister but it would be some years before I would know what to do with his. We were happy to be on the rickety bus the next morning, chuntering toward the little tumble-down fishing port of Sanlucar.

Our instructions, on arrival at Sanlucar, were to "find a fisher-man" and ask him to row us across the river. Apparently, there would be a fleet of fishermen, all in the pay of the Marquess, who would be happy to get this privilege. This seemed a bit unlikely to us but indeed we did find a volunteer and he crammed us and our rucksacks into a little wooden boat and swept us over the wide, quiet waters of the Guadalquivir, rowing cheerfully until we clambered up on the sandy bank of the Borghetto Estate. There stood a lanky man with a rugged face who introduced himself as Manuel Espinar. This we thought, must be "the foreman" so Toni pressed the wadded hundred peseta note into his hand and he promptly disappeared. We never saw him again. Toni told me that espinar meant thorn in Spanish and for years after I only had to refer to a thorny problem and Toni would fall about laughing. Perhaps, however, Señor Espinar pulled invisible strings because half an hour later a tractor – a rare sight in itself – came lumbering out of the forest and we were hauled aboard. First, we rocked our way to the Marismillas Palacio, where we found the Marquess himself, and a small house party, all with spears in their hands, mounted and ready for a boar hunt. Would we like to join them? No we would not. We wanted to set up our camp and start bird watching. In retrospect, this was probably the wrong answer. But we were single-minded little fellows and boar-hunting was not a prescribed activity.

The tractor coughed and stuttered its way out of the forest, across a set of dunes and out onto a flattish prairie where we could see, stretching away for miles and miles the famous marismas of the Coto Donana. The driver took us out onto a long, dry grassy spit of land which poked its finger deep into the marshes and left us there. It was

perfect. We were surrounded by birds: black-winged stilts, little
bitterns, squacco herons... There was a well and a tiny stone house in
the distance where a guard usually lived. He proved to be a kindly
man who helped us dry our sleeping bags whenever the spring rains
poured into our hideously leaky tent. For the next two weeks he was
the only other human being we saw. He found eggs and bread for us
occasionally. Otherwise, we survived on "Stephen Mills's Special
Concoction" of half-cooked rice, quarter-cooked onion and tinned
tuna. It was ghastly. Oh, and porridge with sugar in the morning.

I don't think I had ever been so happy as I was for those weeks.
Every day we explored, walking the long line of the marsh edge for
miles and then turning towards the sea, crossing the grasslands into
the dune slacks and stone-pine forests and finally stumbling out onto
the pounding, empty sea shore. Every day we saw birds that were new
to us and whose identities had to be teased out of the field guide. I
remember a beautiful, huge silvery hawk that hovered slowly above
us, fixing us with owlish yellow eyes. This had us fooled for a bit but
eventually we realised it was a short-toed eagle, so-called because its
back talon is abbreviated so that it can more easily grasp wriggling
snakes, which are its favourite prey. We saw lots of wriggling snakes
ourselves – big Montpellier's snakes, lithe grass snakes and small,
horned, slightly dangerous Lataste's vipers.

One day we found a big boisterous family of wild boars, mothers
and dozens of little stripy piglets, and at least one male, all rooting
through the sparse undergrowth of a little pine forest. Toni, who was
an impressionable boy who had read about the fate of Adonis, gored
to death by one of these monsters, promptly climbed a tree. He
stayed up there for quite a long time while I watched the boars scur-
rying and squeaking around me. He was always a prudent chap but
he came down eventually.

Early spring brings millions of migrant birds to the Coto. They
come from Africa, some resting on their way to Northern Europe,
others staying to breed. One morning we walked down our spit of
land from our tent to find the whole line of the marisma shore had
flowered overnight. There were thousands and thousands of tiny

yellow blooms. Were they the marsh mallows for which Las Maris-millas was named? But as we drew closer and the shimmer of the dew drying in the early morning sun began to fade, we saw what they were. They weren't flowers at all, they were birds, they were blue-headed wagtails. The sight of this sudden glorious inflorescence of tired, courageous little yellow birds moved me beyond words. It was the most beautiful thing I had ever seen. I experienced something similar years later when I was working in the Ngorongoro Crater in Tanzania. Again, it was an early morning, this time in late autumn. I drove down into the Crater to find its dry, dusty bottom painted with wagtails. To add to the Iberian feel, every other flat-topped acacia seemed to hold a black-shouldered kite, as if they'd all flown in together from somewhere near the Coto in a package. Wagtails became my favourite birds. I think I've seen all the world's species and while the blue-headed will always be my special love I do have one other secret love. It's called the forest wagtail. It's rather rare but you can occasionally find it in the great Sal forests of Madhya Pradesh in India. It isn't yellow or pied like most other wagtails. It is every possible shade of brown and fawn like a large tree creeper, dappled and spotted. And it doesn't wag its tail up and down like all the others. It wags it from side to side, which is adorable.

One experience, however, stands out above all others from that first visit to the Coto. It set something moving in me which was to define my life, something which still moves in me today. One morning, far out over the forested dunes, we saw a huge dark, flat-winged bird gliding low over the broken tree line. It braked, flapped upwards and landed on a massive pile of branches wedged at the top of a big stone-pine. Toni and I lay in the shelter of a dune, with our telescope peeping over the top. What we saw amazed us. Sitting on what appeared to be a nest, was a large Aquila eagle, very much like a golden eagle, but a little smaller and almost black, except for its beautiful silver head, white shoulders and bright yellow cere and feet. It was an adult Spanish imperial eagle, one of the rarest birds in the world. There were thought at the time to be only thirty pairs left and we had just found an unrecorded nest. From then on, every day, we returned to study the birds. We saw both parents and, from their behaviours, deduced that they were sitting on eggs. We stayed far away, for fear of needlessly disturbing them, but watching these imperious, critically endangered birds, far out on their lonely tree in that remote and silent landscape made me think. Almost like a novice urged towards a vow of priesthood, I felt there was a meaning here beyond just bird-watching. I wanted to come back and photograph the eagles and in some small way help to save them from extinction. To use photography and words to tell stories that might change the way the world perceived nature and shift the balance of opinion, however imperceptibly, in favour of struggling miracles like these eagles, seemed now to be a worthwhile way to spend my life. I had no idea how I could achieve this. I didn't even own an appropriate camera. But from then on, I would try to follow what Herman Hesse called the faint and slender golden thread of purpose. I developed an idea in my head of The Bank of Meaningfulness. I would judge every project and activity by whether it paid into this special account. Of course, like any youngster, I spent most of my life messing about but bit by bit, with an article published here, a lecture given there, the account began to grow and I realised that anything one did, however small, could make a difference. This, I decided, would be enough for me.

Every spring holiday from school Toni and I would go back to the Coto Donana. We didn't get the chance to visit Las Marismillas again. Instead, we based ourselves in the village of El Rocio on the northern perimeter of the reserve. In the 1960s El Rocio consisted of two dirt streets with a church and a bar. Behind the bar the entrepreneurial owners had cleaned out and enclosed a pig stye, painted the interior white and installed two metal beds. This was our home. The little road from Almonte passed through El Rocio and continued, almost completely untrafficked, to the coast. We didn't often go there because the road ended at a new nascent tourist urbanisation called, ominously, Matalascañas, which means 'Kill the Marismas". Sometimes we hitched there and set off to sleep some nights out in the open in the dunes and walk the main reserve, but mostly we started our days sitting on the bridge outside El Rocio. There we could observe the constant flow of herons and egrets and birds of prey that passed to and fro between the marismas to the south and a private reserve of cork-oaks and reedbeds, called La Rocina, to the north. La Rocina was supposed to be off limits but we spent days exploring it. Eventually we were caught by the guard and at first he wanted to throw us out. But Toni spoke beautiful Spanish and was charming, I tried not to scowl and we became good friends. He loved to sit with us poring over our field guide. He had no binoculars, he couldn't read and he had no training but he knew every single bird that might normally be seen on his reserve. The only mistake he made was that he thought the juvenile, motley brown night heron was a different species from the sleek, grey, black-crowned adult – an understandable slip. He was a kind, clever man and we learned a lot from him about what to look for and what to expect.

One day we were sitting on the bridge when I pointed at a little wood about half a mile away and said "let's go down there and see a golden oriole." I've no idea why I said it. We'd never seen a golden oriole anywhere. They tend to be late migrants, arriving in May when we were always back in school. But they were high on our wish list so we walked to the wood. Almost as soon as we entered, a female oriole, inconspicuous in her green plumage amongst the green leaves, appeared and sat for a few seconds on a branch ten feet above our heads. Then it was gone and we never saw another. It was a tiny incident and I only mention it because it was, I think, the first of many, many occasions when I have expressed a clear and accurate premonition of what I and my companions were about to see. To give one more example, typical out of hundreds, in 2019 I was leading a small group of dedicated tourists who wanted to watch tigers in Rajasthan. At the end of a long India-hot day in the field in which they had been remarkably patient, I announced that, as a reward, they would see a tiger under one of the ancient arches of the famous Ranthambhore Fort. Such things are possible, but I'd never seen one there. Ten minutes later, just before we left the park, we rounded a corner to see just what I had described – a tiger under the arches.

Even more interesting, the tiger we were looking at could be identi-fied, by a sort of dollar sign made by the stripes on its flank, as an old male who hadn't been seen by anyone for more than three years. It was odd. I can't say these things have a meaning. But coincidences of this sort, both with animals and people, happen so often in my life that I am bound to wonder. Is it possible that by clearing the mind and focusing intensely, one can become hypersensitive to signs that are otherwise invisible? I think, perhaps, that it is a form of medita-tion – and we know that strange things can happen when people meditate.

It was hard to get food in El Rocio. The village really only existed for the two weeks in May when it came alive for the famous festival of Our Lady of the Dew. The origins of the festival seem to involve an ancient wooden statue of the Virgin Mary that lived in the Hermitage of El Rocio and was hidden in a tree trunk from Moorish invaders and lost. Years later in a dream, the hiding place was revealed and the statue recovered. The legend gave rise to a massive annual pilgrimage to El Rocio which dates back to 1653 when Our Lady of the Dew was declared the patron Saint of Almonte. Priestly and secular brother-hoods have lodges in the village. Indeed, in the 1960s most of the buildings were dedicated in this way and were entirely empty except for the weeks of the festival. There was a kiosk that sold strange, sugary chocolate and our pension would cook us an evening meal. The problem was that, even though every morning we ordered our food – usually a tortilla or eggs and potatoes or a rarely available strip of meat – our hostess never started cooking until we arrived. This often meant a long starving wait as the delicious smells of onions and garlic drifted into the night but no food actually appeared for hours.

Toni and I left school in December 1970. We had both been successful in the Oxford University entrance exams which meant we were now completely free until we entered our respective colleges – he to Pembroke, I to Merton – the following October. On 8th April 1971, we arrived back in the Coto. This time we were official guests of the biological station and would be staying for six weeks in the Palacio at the heart of the reserve. I wrote in my diary that day "Met

Viggo Ree – our companion – excellent. Should get on v.well." Viggo was modelled on Baldur, the Norse god of light and beauty. He had many abilities. He could climb the long, bare, branchless trunks of pine trees just with his hands and feet, like a Barbary ape. He could ring birds with his teeth. I made films of both these achievements. He could draw and paint anything and he was a taxidermist. Like Baldur, he could breathe life, or almost life, back into any dead bird or animal with his deft skill and his habit of observing precisely. He also had, I was to discover, an uproarious sense of humour with a love of the ridiculousness of things that we all shared. Best of all, he was seconded to the Coto for a year so he would be with us for our whole stay. He would indeed prove to be "excellent'.

Viggo was chief ringer and observer. It was his job to ring-mark as many birds as possible, both breeding birds and migrants, as well as maintain a detailed log of all observations made during his stay, both his own and other peoples' if they could be verified. We were to be his assistants. The weather had been cold and rainy when we arrived, which it can be in early spring even so far south, but the following day it cleared, a warm sun was shining and we spent the afternoon putting up the nets. Wispy mist nets that hang in four or five tiers on almost transparent strings are the main tool for catching smaller birds. But while you or I might easily blunder into one, they are not invisible to a bird that has to rely on its sharp eyes for survival. So they work best if they can be strung between low bushes, reeds or in woodland where they are less conspicuous. But there was a hitch affecting our work at the Palacio and we discovered it right away. Although an area had been fenced as an exclosure to keep marauding wild boar and roaming cattle from trampling the nets, no-one had actually thought to plant any bushes, so these, our "ringing gardens" were less than perfect. But the migration was in full swing and Viggo was anxious to get to work.

When he'd arrived at the Coto the previous October Viggo had found the mist nets that were left to him were mostly shredded beyond use and he'd had to wait weeks for replacements, by which time he'd missed the peak of the autumn migration. These were early days for the Biological Station, and Spanish wildlife research, which has since become in many ways excellent, was then in its infancy. Ornithology was ruled with an iron first by two professors, Francisco Bernis and Jose Antonio Valverde. In many ways they were good scientists but seemed to be nationalistic, not publishing their results outside Spain to the wider scientific community, and they were somewhat tyrannical. Franco's Spain was intensely hierarchical and I suspect if you wanted to get on you needed to emulate the Generalissimo. Dr Valverde was in charge of the Station but he had a full-time job as Professor at the University in Seville. I wrote in my diary "Valverde is rarely present and no-one else is allowed any initiative. Thus for most of the time the reserve is without a boss – ringers are unable to obtain a saw or nails for bird-boxes or staples, poles and wire for fencing-in cork-oaks. The guards therefore do practically nothing all day and never ride round to effectively protect boundaries." When I re-read this fifty years later, I realise how little I then understood about the habitual inefficiencies of the human workplace. But there was a grain of truth to what I'd said.

In the meantime, we made the best of the materials we had. We finished hanging the nets and then stopped to admire a fat Greek tortoise parked under a bush by the well outside our ringing garden. Suddenly Viggo was off at a run and dived into the scrub, emerging with a baby wild boar which, according to my diary "squealed human abominations at us". Well, who can blame it? Viggo, of course, let it go but a few weeks later there was a celebration in the Palacio and someone had obviously done the same as Viggo but not released the quarries. We had baby wild boar, beautifully cooked and I have to admit it was absolutely delicious.

The next morning, we opened the nets before dawn. There was a change in the air, birds were on the move and we were soon busy with our first migration "rush". We caught fifty or sixty birds, mostly garden warblers and blackcaps, and our first wryneck, a weird little brown woodpecker which sat in my hand, turning its neck almost inside out while I filmed it. You need to check your nets every hour. Birds must not be left hanging too long, in case they damage themselves or get nabbed by predators. When a bird hits the net, it drops into a fold that forms under the cross-string. The longer it's there the more tangled it becomes. You have to peel it out legs first, very delicately. An experienced hand can do this in a few seconds but Toni and I were beginners and we and the birds had to be patient. We would put our quivering little scientific specimen into a soft cloth bag, where, deprived of light it would instantly calm down, and then carry it off either to a nearby table or, from the ringing gardens, back to our little office in the Palacio, where we would process it. This meant fixing with specially-made pliers the all-important, tiny aluminium ring to its lower leg. This carried a unique number which we noted down and which would be quoted by any-one who caught the bird again in the future. We carefully weighed each bird, noted its wing length and the details of the moulting of feathers and the state of its fat deposits. Over the last eighty years of ringing effort, scientists have learnt an enormous amount, not only about the routes birds of passage use and the key places that are important to them, but also about their physical responses to the increasing changes in their environments. We knew we would only contribute a few grains of dust to this growing mountain of knowledge, but still it was exciting to be part of such a worldwide venture. For all three of us, however, the highpoint was always the moment when we released a bird and watched it fly, apparently unperturbed, to safety.

This was the pattern of our days for the next many weeks. But on occasions when it was too wet or windy, or even too hot to use the nets, we found other jobs to do. We checked and repaired the bird boxes that were dotted throughout the little woodlands. We tried, if we had the materials, to fence small cork-oak saplings from the ravages of deer or we set off early to walk the furthest sectors of the reserve, ecstatic at this official freedom to roam. We kept an eye on the small spoonbill colony in the cork-oaks by the Marismas and on three Spanish imperial eagle's nests in the reserve and we checked conspicuous pine trees for kite's nests. Viggo, of course, could do his simian trick but for Toni or me clambering up was a more laborious process. But often rewarding. In one tumble-down kite mansion Toni found a tawny owl's nest, with two very lively, well-rounded owl chicks, nibbling on the remains of a garden dormouse. This was apparently only the second breeding record for the Coto so we felt quite proud ringing them. Most of the breeding kites were black kites but we did manage to find five red kite's nests and these were always fun to investigate. Red kites like a bit of avant-garde home decor. In one we found a packet of cigarettes AND a box of matches, which seemed quite intelligent. But the best find concerned Betty Bird-watcher. Betty was one of a small trickle of visitors who came to stay in the Palacio for a few days. She worked for the station in some capacity, I think in publicity, which was anyway a mystery to us. She was kind, a bit vague and wore the complete "expert's outfit" of khaki coat and slacks and "the hat" and because she appeared to know nothing whatever about wildlife, we called her "Betty Birdwatcher". Perhaps we misjudged her, however, because in one nest we found a whole wedge of her love letters that some apparently literate kite had stashed there.

The Palacio has since become a productive scientific station but in those days the only scientist we met was the newly-qualified Dr Fernando Alvarez. Fernando was extremely kind to us and it was always fun to accompany him in the Land-Rover, to help him with his observations, though his research methods did sometimes seem a little haphazard. One of his studies involved red-legged partridges. One night, a week after our arrival, we drove out to investigate where they were roosting. Mostly, they sat in pairs on the edge of the sandy tracks. As each set of birds flew up out of the headlamps, Fernando would call out the location and number for us to note down: "Fuente del Duce, dos perdices, muy interessante observacion." Often the partridges would fly a few hundred yards and land on the road again, only to be added excitedly to the list: "Ah, dos mas perdices, muy, muy interessante observacion'. One unfortunate bird didn't make it onto our list. It didn't fly up and ended instead flattened under our wheels. We wondered mischievously whether this might not be a new sampling method. You drive round very fast at night and count the carcasses the next day. But that first, happy, hilarious night-drive ended in a moment of unforgettable magic. At 11.30 p.m., just beyond the spoonbill colony, there was a flurry of deer and then a neat, pale orange Iberian lynx trotted across the track right in front of us. In those few precious seconds, the four of us joined that very select brotherhood of naturalists who had seen an Iberian lynx in the wild.

Fernando's main topic of research was the parasitisation behaviour of great-spotted cuckoos. This was very interesting. We had all been brought up with our northern cuckoo whose habits were very well-known. It lays a single egg in the nest of a much smaller host. When the egg hatches, the cuckoo chick expels all the eggs and babies of the hosts so they will concentrate all their feeding efforts entirely on the cuckoo in the nest. The great-spotted cuckoo, explained Fernando, is quite different. It chooses like-sized hosts, mainly magpies and azure-winged magpies, it can lay several eggs in the nest and it leaves its young to grow up alongside the foster-chicks. Previous estimates had claimed that 45 per cent of magpie's nests on the Coto were parasitised. Fernando wanted to check this. Out in the field we helped him find nests and number all the eggs in pencil. He would note which eggs he believed would hatch into cuckoos. Magpie's eggs are slightly pointed, pale blue and usually speckled with regularly distributed spots and streaks. The great spotted cuckoo's eggs, Fernando believed, could be recognised as a little greyer or browner and rounder. The chicks were checked daily as they hatched, the cuckoo chicks being immediately distinguishable by having two toes forward and two back, instead of three forward and one back like the magpies. In all, he found 33 nests in his study area. Only three were parasitised giving a percentage of nine percent not 45 percent. It emerged that his predictions of which eggs would produce cuckoos were entirely accurate. So far, so excellent. The study took a more bizarre turn, however, when he wanted to examine whether the cuckoo chicks were more successful than their foster-siblings at eliciting food from the host parents. What he did was tie thread round the throats of the chicks to stop them swallowing, and then quickly weighed the food parcels that the parent magpies had crammed in. This was an inspired, if slightly crazy idea and I'm not sure how productive it proved.

Fernando was a man of infinite curiosity. He was lovely to talk to and I'm not surprised that he became a successful professor and a much-loved teacher. One evening we sat up talking together late into the night over a bottle of rather raw Spanish brandy. When the bottle had nearly emptied, mostly into me, he pointed at it and asked if that stuff didn't affect me? I hadn't actually noticed that I'd been drinking so much, I'd been enjoying the chat, so I said, indeed, that it didn't seem to and eventually went off to bed. Around 4 in the morning, I woke up and was violently sick straight into the well of Toni's guitar, which I had been playing before falling asleep. I must admit this didn't improve its tone.

The weather was warming up now and, in celebration, the bee-eaters began to indulge in spectacular aerial displays right over our ringing gardens, chirruping out their liquid, bubbling calls, and then dashing downwards to their colonial nesting holes in a sand-bank near the Palacio. With their blue breasts, yellow throats and cinnamon heads and their dainty curved beaks, I thought they were the most beautiful things I had ever seen. I could watch them for hours but now a big change occurred. Professor Valverde arrived and the previously dormant human ecosystem burst into life. It was like an old car with flat tires, covered in dust that looks as if it will never work again is suddenly cleaned up, pumped up, filled with petrol and turns into a throbbing Bugatti. Boixu, the head guard, found the keys to a shed we didn't know existed and found, after all, that he did have wire and poles and nails. Chaps on horses appeared, eager to patrol. Everywhere there was bustle and activity. Valverde was in his mid-forties. He was a small man who had contracted tuberculosis as a child which had left him with a pronounced limp. But he was a ball of fire. On that first day he sprang onto the tractor, having piled us and several visitors into the trailer and simply roared off straight into the marshes, swamping coots' nests left right and centre and stirring the whiskered terns into a frenzy. The next day we raced with him in the Land-Rover to inspect some twelve-foot sharks that had washed up on the shore. Valverde was doing his rounds.

But most exciting for us, on 25th April he ordered the erection of an observation tower beside one of the three Spanish imperial eagle's nests on the reserve. Any chicks would be at least two weeks old by now and the eagles would be much more tolerant of disturbance. The day before, one of the guards had checked the nests. Each had originally contained two eggs and of the six eggs, three were barren. These, taken from under the feet of the three live chicks were brought to us that evening to be blown. I'd blown lots of eggs as a child. You make a small hole in either end and use your mouth to blow out the soft yolk. If it is soft. It is likely to be rotten and if you get a mouthful of that it is beyond disgusting. But these were eagle's eggs. Indeed, eggs of one of the rarest birds in the world. We knew they were for the museum but also that they would have a huge value on the black market so I was quite glad that Viggo did most of the work. I didn't want to end up as roadkill under Valverde's tractor.

The tower was put up in stages over the next week, and completed on 2nd May. It stood about ten yards south of the nest and consisted of seven storeys of metal pylons, screwed together and secured to the ground by metal guys. Fifty feet up, on the platform on the top, was a square wooden hide which looked straight across at the nest and, amazingly, was going to be our home for several nights.

I don't think Lola, the cook and housekeeper at the Palacio, liked me very much. For one thing Toni and I had had an epic pillow fight which the pillows lost, puffing all their feathers out of our room into the kitchen. And she had a rather raucous daughter who used to bellow out a song called La Blanca Paloma which I could imitate rather well in hideous falsetto. And I'm sorry to say we used to make fun of the guests. There was one dear old man who must have had a stroke. He couldn't lift his feet but moved in a continuous noisy shuffle, which could be heard along the corridors long before he appeared, which indeed did often take a long time. I decided this was the way to travel and soon all three of us would line up like penguins, one behind the other, and sluff-sluff-sluff up and down the Palacio.

Inevitably, one day we came round a corner and collided with him which caused the sort of childish, painful mirth that can last for days. Except it didn't because the next day we rescued a barn owl that had been stung by bees. We tried to revive it and when it perked up, we tested to see if it could fly in the ringing office. But we'd left the door slightly open and it escaped and flew purposefully down the corridor, nearly decapitating Mr Sluff Sluff as he came round his favourite corner. I doubt that either of them were long for this world. In fact, the barn owl definitely wasn't as it died the next day. Apparently Viggo had been entirely saintly for months until I arrived, after which he acquired a wicked glint in his eye which I'm glad to say is still there fifty years later.

But, despite my justifiably low-standing in Lola's eyes, on the day we climbed the fifty feet to our eyrie at the top of the tower, she had done us proud. We were going to get hungry over the next 36 hours so Lola had cooked us the most mouth-watering, garlic and onion garnered, soft but not runny, Spanish tortillas that I have ever tasted. And they tasted even better with your own Spanish imperial eagle eye to eye thirty feet away. Toni and I did the first stint and an hour and a half after we settled in on that first morning, we were astonished to see above us not two but six adult Spanish imperial eagles circling quite close together but as three separate pairs. One pair displayed to each other and none of them showed any aggression. An hour later one of "our" adults swooped in low from the north and landed on the far side of the nest with an unidentifiable dead bird in its talons. It tore open the prey and then was gone within fifty seconds. Two hours later our pair were displaying above us again, the male, slightly smaller, doing a complete loop the loop. Then suddenly the female was on the nest again. She tore a strip off the prey and ate it and then spent the next fifteen minutes proffering titbits, held daintily on the very tip of her huge chain-saw of a beak, to the hungry chick.

We learnt a lot over the next few days. For one thing, we discovered that the male, sensible chap, had his own rudimentary nest about five hundred yards away. He seemed to do most of the hunting and sometimes brought his shopping to his own platform from where the female would collect it. He rarely visited the breeding nest and if he did, he only stayed for a minute. The female spent hours either in her favourite adjacent tree, or in a cork-oak on the edge of the marismas. She would visit the nest at roughly two-hour intervals to supervise meal times and if it rained, she was very attentive. She would stand on the edge of the nest with her wings outstretched for the chick's protection, while he went on getting drenched because he was never quite underneath them. She was like one of those annoying people who insist on holding the brolly and then let the rain constantly trickle down your neck. If I'd been the chick, I'd have asked her to move two feet closer but I wasn't and she didn't and he went on getting moist. But over the next days he, or maybe it was a she, grew visibly stronger and more eagle like, so obviously a bit of rain was no longer a serious threat. And anyway, I suppose if he'd been really bothered, he could have resolved the stand-off by creeping closer to her.

When there was nothing happening at the nest, there were other things to look at. From that vantage point, high above the surrounding landscape, we could see the grasslands and dunes rolling away to the west. Northwards, in front of us, were a few miles of scrub, the end of the reserve and El Rocio far beyond and to the East lay the Marismas. From here you could see how very, very far they stretched. Or rather you couldn't because their end was too far away to be visible. There, towards that distant perimeter long pink lines of flamingos would rise and fall, like gnats in a breeze, while closer, the egrets, spoonbills, terns and herons went back and forth on their marshy business. In the eagle's tree and in the bushes below us there was always something to catch the eye. A garden dormouse liked to swing in the leaves below the nest. Golden orioles would visit and a kestrel used a branch below the nest as a look-out. If you needed to answer a brief call of nature you could edge out of the back of the hide without apparently disturbing anything. Except I did disturb something once when I inadvertently peed on a great grey shrike that was sunning itself below me. I think I may be the only naturalist in the world who has achieved this feat.

Around lunch-time on the second day there were suddenly two eagles at the nest. The female came first and was bustling around when the male landed. She didn't greet him and he was quite nervous, as smaller male raptors tend to be when their large bone-crushing mates are oppressively adjacent. Two minutes later he was gone and I had managed to catch the whole event on film. Until now, the only camera I had owned had been a Brownie 127 box camera. It only took twelve photos on a reel, had no aperture choices, no form of telephoto lens and was no use for anything except taking pictures of the family dogs. Which is what I'd used it for: golden retrievers in wheelbarrows, on deck chairs, sitting somewhat forlornly on a home-made raft in the swimming pool. But now I had a nifty little super-eight cine camera which shot colour film through a zoom lens. I'd acquired it from my father who had bought it for a most uncharacteristic foray to East Africa. Dad didn't like travel and he didn't like hot places. In fact, the only typical thing about his first and only safari was that he'd manage to time it to coincide with Idi Amin's coup in Uganda. Dad had had to be evacuated in a small plane from the top of a hill in the middle of the night. Now I discovered, much to Toni's amazement if not my own, that at this, the apex of excitement in our careers so far, I had the presence of mind to press the magic button that set the camera running. Not only that, I let the birds come into picture, held steady as they landed, followed them smoothly as they moved on the nest and managed to get them leaving again. From then on, I was glued to my eyepiece. The results, because of the world-beating charisma of the birds, turned out to be quite good and later I nearly wore the film out by projecting it so often. It was only super-eight, it was only amateur and it was only me. But it was a first step.

On 17th May, we took down the nets and Toni and I packed our rucksacks. It was time to go. That last evening, new guests arrived at the Palacio. Among them was a young woman from Norway who was hoping to do some filming for a Norwegian film company. I who had three brothers and no sisters, I who had just spent the last eleven years in English boys' boarding schools, knew absolutely nothing at all about women. Of course, I had friends who were girls but I liked them because they enjoyed talking about ideas and poetry, not because they were girls. But now, as I was introduced to this woman and shook her hand, my mind already on tomorrow's journey, I looked at her and promptly disappeared into her wide-spaced blue eyes. It was several years before I emerged. Her name of course was Lone.

3

HESTETUREN

After leaving the Coto, Toni and I spent a few days watching vultures in the desolate mountains round Grazalema, eating bread soup and then I went home to England. I resumed a little "teaching" job I'd been given at a happy little day-school just outside Oxford. I'd been to Josca's myself as a very little boy prior to being interned in Dotheboys Hall and I knew it had a carefree ethos. I was supposed to instil in my victims a little Latin, History and English grammar – all subjects, of course, very dear to my heart. But what we all preferred was the occasional lesson called "Defenestration." I taught in a big ground-floor room with large sash windows looking straight out into low soft bushes and the garden. It was the bushes that gave me the idea. I would open the window to its full extent and the boys would line up and run at me. It was my job to fling them out through the open casement into the shrubbery, awarding them full marks for a clean flight and deducting points for collisions with the woodwork or breakages. But at last, our glad frolics ended, the summer term came to an end, I had passed my nineteenth birthday and I needed to make plans for my last months of freedom before university.

I thought it might be fun to travel with my other school friend, Mike Garner and our chief drinking companions, Mike Robinson and Giles Morrison. Mike Garner had proved a fearless nomad when, a few summers earlier we had won a little travel scholarship from school and gone to Crete. We had lived on a pound a day between us. We had visited the tomb of my hero, Nikos Kazantzakis (who wrote Zorba The Greek among other interesting novels), we had camped out in the unguarded ruins of the Minoan palace at Phaestos, hardly known about in the 1960s, and we had slept under the stars on the chequered marble floor of the Roman law courts at Gortyn. There the scops owls had called all night from the dark pillars of the resinous cypress trees surrounding the courts and on the amber wall of the ancient Doric law tablets a barn owl had settled in the moonlight. And we had talked into the early hours about how to make the perfect cowboy film.

A new journey together could be exciting. But then something strange happened. I received a thick letter from Norway. It couldn't be from Viggo. It wasn't his writing and anyway he was still in Spain. I opened it to find a love letter. From Lone. How could this be? We had only talked for an hour. Then we'd shaken hands. That was it. How could she possibly be feeling what I was feeling?

A week later I took a student flight to Norway. Lone had promised to meet me at the little rural airport where we landed and as I waited for her, I began to absorb the special beauty of my new surroundings. I admired the little red wooden houses that stood on uncircumscribed plots unmarked by suburban fences. Everywhere huge rocks pushed their way up out of the soil. This was very different from the stiffly owned landscape of southern England where I'd grown up. Here nature was still the landlord and I already loved it.

I waited and waited but Lone didn't appear. The airport emptied until only I and a quizzical looking taxi driver were left. We had no phones. The only address I had was a postbox number and a village, Hølen, so I got into the taxi and asked him to take me there. We drove and drove and my life savings ticked away on his meter. At last, many miles south of Oslo, he stopped at a gas station and said, apologetically, that this was the best he could do. I emptied my last bag of doubloons into his hands and stepped out into the dark and the rain. In the hedge by the road, about a hundred yards away, was a large wooden electricity junction box. This looked promising and when I prised open its cobwebby door, I found that all the lethal contraptions seemed to be safely above waist height and that below them was a sizeable, empty, dry space. I lay down there and fell fast asleep.

The next morning, I walked back to the gas station which I now saw had a little café at the back. Inside, were half a dozen red-eyed, rustic regulars so I asked if anyone knew where Lone Gunvald-Teilmann lived. Perhaps alarmingly, they all knew. The last house, right at the top of the hill. Well, it would be wouldn't it? As I trudged up the steep road, I looked up into the late summer leaves of the tall trees on either side and I saw a nutcracker. It was the first time I'd ever seen this elusive, speckly kind of crow so by the time I reached the summit I was in a good mood and there, sure enough was an old barn, a small paddock, a cheerful looking horse and a grassy avenue leading to my fairy-tale wooden house. Full of anxious, ecstatic anticipation, I knocked on the door. Nothing happened. I knocked again. Still nothing, then perhaps the faintest stirrings, then nothing again, and then finally, after at least five minutes the door opened. There stood a very sleepy Lone, lovely in her nightdress, with that very special look of astonishment that you always find on the faces of people who are not good with dates.

Living with Lone was quite entertaining. She was absolutely convinced she was going to die young, a fear reinforced by troublesome, repetitive dreams. These were invariably heralded by the same bars of menacing nightmare music. The unearthly harmonies would suck her down into a long tunnel from which the light, visible at first at the far end, would, as she moved towards it, slowly fade. Her divorced father had died of lung cancer at the age of 47. She barely knew him but she idolised him and she kept a photograph of him. He looked disturbingly like her, the way Liv Tyler's father looks weirdly like Liv. He'd been a doctor and he stood, relaxed in the photo, sucking sweetly on the pipe that killed him. I think Lone was influenced by Albert Camus. She told me how in 1960, as a penurious teenage film student in Paris she had stood on a cold January day staring hungrily through the window of a bountiful fruit shop. A strange man had appeared at her side, insisting that she go in and buy whatever she wanted. His manner reassured her so she did. She bought a huge basket of delicious fruit. He paid, turned to her and said "Today, Albert Camus has died." Then, having made his existential gesture, he had walked politely away.

If the cacophonous tunnel didn't get her then she was afraid that nuclear war would. It is true that we all had a nagging background fear that the Cold War could end badly. But for Lone this was nearer a certainty. One morning we woke quite late to what seemed to be an eerie silence. Even I had to acknowledge it because no birds sang. We looked out of the bedroom window and nothing was moving. No customary distant tractor, no-one walking on the road at the turn of the wood. It was very quiet. Lone announced that there had been a nuclear strike and we were the only survivors. When I suggested that the pickled chaps down at the café looked as if they could withstand any amount of radiation, she was unamused. Only when I reminded her that it was Sunday did she reluctantly admit that we might after all have a few more years of life left to us.

When we first started living together, Lone was not on good terms with her mother, Gori Gunvald. I like to think I helped to put that right. When I was finally allowed to meet her a few times I found Gori extremely interesting. She was a psychologist, small, dark and wiry, Danish-born, highly intelligent, an intense listener and talker. She lived in a fine wooden mansion in a beautiful, wooded part of Oslo, close to the little train that would take you up into the open forests and ski runs above the city. Her second husband, Lasse Conradi, was the big boss of Norsk Hydro, one of Norway's major state companies. He now lived in Haugesund on the West coast but they had two lofty sons who were completing their studies and were still more or less based with their mother. Gori was an insomniac. To help her sleep she had insulated her bedroom door and added an outer door for extra silence. But on many mornings, she would emerge desperate and grey with fatigue. Gradually I learned a little about the probable cause of this trauma. For ten years, from 1952-62, she had been the state psychologist at a government-run institution for troubled girls called Bjerketun. During her professional visits there she began to suspect and then uncover a web of appalling abuse. She took her worries to the Director but nothing was done. Then she went to the ministry and nothing was done. Finally, she took the step most loathed by apparatchiks, time servers and shameless conformists everywhere, she went to the press. The subsequent scandal buried Gori's career. She was blacklisted from all state work and had to subsist on private consultations. But a few years before I met her, she published her own, scrupulously documented account of the affair in a book simply called "Bjerketun". Slowly the tide was turning in her favour. The book became something of a classic and people, especially members of burgeoning women's groups, began to visit her – people from France and Germany and beyond. I would sit sometimes at her table listening to conversations going on in four or five languages, all of which she, and Lone, were following. It must have been exhausting and indeed on one occasion I remember asking everyone to leave because I was afraid she was going to faint. Eventually, Gori would receive some of the credit she deserved. Among other things, a prize was named after her and she was elected as Chairperson of the International Council of Psychologists.

That blissful summer of 1972, a summer of hard work and reconciliation, we borrowed the top flat in Gori's house and finished editing the Oxford film. Over the previous year we had been together and we had been apart. Now we were happy and together again, we had sprung Frøy from captivity and it was time to prepare for The Big Journey – to the West and then to England. First, we had to paint the cart we had rescued earlier from the famer's barn. We decided on a colour scheme of rich, navy blue, with all the trim highlighted in deep yellow. Our paint strokes were not particularly professional but we were very proud of the result. The cart could have been lifted straight out of "The Wind in The Willows" which has always been one of my favourite books. Then we had to cadge some second-hand harnesses and soften them with unguents and polish. We needed super-rich oats as fuel for Frøy and a decent nose-bag so he could munch as he walked. We had a small tent, two sleeping bags, my little camping-gas cooker, a pot, a frying pan and a kettle. What else? Oh yes, a film contract and then all the professional paraphernalia that would entail.

When we were ready for a dry run, we hitched Frøy to the wagon and trundled down to the TV station at NRK. Who could resist us? There, on the strength of the successful delivery of our first venture, Ada Haug now agreed to commission us to make not one, but two films. The first would be Hesteturen and the second would be called "Utsira: Island of Migration" which we would make after we reached the West coast.

A few days later we waved good bye at Gori's gate and set off, riding in state out of Oslo along the road towards Drammen and the wild countryside of Telemark that lay beyond. Stowed aboard we had on one side of the cart our meagre camping gear, our first night's rice and tuna and a big bag of oats for Frøy. On the other were fifty tins of black and white film, our Bolex camera, a Tandberg tape-recorder, tapes and microphone and an unwieldy, slightly suspect tripod. We felt utterly magnificent.

The first thing we noticed was that the iron-rimmed wheels made an appalling noise on the tarmac road. We rather doubted whether this would make a suitable soundtrack for our film idyll. No wonder horses had gone out of fashion when tarmac appeared. The whole population would have gone deaf. I began to feel even more admiration now for my beloved Romans building their stone roads and whacking natives even after listening to this racket every day. We tried to steer for grass verges and softer ground wherever possible and later we altered course to use forest tracks, but still there would be a lot of tarmac.

The next thing we noticed was that the machinery inside Frøy was having to work overtime to process the high-energy fuel we were feeding him. The inevitable bi-product was a dense, warm cloud of ripe methane that coalesced precisely where we were sitting and rendered normal life impossible if not comatose. We decided that it was equally dignified to walk beside him, holding his bridle. This lightened his load and he preferred it. He thought it was more democratic.

The third thing we noticed, about five miles out, was a horrible clunk and a thud and we turned round to find the harness had broken. One thing Lone had taught me was how to swear in Norwegian. "Fuy faen y helveter, pokker, piss, mukk, loet." She would take me through this mantra patiently word by word until I was fluent, which I still am. It sounds harmless to me and I always use it when I'm cross. But not with my Norwegian friends because it is very, very rude. Now, however, was an appropriate occasion and we both jumped about mantra-ing energetically. Twenty years earlier there might have been a leather-worker in every village but now we were on our own. There was nothing for it but for me to set up camp and stay with the horse while Lone hitched back home to fetch our spare harness. Frøy and I stood mournfully together as she disappeared, and then, as we often did subsequently, we spent the night in comradely contemplation of the constellations. It was a testimony to our skills in judging leather that the spare harness we had rejected and left behind would last us the rest of the journey and beyond without further mishap or the need to swear.

The next morning, when Lone was back, we began to focus on filming. We were still using our clockwork Bolex. This had a lens turret with space for three lenses so you could click from wide-angle, to closer, to telephoto to allow the variations that film montage requires. The camera itself was basically a lightbox with a clock inside it. A Swiss clock but still just a clock. You wound it up and it whirred your film past the lens aperture at roughly the right speed to synchronize with human movement. Fully wound, the mechanism permitted a maximum of thirty seconds of filming before it needed rewinding. This meant your shots needed to be concise and you had to remember to keep the camera wound up or you wouldn't be ready when something interesting happened. These were limitations, but actually being concise and being prepared are excellent film-making habits. The film was loaded on daylight spools, consisting of two black circular disks joined by a central axle round which the film was wound. The big advantage for beginners was that these could be loaded into the camera in daylight with only the outer few frames being sacrificed to the light, allowing you to see exactly what you were doing. The downside was that for two spools to fit inside the camera housing, so the film could wind from one to the other as it was exposed, the spools had to be small. Each one carried 100 feet, which gave you just two and a half minutes of filming. Again, you had to remain alert or you could run out of film half way through a shot or have insufficient footage to capture an important moment.

Our story, however, was simple and could easily be told within these practical constraints. It was the classic story of a journey: who we were, what we saw, where we went, how we got there. The piquancy was added by the horse and cart and the looming problem of the mountains and the North Sea and how we would cross them. We filmed our campsites and our funny meals and Frøy sneaking up behind me and ever so delicately leaning over my shoulder and nicking the sandwiches I was making. Lone of course had seen him coming but I was taken completely by surprise. I thought he'd come to give me a nuzzle. We filmed the landscape and the shadow of the cart ploughing past on the ground. We filmed occasional piles of litter and streams that looked polluted and offended our sense of the value of nature. We filmed barking dogs and the bevy of laughing children on bikes that always emerged from any new village to escort us through. People must have tipped off the local newspapers too because as we approached the main towns, first Drammen, then Kongsberg and later Notodden, press photographers appeared to document our progress. I think we were in all the papers from Oslo to Haugesund.

There are very few scenes in the film where Lone and I are both in the picture together. Obviously for those shots we had to find someone else to hold the camera and most of the time there was no-one else around. So we realised that the real hero of the story had to be Frøy and the film became Frøy's journey more than ours. Perhaps this went to his head. One evening we'd been invited to set up camp in someone's "garden" while Frøy munched the rich grass of the verge. Suddenly he had a change of plan. He decided enough was enough, pulled up his stake and started walking purposefully back towards Oslo. By now Oslo was a very long way away. This had to stop. I walked determinedly after him, offering him all sorts of inducements, Hollywood contracts, extra oats, anything if he'd just come back on board. But he was adamant. However fast I walked, he walked just a teeny weeny bit faster. I was never going to win this race. Luckily a car came along which let me flag it down. We drove unobtrusively past Frøy – I didn't want to spook him – and then after a fair distance I got out and quietly waited for him. I didn't move, I just stood there. He came on at a pace, still the King of all Frøys, and then gradually the spirit of rebellion ebbed out of him. He walked slower and slower, coming to a stop right in front of me. He'd given up but his expression was priceless. It said "you cheated."

It was now early September. The days were shortening and the nights growing colder. It was romantic, snuggled up in our little tent, falling asleep to the sound of Frøy munching the grass outside. One night I woke to check on him. He was standing nearby, a black silhouette, just visible against a dark sky. And then strange lights appeared, like the beams of search lights, long white fingers playing back and forth above the northern horizon. They almost looked like the distant headlamps of cars, but even Norwegians can't sit their cars back on their haunches and aim the headlights straight up in the air and anyway, there were no roads to the north. Up, up into the silent invisible sky, pale flashes soared and splashed and spangled. Some were faintly tinged with green and then we realised what we were seeing. This was the season's first inflorescence of the Northern Lights, rarely seen so early and so far south. After a few minutes the light-show faded to black but it left us with a feeling so intense – of connection to nature and to each other – that our journey seemed to have been endowed with extra meaning.

The road that rolled out in front of us had to be gathered in, step by step. It was a laborious process. The wheels of the cart rattled round and round, like giant spools, winding our route onto their axles. This was very different from travelling by car, or even by bicycle. Nothing sped by, only the happy hours. A tree at the turn of the track would take ages to reach us, a stream might bubble beside us for the best part of a day. But all the while, mile by ominous mile, the looming mountains moved towards us. West of Notodden the gradient began to steepen. On shorter stretches of hill we would get behind the cart and push to take some of the strain off Frøy. But the cart had no brake and eventually we had to summon the cavalry. We had always known that we were not equipped to cross the high passes so we had included some modest transport costs in our vanishingly small budget. Our circuitous route had covered a little more than one hundred and seventy kilometres and taken a little less than two weeks. Now we wheeled the cart up the ramp of a robust lorry. Frøy was not keen to follow. He thought you should put the horse before the cart, so we had to stretch a wide strap behind his back legs and urge him aboard. Then we squeezed in beside the driver in his cramped cab and he ground through the gears out of the hills and into the bare mountains, with their snowy peaks, on a road that wound down into steep gorges where our cart could have never gone. We watched the postcard landscape slide safely past and we felt mostly wonder and relief. But we soon found ourselves missing our old snail-paced life and the sweet companionship of the open road.

In Haugesund we had a rabbit to take out of a hat. The hat was Lone's step-father, Lasse and the rabbit was a boat. Lasse had agreed that if we could get our horse and cart to Haugesund, he would arrange transport to England on one of the tankers that Norsk Hydro operated. So now we stayed with him for a couple of days while we organised this next leg of the journey. We would need a padded crate to be knocked together for Frøy, in which he could be safe but comfortable and we would need a boat with a decent crane to lift him and the cart aboard. Embarkation was fixed for after 5th October – nearly three weeks away.

In the meantime, we had another film to make! Viggo had recently discovered some interesting papers during his researches in the National Museum in Oslo. They were accounts by several Norwegian ornithologists in the company of the English naturalist and adventurer, James Chaworth-Musters, of expeditions they had made to the island of Utsira in the 1930s. Those were the early days of the serious investigation of the phenomenon of bird migration but not much was yet known. Utsira lies about 10 miles off shore, due West of Karmøy, near Haugesund and Musters and his friends suspected that it lay on the path of a regular southerly, autumn migration route that might begin all the way up in Western Siberia. They thought their theory could be proved if they visited Utsira during migration and found six target rarities that would have originated in Siberia. The six species they selected were yellow-browed warbler, red-breasted flycatcher, two-barred crossbill, scarlet rosefinch, Richard's pipit, and either barred warbler or rustic bunting. At that time, theories had to be proved by the taking of specimens. Musters and his friends went off to Utsira armed with shotguns and enough cartridges to satisfy a Mexican bandit and one by one they quite quickly "collected" five of their six rarities. For a while, the tiny yellow-browed warbler eluded them but one day they found it in a cottage garden. There was just one problem. It was sitting in front of a cottage window and one of the Norwegians, who had his gun with him, was loathe to shoot. "You shoot the bird" said Musters "and I'll pay for the window". So it was that their thesis was upheld, at least to their own satisfaction.

Viggo had decided that it would be extremely interesting to try to repeat this exercise, not with guns but with mist nets and rings. He therefore assembled a small band of suitably experienced young naturalists and we were invited to join them. This was to be the now famous inaugural Utsira ringing expedition, the first of several he would lead to Utsira over the coming years. On 20th September Lone and I landed at the little ferry terminal at Nordvik. There are two harbours on the island, called, imaginatively, Nordvik and Sørvik, with a church half way between on the island's only road. Viggo and our new "ringing station" were down in Sørvik, so we hoisted our rucksacks and camera gear, and started plodding south. We didn't have to plod for long. We could see most of the island from the road, because it's only about one and a half miles across and it's roughly round. When we reached the church, the focal point for the fishermen and farmers who eked out a life there, we found one of the island's only mature deciduous trees. It was a large sycamore (two together in fact) pressed up against the leeward gable of the church. Whenever they had poked their leafy noses round the edge of the building they had been cut off by the constant wind. Finally, they had given up all attempts at exploration and had settled for being a single tree in the exact shape of a church. It was a wonderful example of natural topiary. But it was also a warning. Utsira was a land of tough love.

Our new home was a large wooden fishing warehouse. On the first floor was a spacious room with a wooden floor, a table, a scattering of old sofas and windows looking straight out onto the tiny harbour. A ladder outside led to an attic where Lone and I installed ourselves for romantic privacy – which was occasionally disturbed. Viggo had arranged our headquarters with the owner, Johannes Klovning, the island's only entrepreneur. I remember visiting the grave of Mr and Mrs Klovning. There were dozens of them, stony little tombs in a stony landscape. Most of the people on the island seemed to be called Klovning. The lodging was perfect. The others in our party had already been there a week and had settled into a regular pattern of work. Sigurd, an excellent photographer with a Hasselblad, the most expensive camera I'd ever seen, would roam the island for images. Freude, a quiet, serious-minded law student, mostly helped Viggo, and then there was Baust. Baust was a policeman. He had a gun with which he was waging a silent war against feral cats. At least, Baust was silent. He would disappear just after dawn and the silence would continue, perhaps for an hour. And then there would be a hideous bang and Baust would return much more chatty.

A couple of times a week the shrimp boats would come into the harbour. On still days we would hear the slow deep tok tok tok of their little diesel engines as they rounded the last rocky fingers of the island and we would rush to the tiny quay where they tied up. Those shrimps, straight from the sea, cooked on board and spilled into large brown paper bags, five kroner a kilo, were among the best meals I've ever had. Hungry young friends, sitting together sharing fresh bread spread with a film of mayonnaise and piled with more shrimps than you've ever seen: we knew this was happiness.

We all helped with the ringing. The days were long and tiring. Nets to be hung. Birds to be gathered and processed. Notes to be written. There was always someone asleep on a couch. We focussed on one of the very few small conifer plantations on the island. Utsira must have looked a bleak prospect to tired migrants passing overhead at two thousand feet, looking for somewhere safe to rest their weary wings and reprovision their empty larders. So when they spotted our little bank of dark trees nestled among the rocks below, their hearts must have raced. I will never forget the roar of a thousand wings as a tight flock of redwing thrushes plummeted from afar, filling the trees around me one day as I worked the nets.

For the film we wanted to make, Lone and I had acquired a small boy. Vidar Thorsen was the ten-year-old son of a friend of Lasse's and he bravely came out to Ultsira to see the ringing and to help us. The plan was to repeat a sequence I had previously shot only in amateur super-eight format on the Coto Donana. Bird ringing was not much known about at the time and I don't think it had ever been shown on Norwegian TV. We filmed the whole process, firstly selecting the right location, preparing the ground and hanging the nets; then catching the birds, disentangling them, ringing and measuring and finally releasing them. The difference now, was that we were filming professionally and we had our star, Vidar, who Lone suggested should stand in for the entire audience as the pupil learning the process. It was a good idea and Vidar was perfect. He didn't act. He watched and nodded and behaved entirely naturally and we wrapped up the film's core in a single day. The rest, the story of migration, the island and why birds come there, we could complete at a relaxed pace over the coming weeks.

One day Viggo came back to the harbour house in great excitement. He had seen one of Musters's rarities. Out on a stretch of rocky pasture he had spotted a two-barred crossbill, a large finch with two prominent white lines in its wings and a pair of pliers as a beak. It was a long way off but he quickly took a photograph for the record. Then he crept closer and took another. Closer. Snap. Closer still. Snap again. Soon it was just a few feet away. Big snap. And then he walked forwards and picked it up. Now he took it out of the ringing bag and showed it to me. It was a young female and it was love at first sight. For both of us. I called her Koulouria, which my beloved Cretan music teacher had once told me was Greek for seedcakes. Koulouria didn't want to fly. Every day she ate about four tons of bird seed out of my hand and then sat on my head. Whenever I came back into the ringing-room she would flutter up to sit on me. I was mostly beard and hair in those days so I suspect I was the one in the group who most resembled a nest. Day after day she ate her hearty meals and day after day she lost weight. There was no saving her. At last she curled up in my hand and died. Very often, if a bird perks up so visibly after a trauma, they survive. But we suspected that somewhere on her travels she had picked up a poison, probably an organo-phosphate or DDT which were still in use as pesticides, especially in the lawless lands she'd come from. The seeds of death must have already been inside her when Viggo had picked her up. I should have called her Sporoithanatou.

The ringing was successful. We caught several more of the famous target rarities, although "our" first barred warbler was eaten by one of the cats Baust had carelessly forgotten to shoot. We even caught a woodchat shrike, which I knew well from the Coto days. This was only the second record for Norway, though it turned out to be a weird subspecies from the East which I wouldn't have recognised. On our last full day, we spotted a red-breasted flycatcher, a peaceful little fellow with two charming white spots at the base of its tail. This was a prime goodie. Now if there was one thing I was good at, it was making birds and animals go where I wanted them to go. The flycatcher was sitting on a stone wall. Our nets were about seven hundred yards away. So I lined up the team and then, by manipulating the wingers, the chaps at each end of the line, urging them forward or holding them back, we were able to deflect the flycatcher like a billiard ball. It went like a dream. It flew down the wall. It crossed the next field. Finally, it was sitting on a gorse bush within thirty feet of the net. This last push, I whispered, required great delicacy. None of Baust's loud bangs. We inched forwards and then it happened. That magical, never-to-be-forgotten moment. My very first red-breasted flycatcher, a bird I'd always wanted to see ever since first looking into Witherby's celebrated Handbook of British Birds, flew like an arrow from my heart straight at the net – and perched on the top. It sat there watching us for a few seconds and then it flew away. We never caught it. In fact, we never saw it again.

We left Utsira on 5th October. Our film was finished and we now faced the unknown challenge of getting Frøy onto a ship for England. This happened a couple of days later and turned out, in its way, to be a spectacular event. Haugesund had an industrial shipping port, a noisy, busy place where no-one much would notice a little cart being hoisted high in the air and swung out over the water but to us, the sight of its gold trim and yellow arms, waving forty feet in the air was slightly intimidating. The cart clattered down onto the deck of the tanker and then it was Frøy's turn. Lone, slim and lithe, slipped between the bars of his crate and squeezed in beside him to give him a last soothing rub with the brush before he went aerial. I thought this was a brave thing to do but I guess she knew Frøy, how gentle and affectionate he was, and that this contact would settle him. Then he too was up and away. Our hearts were in our mouths in case the crate would tip or jerk but the crane operator knew he had a living being at the end of his cable and he landed Frøy aboard, smoothly and the right way up.

At the beginning of the following summer, we saw a bit of Hesteturen when we took the ferry from Norway to Denmark. It was, by coincidence, the evening of its first transmission and the television was on in the boat's cafeteria. Lone and I were not very interested in clothes so we were wearing the same sweaters and jeans that we had worn in the film. Perhaps the conspicuous Norwegian patterns would have stood out on a British boat but here no-one noticed that the beautiful young couple standing beside them were the same people they were watching on the film. I love making films. I love bringing an idea to life, seeing the adverts in the schedule, even reading the reviews, but I've never really liked watching my own work. One of my regular editors, Peter Gahan, used to quote to me that "a film is never finished, it is only ever abandoned." Watching my films, I saw only the faults and the disappointments. But perhaps a forty-year gap makes a difference. Around 2012, I wrote to NRK, they kindly sent me some DVDs and I sat down to watch Hesteturen again. I expected to find it the most boring film ever made: 45 minutes of unrelenting clip-clop and rattle rattle. But it wasn't. It was sweet and delicate and it brought back the wonder of those weeks of travel. Apart from my unrecognisable youth and Lone's memorable grace, one thing stood out. This was the personality of the horse: mischievous, long-suffering, companionable. The last scene summed it up. When we'd finally arrived in Oxford, we had taken Frøy down to Port Meadow. This is a famous expanse of damp, common pasture land between the North-West edge of the city and the River Thames. There, tradition has it that the free folk of the nearby village of Wolvercote have the right to graze their horses free of charge. We thought it would be nice to make Frøy a Free Man, so we released him on Port Meadow and the film ends as he walks up to a little group of local ponies, touching noses with them before they all trot off out of picture. An hour later we had rounded him up again and we were on our way to our cottage in Garsington where he would live in the little back garden. But a point had been made. This was Frøy's film.

After the success of that first ringing trip, word began to get out that Utsira was a very interesting place. By the time Viggo had finished his researches it had become famous among bird watchers. In 1992 an official bird station was established there, associated with the Stavangar Museum and it is now probably Norway's foremost bird observatory. It is a pity, therefore, that our film, the first TV film to be made about the island and its birds, has disappeared. NRK cannot find it in their archives. I don't have it but a copy is probably still out there somewhere, in someone's garage or in a suitcase in a basement, and in flickering black and white those bleak landscape scenes may still exist, with little Vidar learning why we study the migration of birds.

4

IN SEARCH OF THE SPANISH IMPERIAL EAGLE

In mid-October 1974 I was camping under the spiny peaks of the Sierra de Guadarrama, about fifty kilometres North of Madrid, beside the sandy edge of a huge lake, the Embalsa de Santillana. I'd finished my first degree at Oxford and on 2nd October I had hitched to Germany to pick up a Novoflex lens. The manufacturers had kindly offered to give it to me for free to support my researches, but I had to pick it up in person direct from the factory. Then I'd hitched down through France and now, here I was, sitting outside my tent alone, licking my wounds. Lone and I had broken up. I was too young. Our lives were at different stages. We wrote to each other. We thought about each other. But we never met again. And she would be proved right. She did die quite young, of cancer like her father, just a month after her fiftieth birthday. I've always been very lucky with companionship but she was my first love and that autumn in Spain, watching the flames of my solitary campfire, I was full of sorrow.

But I was back into the consoling rhythm of bird ringing and that gave solace. Toni had discovered Santillana as a child, driving out for walks with his parents. Now I was beginning to document the area more systematically. There was a notch high up in the mountains where the streams gathered, flowing down towards me and the little bramble and willow clad valley where I had placed my nets. The migrating birds, heading south now, funnelled through the notch and along its spilling streams so my little valley and the wide sandy beach of the lake where I had my tent became busy feeding stations for them. I caught a lot of garden warblers, small, neat beige-coloured birds whose rich burbling song I knew from the woods at home. They are mainly insect eaters but here their beaks were stained by the tell-tale dye of late sugary blackberries. I discovered that the average garden warbler weighed eighteen grams. One day, however, I took one out of the net that felt like a lead ball in my hand. When it hung in its bag from my scales, I saw that it had pulled the spring down to read a whopping 32 grams. Gently I parted its breast feathers with my breath to reveal fat deposits that would make a Michelin man proud. This little fellow was loaded like a dam-buster bomber for his journey to Africa. I was fascinated by the thought that a little bird could nearly double its weight by feeding so avidly. Did this really give it a travel advantage? At what point did the valuable extra fuel get too heavy for the infrastructure and begin to reduce its flight efficiency? I knew I would probably never know the answers but I liked the questions.

After each round of the nets, I would walk down to the dry lake shore to look for driftwood. I'd haul back a tangle of sun-whitened branches to my camp for my night-time fire and then I might walk up to the village. The little white row of houses that comprised Manzanares in those days included a small shop. On my first visit there I noticed with delight that on a dark shelf behind the little wooden counter stood a line of exceedingly hopeful-looking tins. From what I could see in the gloom, their contents would provide me with a sufficiently varied and convenient diet for many days to come. There were tins of beef stew, and strogonov and mutton stew and chicken. I bought a dozen and that night I lit my tinder-dry fire and as the sparks flew up to join the stars, I decided it was time for my first gourmet meal. I chose a mutton stew but when I'd pried open the jagged lid and poured the contents into my dented billy can I was a bit disappointed. There wasn't any mutton. In fact, there wasn't any stew either. All I could see were hundreds of round, hard pinkish pellets in a pinkish sauce. These were garbanzos, Mexican jumping beans. Oh well, I could close my eyes and think of England and its baked beans, so I cooked them up and polished them off. The next evening, for variety, I chose chicken. Same result. No chicken, just garbanzos. And the next night, no beef, just garbanzos. No strogonov, no nothing. Night after night I had to eat garbanzos. After this cata-strophe, for some reason, I cheered up. I wasn't exactly walking on air – while I was in a way – but the whole ridiculousness of it made me happy. I lay in my sleeping bag at night on the hard ground wondering if all the tins in the shop contained only garbanzos. I was sure they did. What about all the tins in the Province of Madrid? The whole of Spain? Had I uncovered the beginning of the great garbanzos conspiracy that would one day propel a new generation into space and beyond? The next day I woke feeling much happier.

Every weekend I received visitors. My ringing effort was co-ordi-nated by the Sociedad Espanola de Ornitologia, the SEO. They supplied the rings and my results were logged in their archive to be shared, eventually, with the outside world. As part of my remit, I had agreed to be a spectacle for novices and to give a bit of encourage-ment to those with a real interest. Spain was at a turning point. Franco would only live a few more months and the country and espe-cially its young people, were emerging from political hibernation. At first, I used to laugh at my new audience. Most of them knew nothing about nature but they would arrive all dressed like Felix Rodriguez de la Fuente, Spain's new television naturalist who published a nature magazine with a picture of himself on every page. They looked very dapper with their serious hats, their brand-new parker coats and beautiful never-before-worn leather hiking boots. They must have been disconcerted when they found me in my usual mess, my decaying gym shoes and faded rugby shirt, though when they saw the nets strung across water and under bridges, they probably realised the value of less formal wear. As I got to know them, however, I stopped laughing at them. They had understood that the environment was a legitimate ground on which to express political dissent. Spain up till then had no real public tradition of environmentalism, indeed it had been one of the things that had disappointed me. There were very few nature reserves, an economy that relied too heavily on tourism and corrupt developments and no encouragement to be interested in animals and birds. But now they had Felix's films and I saw that just by showing people things you could nudge them in a new direction. Indeed, it was a tragedy that Felix was killed six years later in a helicopter crash in Alaska. But by then the groundwork was laid. In 1992, the area above me, where my birds were coming from was made into a National Park. The SEO, which then had a handful of members and just one employee, now has fifty staff, eight thousand members and is involved in widespread conservation work. Those naive youngsters, escaping by bus from Madrid and their parents, to watch me work and help me, on those long-ago Saturdays, went on to change their world. And in my small way I helped to change them and provide them with the first basic evidence to justify their push to establish nature reserves. From small stones mountains are made.

Bird ringing was always interesting. Toni and I had conducted a reconnaissance ringing trip to Santillana earlier in the summer. On 31st July we had caught a common sandpiper, a small brown and white wading bird, with a ring already on its leg. To catch a bird wearing someone else's ring is always exciting. It means extra information. We could see immediately that this was a British Museum ring, which was good news because that meant the data would be properly documented and fairly swiftly accessed. In due course we discovered that our sandpiper had been ringed as a breeding bird that spring at a lake in Kent. Not only that, but I had actually met the ringer, Mr. Harrison, when, as a schoolboy, I had been Town Secretary of the Oxford Ornithological Society. In the late summer of the following year, I would do a second long stint at Santillana and I caught the same bird at the same place on the same date – only exactly a year later. In the meantime, it had presumably been down to Africa, back up to Kent to breed and was then heading south again.

All that autumn of 1974 I waited for the cranes. I knew that huge flocks of these spectacular birds gathered in Sweden after breeding in the hills and swamps of Scandinavia and then headed south, stopping in Germany and France before crossing high over Spain on their way to the Coto Donana and Africa. At some time, some of them must pass over me. I had never seen a crane and I looked longingly up into the clouds every day. On 1st November, Dr Arauco, the good-natured secretary of the SEO came out from Madrid with a fresh stock of rings for me. When I asked him about the cranes, he said it was too late for them and I must have missed them. But the very next morning I heard a mournful, vibrant trumpeting and there far above I saw a thin V-formation of birds. Long necks outstretched, long legs reaching well beyond the tails behind. Arauco was probably right. These were the last stragglers of the great congregations that would have passed over weeks before. I counted them. There were just 22. But 22 cranes were good enough for me.

Buoyed up by the cranes I began to scour the distant mountains every day and a few days later I saw something else interesting. I spotted two adult Spanish imperial eagles. I saw them again, several times, behaving very much like a pair. I hadn't expected to see them here. Could this be a northerly outpost of "our" eagle? This got me thinking, not just about the eagle but about myself. What was I going to do with my life – or rather not "what" but "how"? I knew I didn't want a job. I wanted to keep my freedom and, like a lot of my generation, I wanted somehow to influence the world around me. I knew I wanted to use film as a medium of change but I was a little technophobic. The films I'd made with Lone were the works of beginners and I didn't feel ready yet to progress on my own. I would come back to that, I hoped. In the meantime, I wanted to spend more time in the field and find out things that would be useful for the conservation of species or places. To do that I realised I would need to search for grants and scholarships and sponsorship and to have a chance of earning any of those I would need to come up with some pretty coherent plans. All of which brought me back to the eagles, circling the faraway peaks way above my little camp.

It was assumed at the time that outside Spain, the Spanish imperial eagle also had a stronghold in Morocco. No-one knew how many pairs nested there but a suitable landscape of cork-oak forests and wooded hills was said to exist and the assumption was that they supported a viable breeding population. Indeed, Toni and I had rather suspected that the supposed existence of the Moroccan birds had furnished an excuse for the Spanish authorities for their lackadaisical approach to the bird's conservation. The eagle was, after all, one of the rarest birds in the world but very few people in Spain seemed to know or care much about it. Now, as I sat alone by my campfire at night, I began to map out a project. We would go to Morocco, Toni and I, and visit all the locations where our researches – yet to be done – told us that eagles had been recorded. We would visit all the likeliest habitats. We would conduct interviews across the eagle's assumed range with forest personnel and interested parties and we would make a general survey of the environmental conditions that could affect the eagle and other species of raptor. If we found it, we could use the information to exhort the Moroccan authorities to strengthen its conservation. If we didn't find it, we could use that as a wake-up signal to the Spanish government that the only eagles left were the handful for which they had responsibility. Provided we did the work to the best of our ability, whatever result we achieved would be useful.

By late November I was back in Oxford, reading old bird reports in the ornithological library of the Edward Grey Institute and puzzling through old maps in the Bodleian. It's hard to imagine how laborious even quite basic research could be in those days before the internet, especially if you were an outdoor type who didn't have mould growing on your eyebrows. But I was able to produce a decent short-list of possible eagle sites in Morocco and I wrote an expedition plan. Things were firming up. And we had two new personnel. Toni's girlfriend, Juliet, said she's like to come. Juliet Sparkes had been born on a tea plantation in Sri Lanka and she liked adventures. Her father was the secretary of the British Olympic Association so she had some good suggestions about sponsorship. And I had a new friend too. Carol Merriman was aptly named. She was very pretty and feminine and with her dainty eye-shadow she looked like butter wouldn't melt in her mouth. But she had a wicked sense of humour, she encouraged outrageous behaviour with her hilarity and I knew that if anyone could keep me from growing gloomy, it would be her. We all settled down to write begging letters. We wrote to industry and institutions, charities and trusts and, as a very far shot in the dark, I applied for a Winston Churchill Travel Fellowship. Tate and Lyle offered us as much sugar as we needed for the expedition. That wasn't really much help. I did entertain the thought of asking for a truckload and selling it in Morocco but that wouldn't have been in the spirit of the agreement. Zeiss gave me a superb pair of binoculars, which I still have. Otherwise, our enthusiasm was greeted with a deafening silence.

Until, that is, we received a letter from the International Union for the Conservation of Nature in Geneva. The IUCN, which had helped to save the Coto Donana, had an interest in the future of our eagle and they announced that they had authorised a grant of $1000 to us through the World Wildlife Fund. This was a massive boost to our plans. A few days later we received a package of documents, flyers and large cheerful panda stickers for our luggage. There was no going back now. Toni went home to Spain to source a car, while the rest of us wrote our last wills and testaments and booked the boat from Portsmouth to Bilbao.

Then something surprising happened. An official notification arrived telling me that, out of the hundreds of applicants, I had been short-listed for a Churchill Fellowship. I was asked to report for an interview at Queen's Gate Terrace in a week. This meant a journey to London, which was alien territory. This meant I had to comb my hair. This meant panic.

The selection committee was chaired by Sir Peter Scott, the famous son of the legendary Antarctic explorer. Peter Scott had founded the Wildfowl Trust at Slimbridge, he had saved the Hawaiian goose and he had been a hero of mine since I'd found my first linnet's nest when I was three. He had also been the person to whom I had written, four years earlier, about my concerns over how the Coto Doñana was being run. Would he remember? If so, I feared it would count against me. Nobody likes an arrogant twat and perhaps that's what I was. Worse still, I was now telling the board that, whether I won an award or not, I was going to look for the eagle in any case. A Fellowship, I explained, would allow us a longer trip and enable us to carry out a more thorough search, but whatever happened we would cover the core potential habitats. And because the eagle was an early nester, we needed to leave several weeks before the Fellowship results were published in mid-February.

The next morning the phone rang in my parents' hall. It was the secretary of the Trust to say that I had won a Fellowship but please not to tell anybody until the official announcement. In the meantime, the Trust would organise the paperwork and travellers' cheques. So, after all, we wouldn't need the lorry load of sugar. I also learned that two of my friends had received awards. Kate Lessels was off to Iran to ring birds and David Macdonald to the Sinai Desert to study foxes. Both would go on to have distinguished academic careers and David made a monumental contribution to conservation by founding Wild-Crew, Oxford University's outstanding Department of Conservation Biology.

On 26th January our train pulled into Madrid's spectacular station, which Toni was always boasting had starred in the film Nicholas and Alexandra, and there was Toni with a broad smile, waiting for us. Our joint luggage and equipment covered the entire floor of the main room in Toni's parents' flat. Somehow it had to be sardined into the little can on wheels that he had bought as our expedition vehicle. This was a very small, ancient, cherub-white Renault 4, which, he had been assured, ran like a dream. Toni had decided that most of our gear could go on the roof, in a huge red tin trunk that he had bought for the purpose. This, I suggested, would make the car an unwieldy sort of mobile hamburger with the two buns only loosely connected and we, the meat, very much exposed in the middle. The trunk would have to stay behind. So too would the girls' party dresses and indeed most of their junk. I was adamant. I see, however, from my diary that later, on the way south, Toni threw my cushion out of the window, so we must have all made sacrifices. I did keep my slippers though.

Toni's parents, Michael and Meli, were probably as worried about him now as they had been years ago when as children, we'd first set off for the Coto. But they were good sports and on our last night in Madrid they treated us to a huge Chinese meal. I know this because, for the next 6 months, Carol and I shared a diary, taking it in turns to write. Most of my entries are about birds, landscape, or occasionally bureaucracy. Carol's are all about food. If I need to analyse our expedition diet I can just look for pages in her hand.

On 1ˢᵗ February, we crossed the Straits of Gibraltar from Algeciras to Ceuta and began to study the landscape and search the skies. Just south of Tetouan we noted small stands of pine trees and then a large eucalyptus plantation where a pair of goshawks were displaying. This was later revealed to be an unusual observation. The next day we broke down. When all the little bits and bobs that make a car go round were laid out on the mechanic's bench, the culprit was identified as a small plastic cog. To me this looked like the sort of thing one could easily do without, but no, apparently this was a sine qua non for a Renault 4. Not only that, but as our car had been built in Spain, this was a Spanish cog. Here in Morocco, they had only French cogs. Needless to say, les bloody cogs Francais went in a different direction from Los Spanish cogs. Well, they would wouldn't they. Toni shrugged, walked outside and hitched a lift back to Spain, in search of a car graveyard that might contain, somewhere interred among its piles of scrap, a cog of the right order.

The girls and I were rescued by Merson. I'm not quite sure who Merson was but I think he must have been a relative of the mechanic. I can, however, thanks to our culinary archivist, tell you that we had "a nice dinner of mince, tomatoes, onions, asparagus, figs, nuts and chapatis" prepared by Merson's step-mother. I do remember that she and the other ladies of the house had fun dressing the girls as Arab ladies. This was not an outstanding sartorial success. The robes had to be put on over their already bulky jeans and sweaters and after the application of some fairly hideous mascara, they ended up looking like a pair of large rolled up carpets with barely human heads sticking out the top.

The next day I chivvied them outside to look for eagles and the day after, Toni arrived, with the little plastic key to our future mobility. We said goodbye to the mysterious Merson and for the next week we searched the landscape from Larache to Rabat. Rabat was the capital and we had business there. We clocked in at the British Embassy so they would know who we were and what we were doing. Then we went to "Eaux et Forêts", the Forest Department whose co-operation we were going to need. Our contact was M. Laudie. I didn't really like M. Laudie. It was hard to make him interested in Spanish imperial eagles. For several days we sat among the flies, outside his office, and while Carol and Juliet apparently found a good place to scoff doughnuts in town, we waited for the essential piece of paper. At last it came. I still have it. It introduced me as "working for the Wild Word Fund and the Winston Chunchill Trust" and required the reader to render me all possible help. Later I realised I might have done M. Laudie an injustice because his scrap of paper ensured us free board and lodging throughout Morocco's forest network.

Our final set of meetings was with Michel Thevenot, the department's zoologist. I don't think he was very impressed with us at first. But we kept chipping away and at least he was knowledgeable about birds. He didn't hold out much hope of our finding eagles. In all his years of service he'd never heard of an actual breeding pair. But he could see what we were trying to achieve and eventually he helped us devise a much more detailed itinerary that would take us from forest post to forest post in all the key areas we needed to visit.

For the next four months we worked hard. We camped in forest clearings or, more often we stayed with the foresters in their little stone houses. One night we nearly died. It was very cold and had rained most of the day. Our spirits were drooping and, when we went to sleep, we asked our host to leave the tripod of coals in our room for warmth. He was most unwilling but we persuaded him. In the middle of the night, I woke up with a vicious head-ache and was violently sick. I woke the others and one by one they all exploded too. It was a terrible mess. Now we understood what the forester had been trying to tell us. We had carbon monoxide poisoning. Would the others have woken up if I hadn't? All the next day we sat immobile out on the hillside, looking for eagles and feeling like death.

A week later we stayed with Azzouzi. He was a sensitive man, perhaps the only literate person for a hundred square miles and he was achingly lonely. He wanted to talk with us about poetry and philosophy and he wanted us to hear his favourite music. He only had two records: Beethoven's Violin Concerto and Tchaikovsky's 1812 overture and he thought they had both been written in the same year. When he put the Tchaikovsky on his gramophone, it became clear that he'd always played it at 45 revolutions per minute not 33. As we listened to Napoleon galloping across the steppes at 200 miles an hour and firing his canons like machine guns, we didn't have the heart to tell him he'd been listening to it at the wrong speed. Instead, we sat outside, looking down over the wide forest terraces while he made us lunch. He served us wrinkled black olives, fresh, rich olive oil and newly-baked unleavened bread. I thought I had never liked olives, but sitting there with that gentle man and his biblical meal, I experienced something of a Pauline conversion. I suddenly understood why for thousands of years men had pressed the oozing oil from the ripe fruit and left some intact, to shrivel slowly into their dark skins and why they had burned wheat dough on flat discs over hot fires. Every mouthful was magnificently simple.

Another forester I remember was Chaffiki, a mercurial character, full of jokes who could suddenly turn sour and cross. He had a huge henchman called Ahmed who hardly left his side. His forests most resembled the terrain where we'd seen our eagles in Spain – low lying, sandy and dotted with cork-oaks. Here we were able to explore in his Land-Rover which saved us time. One day we had a puncture. The ground was soft and there was no jack so Ahmed decided that he and I could lift the back of the vehicle while Chaffiki quickly changed the wheel. I was a powerful young man and I had lifted small cars but there was no way I could pick up a Land-Rover. Nevertheless, "we" did it. I think Ahmed was the strongest man I'd ever met.

Everywhere we went, we asked the foresters, their workers and the villagers whether they had seen our eagle. We had pictures and descriptions and some of them clearly understood what we were looking for but absolutely no-one seemed to have seen a Spanish imperial eagle. And nor did we. We saw other raptors, mainly the smaller short-toed and booted eagles but no sign of our quarry. In early May we arrived in the Rif. This was core terrain, high hills with superb deciduous forest and here we decided to split up for some days to increase our coverage. Jules and Toni took the car and Carol and I stayed in a stretch of prime forest that we planned to explore with the help of the forester there. His name was Ali and over the next week we would get to know him rather well.

Ali had a problem that made him sad. Ali's parents wanted him to get married. They had found him a lady, whom he had never met, and now he was facing the loss of his frolicsome bachelor life in the forest, a prospect that he couldn't bear. He told us all this, looking at us with his big soulful eyes, on our first evening. He was, he said, determined to make the best of these, his last happy days on earth. So, the following night he invited what he called, excitedly, a "Folk-Lore", a small band of traditional musicians, to come and perform for us. The Folk-Lore consisted of three players and a dancer. The instruments were primitive: a sort of viol with almost no strings, a banjo similarly unequipped and a skin drum. The dancer was striking. She was very slim and handsome, rather lightly clad for an Arab lady, and her teeth were, alarmingly, all made of silver. The Folk-Lore lined up before us, smiled and bowed and began to play. They were astonishing. The volume and complexity of harmony and lilting sound that they produced from those unpromising sources was truly wonderful. We felt ourselves enveloped by the alien yet seductive tones, and then Ali seized a tea tray and stood up to dance. Ali was extremely fat. He was a mountain of blubber. Years later, when I was working in Sri Lanka, I was told that if you said to a lady that she walked like an elephant this would be accepted as a great compliment. And indeed, I had learned by then to appreciate how daintily and with what grace and elegance an elephant swung its hips as it walked. So if I tell you now that Ali danced like an elephant you will understand what I mean. I was moved by the monumental beauty of his steps and all the while he kept time with an intricate counter-rhythm tapped out on the silver tray.

I suspected the beautiful lady with the tin-opener teeth may have been intended for me. Ali's ponderously beautiful dance was certainly aimed at Carol. He had fallen for her – as most people did. Later, she told me that whenever I was out of sight, he would make an amorous lunge at her. Fortunately, his great bulk helped to keep most of him at bay but then he came up with a subtle strategy. He invited me to accompany him, by mule, while he made a full day's inspection of his forest. Ali was good company and his men liked him. So did I. We had a great day together, checking forest works, stopping at huts for picnics or hot sweet mint tea and I was able to interview dozens of forest workers and survey miles of woodland. In all, we covered 42 kilometres but as we finally turned for home in the twilight of the evening, I began to feel very sore. I was not a seasoned rider like Ali and I now discovered that there were parts of me that had never been rubbed quite like this before and probably were never supposed to be. For the last few miles, I had to hold myself off the saddle with both hands and when we got back to his house, I had to walk everywhere with my feet nearly a yard apart. This handicap gave him a definite advantage in his pursuit of Carol and apparently, he did manage to land a couple of smacking kisses before we took our final, affectionate farewell. My legs didn't get back together again for several days. I called it "Ali's revenge".

Another source of amusement during our expedition was the car. We enjoyed being together in it, bumping along sandy tracks. We loved its panda stickers and its orange tarpaulin and we liked taking photographs of it in remote locations. On the whole it did very well, but once a month or so it would take a little holiday. On one occasion we had to push it to a garage because, while the engine was purring happily, the wheels were not connected to it. The only mechanic we could find was a ten-year old boy. He quickly discovered that a connecting pin had fallen out of the axle rod. He searched the garage until he found a likely-looking screwdriver which he hammered into the empty hole, sawing off the handle to create a perfect replacement. We were very impressed by his presence of mind. He charged us a pound and the screwdriver held for the rest of the trip. Another time we noticed smoke seeping out from behind the dashboard. My experience of French cars, before and since, was that, while they have charm and sang-froid, their electrics can be eccentric, so we thought it prudent to get it checked. This time the mechanic took a look, shrugged his shoulders, disappeared into his store and emerged laconically with a fire extinguisher which he donated to our enterprise.

Before our adventures with Ali and the beautiful forests of the Rif we had taken a break from woodland research to head south, to the Sahara. This meant crossing the Atlas Mountains. The car didn't like this plan at all. Part way up it petered to a halt. Carol and I were behind in a camper-van, with a local ornithologist, Jean Pineau, his partner Anny and their baby. We watched with amazement as a lorry reversed towards the stricken Renault, spilling out its load of seasonal workers who put their shoulders to the little car and got it going again. A few kilometres further up, the Renault slowed again and again the men jumped out of the back of their lorry to push. This happened over and over, all the way up to the top, where the Renault seemed to get its breath back and we never had trouble again.

Jean had spent a lot of time looking for raptors in the North of Morocco. He'd never seen our eagle but he was very gloomy about its prospects even if we did find a breeding pair. Most raptors' nests he had found got robbed and he said levels of persecution were very high. But for a week or two our minds were on a lighter subject. Jean had brought rings and nets and it was our plan to find a suitable oasis in the Sahara and ring migrants under his license. Together we drove down deep into the Draa Valley and set up camp in what seemed a perfect spot, a little isolated grove of fruit trees with lush corn growing underneath, surrounded by miles of bare sand. On our first morning a friendly boy arrived from the nearby village. He started up a pump and water suddenly gushed from a little standpipe. He took a quick shower and then opened and closed dozens of little mud gates with his hands to guide the water through a maze of little channels like the moats on a child's sand-castle at the seaside. The wealth of the village grew in that little oasis but we were allowed to tramp all over it, putting up our nets and controlling their contents. We took excruciating care not to damage their delicate irrigation system but the village didn't know that when they gave us permission to work there. Up north, whenever we had camped away from the protection of our foresters, we had been troubled by thieves. I used to lay trip wires at night, hung with tightly attached pots and pans, all round our tents, to alert us to intruders. I always collected a pile of rocks to hurl if I heard the pots rattle, but the robbers always escaped with some sort of trophy – our wash basin, our fruit, our towels. In the desert, however, the people were different. You could feel it. One day a group of teenagers crept out of the bushes and surrounded us. The girls were fascinated by Carol and Jules. They wanted to touch them and hold their rings and bracelets. These all came off in a flash and were passed round and tried on with great excitement. But then everything was respectfully returned and replaced as you knew it would be.

After Jean and Anny left, we continued ringing for another week and I see from my notes that we caught only the second Isabelline wheatear to be ringed in Morocco. But we too had more serious work to do so we decided to make one last loop into the southern desert before turning back towards eagle territory. We got as far south as Sidi Ifni, a little desert coastal town that had only recently been ceded by Spain. This region was still known as the Spanish Sahara and there was a certain amount of warlike tension in the air. On the outskirts of the settlement, we found a group of common sandpipers feeding in the sand. This was the same species that I'd caught carrying Mr Harrison's ring the year before at Santillana. I liked common sandpipers so I settled down to photograph them. High on the hill behind, there was a small mud fort. I had even looked at it through the lens thinking it might be an ancient ruin of interest, but it seemed to be a modern fortress with soldiers so not one for my collection. It was very, very lucky I didn't photograph it.

A big car pulled up and a rough-looking man got out and asked what we were doing. We explained about common sandpipers and he went away, apparently satisfied. Not so, however. Ten minutes later he returned with two policemen and we were arrested. We spent several hours sitting in a hot room in the police station before they announced that we were to be taken two hundred kilometres north to the "Hotel de Police" in Agadir. Even I knew that this would not be a nice hotel and there would be no passing go and no collecting two hundred pounds. An additional problem with this plan was that we would have to leave our car and we would have to abandon Jules. She had been ill that morning and had stayed back at the house we were using. But as it is well known that spies never get sick, she had not been arrested or even inquired about and now she would have no idea what had happened to her friends.

In Agadir, they were positively hostile to common sandpipers and were unimpressed by either the Wild Word Fund or the Winston Churchill Trust. Carol was locked up in a carpeted room with several unfortunate girls who had been caught not carrying their papers, most of them with nothing to sell but themselves. Toni and I however, were dispatched to the dungeons. Our cell was an underground room, with a stone floor and no furniture. There was a small barred window, open to the air, high up in the far wall. If you ran hard at the wall and jumped, you could grab the bars and, for as long as you could hold on, you could do a spot of bird watching in the little patch of sky visible above the prison. That way we saw our very first pallid swifts. At one point, I'd just finished and dropped down and Toni was just starting his run-up, when he stopped and said that if we were in the zoo, all the visitors would be very happy. Why's that, I asked. Because, he said, both the animals are moving about at the same time.

We stayed there for four days on bread and water. Every day we were taken upstairs for interrogation about sandpipers. Our ornithological seminars didn't seem to progress very far. The only thing that changed each day was that the vicious looking man who didn't ask the questions inched a bit closer. Boy did he want to punch us. On the fifth day, we were escorted to a different room where we found Carol. She looked a bit tired but she soon rallied when a big plate of eggs arrived for us all. Now it had been my experience, after, for instance, eleven years of boarding school, that a plate of eggs usually presaged a general improvement in conditions. And so it proved. After our meal – which curiously, Carol didn't record in her diet sheet even though it was, in its way the best meal we'd ever had – we were introduced to the Chief of Police. He was dapper and friendly and full of apologies. They had developed my film and indeed had found only sandpipers. No fortress, no soldiers. He gave me back my camera and my big lens, though not sadly the film, and we were free to go. In the package I had received from the Churchill Trust, I had found 500 cute little visiting cards with my name on. Here at last was an opportunity to use one. As he held out his hand to shake mine, I pressed one into his hand and said, as I thought any spy would, "ma carte de visite."

I can honestly attest that when inmates leave prison, they stand around outside, blinking their eyes and wondering how they will ever catch up with this new modern world they have stepped out into. Well, okay, we had only been inside for five days but we were definitely disorientated. We'd never meant to come to Agadir, we'd lost Jules and we had no car. Toni now manfully decided to hitch straight back to Sidi Ifni while Carol and I looked for a really nice hotel where we could all celebrate when we got back together. I felt very guilty that I'd got them all into trouble but Carol soon had me laughing. She told me she had made friends with all the prostitutes and they had all learned a lot from each other. She'd spent the days teaching them English.

When Jules and Toni joined us the next day, we sat down to our first proper restaurant meal and Jules told us what had happened to her. She had received a message about where we were and had gone straight away to the main post office and phoned the British Consulate, seven hundred miles away in Casablanca. The phone was answered by the consul's maid who spoke only French. Jules was the one member of our team whose French was not quite comme il faut so the conversation had gone badly. Jules had ended up summoning her sole phrase, shouting je ne comprends pas and slamming the receiver down before bursting into unJules-like tears of rage and frustration. This happened every day, much to the amusement of an ever-growing party of sadists who headed for the telephone exchange as soon as they saw Jules leaving the house, where we'd been staying. Eventually, however, she had managed to speak to the Consul. He had promised to lobby the Procureur du Roi on our behalf but because this was the government's most senior law officer it was a delicate matter. He had explained that, while even a very junior official can arrest you for spying, only a very senior one can take the responsibility of releasing you. It could take weeks, even months. After that story we agreed that five days had been a doddle and we'd better get on with looking for eagles.

We left Morocco six weeks later, on 9th June. By then we had done our best to cover most of the Rif. We had witnessed the migration of thousands of honey buzzards, gliding in parties of several hundred, through the misty wooded passes of the Rif Mountains. We found beautiful forests full of firecrests, flycatchers and nuthatches. We saw vultures and long-legged buzzards and smaller eagles but we never found a trace of the Spanish imperial eagles that all the books said were breeding there. Before we left, however, we did find the most beautiful place in Morocco. In late May we worked our way up towards the Mediterranean coast. The forester there was a football enthusiast and we spent our first night with him extolling the wonderful skills of Johan Cruyff and discussing the relative merits of Barcelona and Leeds, who were heading for a clash in the European Cup. Fired by comradeliness, he decided to share a secret with us. The next morning, we drove down a long, winding track, descending all the while through the forest until it ended beside a picture-book cottage. This was completely empty. It had a tiled roof, a wooden balcony and the floors were cool marble. And best of all, its windows opened out onto a completely deserted fairy-tale bay of yellow sand

and blue sea with the Mediterranean lapping the beach not ten metres away. Here he said, smiling, we could stay as long as we wanted. It was like a honeymoon and a reward for our long months of work. For a week we swam and lay in the sun. We paddled our camping lilos out to the little island just offshore and at night we slept on the balcony under the stars listening to the knock knock knock of the red-necked nightjars.

The bay must have been teeming with sardines. Sometimes they would boil to the surface setting off a feeding frenzy of thousands of gulls and shearwaters and gannets. Schools of dolphins would slice their way in from the open sea and then the pilot whales would arrive, up to a hundred of them, circling the bay relentlessly. On the island, a pair of ospreys – scarce breeders in Morocco - were building a nest. They went back and forth to the forest behind us, emerging with sturdy branches held lengthways in their talons, which they crammed onto their already conspicuous pile of unruly sticks. There were two other nests nearby but they appeared to be unused. And, as we lay on our backs, joyful after swimming, we watched the continuous spring migration of the storks and raptors heading north. They would reach the coast in the sky above us and then always turn West, presumably following the line of the shore until it swung up to Gibraltar where they could cross the sea at its narrowest point.

Our last couple of days we spent with Jean Pineau and Anny at their home near Tangiers. Jean helped us go through our notes and organise our reports that would later be published in Oryx, the journal of the Fauna Preservation Society, and by WWF. Discussing with him helped me harden up my theory that all modern records of Spanish imperial eagles in Morocco were likely to be migrating birds. They were mostly of immatures and mostly observed either in March going north or October going south. He agreed with us that our failure to find any signs of breeding was significant.

A year later I attended the formal awards ceremony for my Winston Churchill Fellowship. The hefty, solid silver medal, embossed with the gruff features of the great man and duly engraved with the details of the much lesser one, was presented to me by HM

Queen Elizabeth the Queen Mother. As I loomed over this tiny little old lady I kept saying to myself "don't crush her hand, don't crush her hand;" but she looked up at me, sparkling and dauntless and asked sweetly "And how is the eagle?". And I replied "I'm sorry to say, madam that the eagle isn't. In Morocco, I've declared it extinct."

5

"SAVING" THE EBRO DELTA

It is harder to prove a negative than a positive and it is harder to prove that a species no longer exists than to find evidence when it does. The last known tiger in Java, for instance, was shot in 1984 but rumours persist even now that there might still be one lurking, however unlikely, in the few scraps of forest that remain on the island. Our clear assertion that we could find no evidence of a viable breeding population of Spanish imperial eagles in Morocco was not proof of its extinction. It did, however, shift the focus of its future conservation firmly to Spain. Legislators, biologists and enthusiasts began to take serious proactive measures to improve the bird's chances. These included much better protection, the repair of nests and even supplementary feeding and reintroductions. By 2012, they were reporting a total population of 324 pairs, including six in Portugal. This would represent a ten-fold increase.

Our work in Morocco proved to us that we could make a difference, that we could start a ball rolling. So when I received a slightly hyperbolic letter from Toni in early 1977, its contents didn't seem as nutty to me as they might otherwise have done. Over several scrawled pages of foolscap, he frantically outlined a new appalling plan to destroy Spain's Ebro Delta. The Rio Ebro, famous in its upper reaches, for Rioja wine, flows out to the Mediterranean past the little fishing village of Amposta in the province of Tarragona. There it flowers in its last miles into a wide marshland of lakes and reedbeds, ending in two great spits of sand thrown up to the north and south of its final exit. In the 1970s this was known only to the province's eel fishermen and hunters but birdwatchers were just beginning to suspect its superb potential for wildlife. Now, however, the authorities had come up with a huge tourist scheme, a sprawling urbanisation with four thousand tourist dwellings, a heliport, boating facilities, cafes and restaurants and all sorts of monstrosities. So, like Don Quixote, I was to jump on my white horse, ride through La Mancha to Tarragona and knock over these hideous windmills – in a word, Toni wanted me to come immediately and save the Ebro Delta.

It was a grey, February day in Oxford when I received the letter. It had been grey, miserable and gloomy for months – the most depressing winter I ever remember. It wasn't cold but the sun never, ever shone and most days there was a dull drizzle. I won't say this made a difference, but I have to state the facts. I was supposed to be writing a thesis on Shakespeare's Problem Plays. My supervisor for that first year was John Bayley, the novelist Iris Murdoch's husband. I had read all her books and he was a delightful man with an endearing stutter. He would listen with half an ear to my theories about Lucio, Parolles and Thersites and the influence of Montaigne on their creation but he really perked up when I talked about birds. I once told him, for instance, that hobbies, small, shy falcons, were much more common than people generally believed. I met him years later and he still remembered this, though not so much about my thesis. Gradually the Ebro Delta began to take over.

Carol had wisely gone off to law school and I had less wisely let her slip out of my life. On the day Toni's letter arrived, however, I had a visitor from America. Her name was Susan. An elderly classics professor once revealed to me the true art of exploring a museum. Never try to see everything, he told me. Instead, fix your eyes on just one object of beauty – and then follow it from room to room. I'd had no doubt, a year earlier when we'd met, that the most beautiful object in the Picasso Museum in Barcelona that day was Susan Gillette. Susan was a striking redhead from Illinois and a few months after that first meeting, we were camping together on Isle Royale, in Lake Michigan, looking for wolf tracks and photographing moose. Her family were in publishing and in that summer of 1976 a small company grant had enabled us to drive round the Western states, camping in the vast National Forests of Montana, Wyoming, Colorado, Idaho and Oregon. I wrote an article about the trip for Nigel Sitwell's Wildlife Magazine. We even went to Maui, in Hawaii and camped in the Crater of the Haleakala volcano so I could photograph and write about the Hawaiian geese, the same ones that Peter Scott had helped to save.

So now I asked Susan if she'd like to be Sancho Panza and ride with me to rescue the Ebro Delta. But first I needed to formulate a serious strategy and try to raise some basic funds for the trip. Because the Delta was so little known at the time, I had to trust Toni's information and my own hunches as to what diversity of species such a magnificent landscape might contain, but there was not much to go on to incite wider support. I needed to go there first to gather the evidence for any sort of international campaign. I turned for help to the Fauna Preservation Society. FPS (now called the Flora and Fauna Preservation Society) had been founded by Richard Fitter, a greatly respected British naturalist and his wife Maisie was the editor in chief of Oryx, the conservation journal that had published my Moroccan report and my paper on the Hawaiian goose. Much of the day-to-day work of running Oryx and the society was carried out by David Helton. He was something of a rare species himself: a quiet Texan, and I liked him immensely. Any visit to Regent's Park Zoo, where FPS was based, had become an excuse to visit David. He was wise, humorous and helpful. He immediately saw the potential significance of the Ebro Delta, he reserved space in Oryx for a future report, he offered to help with wider publication and FPS approved a grant towards our travel costs. Armed with this backing I was able to secure a Vaughan Cornish Award from Oxford University which doubled our fighting fund. This only amounted to a few hundred pounds but it would be enough to pay our fuel and food so we saddled Brutus and headed south.

Brutus was a middle-aged, long-wheelbase, diesel Land-Rover, with a truck cab. I had bought him from a family friend, Guy Pickford, who just happened to be a world expert on old Land-Rovers. Guy's Land-Rovers didn't let you down and he'd managed to find a rare blue canvas cover for the back that had plastic windows. I thought Brutus was the best vehicle on the road and the next months of travel, camping, research and campaigning would be some of the happiest of my life.

On our slow way through France, we rested for a couple of days at the house of my brother David's in-laws. His wife Christine was French and her parents lived in the picturesque village of Belfort du Quercy in the Lot. Rene, her father, had been the manager of the famous Carlton Hotel in Cannes and he always served delicious wine of obscure provenance. But he had a sadness in his past. As a young man during the war, he had failed to co-operate with the Nazis and had ended up in the notorious concentration camp at Dachau. This had left him with what I took to be a profound stillness inside, a resourceful, charismatic gravitas which I found inspiring. It felt good to have him on our side.

Further south, we camped in a vineyard and woke in the morning to find ourselves surrounded by laughing workers who'd come to weed the vines. The following night we camped on the edge of a farmer's field and he asked the next day very sweetly, 'Vous avez bien dormis?'. I think our happiness was disarming. In early May we arrived in Barcelona, steering Brutus with increasing difficulty through its maze of narrow streets. Toni now lived in a dark third floor flat, in the old part of the city and it was time for a council of war. Like all armies fighting out of their depth, we needed a serious ally. Xavier Ferrer had won the Philips Young Scientist of the Year Award a few years earlier for a pioneering study of the Delta's birds. He already knew how important the area could be and he offered to be our guide for a couple of days, so we drove the next two hundred kilometres together in convoy. When we arrived in that flat land of dykes and reedbeds, Xavier explained that he had to take some water samples. He was doing a study on the plant life of the Delta's lagoons which would later form part of his doctorate on the ducks, so we had a spare half hour before our tour could begin. I see, from my notes of that day, 12th May 1977, that in those minutes while we waited, we saw 40 red-crested pochards, ten purple herons, three gull-billed terns, a water rail, a little bittern, 24 black-winged stilts, three marsh harriers, four singing savi's warblers, 15 reed warblers and two great-reed warblers, ditto singing, a cuckoo and 20 black terns. It was already clear that the Ebro Delta had to be a nature reserve, not a tourist city.

Xavier was an unusual man. He was my age, with dark eyes that danced with enthusiasm for the intricacies of all living things. He was precise in his science, very knowledgeable but also gentle and kind. He said to me, in his halting but expressive English, that people like us, with this deep-grained love of nature were rare – as we did seem to be in those days – so we must stick together. "We are a family", he said, "the international family of naturalists." A quarter of a century later, in a tiger reserve in India, I heard Catalan being spoken as a jeep drove past. In it were four young men with enormous cameras. By then I was quite well-known myself in tiger areas, so I took the liberty of stopping them to ask if they knew my friend Xavier Ferrer. When they heard I knew Xavier they grew very excited. "Professor Ferrer, he is our guru", they said "so we are happy to know anyone who is a friend of his." Xavier loved to teach. In February 2020, he and I, with our partners and friends, took a flat-bottomed boat through the reedbeds of the Albufera de Valencia and he was still teaching me about the macrophytes of Spanish reedbeds. But that's families for you.

Xavier showed us the lakes and reedbeds, the canals with their big wooden eel traps, the irrigated fields of artichokes and the great spits of sand, each many miles long, pushed out by the indefatigable river. He introduced us to the guard on the private hunting reserve on Buda Island and he taught us how to navigate the labyrinth of tracks, some of which went somewhere and most of which did not. He also gave us a book. El Systemes Naturals Del Delta De L'Ebre had just been published, in Catalan, by the Institute of Catalan Natural History. It was a detailed study of the whole ecosystem, with a large part devoted to fish, since fishing had long been a staple cottage-industry on the Delta. But there were sections on flora, invertebrates and birds, this last written by Xavier himself. It provided us with an irrefutable arsenal of facts and it also contained a worth-its-weight-in-gold, wonderfully detailed map showing the topography of every hectare of the Delta's three hundred and fifty square kilometres.

For the next four weeks we camped on the Delta, photographing the landscape, its birds and its other wildlife, recording everything we saw so that, in our report, we could bear witness to the bountiful world of this little-known paradise. Brutus was our palace on wheels. He was quite a simple palace. I'd cut two large boards to lie across the rear compartment. These provided a cosy sleeping area under Guy's completely waterproof cover. But, most ingeniously, I thought, the boards could be slid back, one over the other, so we could cook in the revealed well and sit comfortably to eat our meals and write our notes. The whole invention had involved one large plank and a saw but I was very proud of it. Brutus could go anywhere. On the damp sand we could drive the twelve kilometres up the shore to the tips of the sand spits, Fangar to the North and Banya to the south, and camp far from anyone. Or we could tuck ourselves under the pines on the edge of the dunes, or by the big salinas with their flocks of wading birds, or, on still nights, right on the edge of the sea with the water a few feet away. Susan was a resourceful cook. She would slip off into the fields and I would come home to a delicious meal of fresh artichokes cooked in a sauce of tarragon. She would make spaghettis that would make a Bolognese proud or cook fish from the fish traps. The empty beaches and the deserted Mediterranean were our shower room. She loved to swim and I would photograph her, rising from the waves like Boticelli's Venus, only more beautiful.

Only once were we disturbed. One night, quite late, a Guardia Civil shone a torch under our tarpaulin and I told him in my best and most authoritative Pigeon-Spanish that I was there studying birds for the Spanish Ornithological Society. I don't know whether he was impressed or just flummoxed but he went away and we were never bothered again.

I spent many days hunched in my portable hide out on the marshes. On the well-tried photographer's principle that birds can't count, Susan would accompany me to the hide, give me time to get comfortable or pick up the stuff I'd accidentally dropped out of the window, and then she would depart, taking the attention of anxious birds with her. For a while the large green bump in the middle of their habitat would be a cause of mistrust but provided its contents didn't move too much or make inappropriate noises, the birds would forget me eventually and I could add them to my portfolio: terns and avocets, stilts and gulls, pratincoles and plovers, all busy nesting. When I'd finished for the day, I'd hang a cloth out the back of the hide and when Susan saw it she would come and retrieve me, fooling the birds again. I've always loved working in my hides. I love the intimacy that you can establish with your subject and the possibility that you see something surprising or even new. I love the meditative effect of being quiet and alone and concentrating. I also like the fact that no-one can get to me – no fax, no phone, no lawyer's letters – and that while everyone thinks I'm working terribly hard I may actually be just having a little delicious day-dream.

The more we saw of the Delta, the more convinced we were of its potential. Xavier had already told us that the ninety-odd pairs of sandwich terns on Buda island represented the only colony in the whole of the Iberian Peninsula and that the Delta's large breeding population of around fifteen hundred common terns was also almost unique. There were other red-letter species, like squacco herons, moustached warblers and slender-billed gulls and the fifteen hundred breeding pairs of red-crested pochards might already be of global importance. But what struck me, as I travelled up and down the long expanses of empty beach and looked at the great salinas and lakes was that this amazing landscape could get even better. It was obvious that birds bred most successfully on the lake islands and the more distant sand points, where they were least disturbed. What would happen if disturbance could be reduced over the whole Delta?

We photographed a resident flock of around a hundred flamingos in the salt pans. They stayed there the whole year round, apparently but they didn't breed. Why not? I knew that in the Camargue, in southern France, recent improved protection measures and an imaginative initiative to build fake nests to incite breeding had been very success-ful. Was this a big enough flock to seed such a revival here on the Ebro Delta? And on the most isolated stretches of beach, we'd noticed another interesting species, one that was new to me: Audouin's gulls. We saw them every day, foraging off-shore or sitting quietly on the sand. Audouin's gulls are large, pale gulls with big red beaks and dark, grey-green legs and at the time, they were very rare, found only in or close to the Mediterranean. The world population in the late 1960s had been estimated at just a thousand pairs. Audouin's gulls are specialist fishermen. The Ebro bay was full of fish. Was there a chance they might breed here?

I wasn't sure about the Audouin's gulls. I didn't know enough about them, but I noted their presence with interest in my report. I did have higher hopes for the flamingos, however, so when we finished our work and summarised our conclusions for Xavier and Toni, we drove north to France and the Camargue, the big brother of Europe's river Deltas, where the Rhone fans out into the Mediter-ranean and wild horses famously gallop through the marshes.

Our goal was Tour du Valat. Established as a research station in 1954, it comprised three thousand hectares of prime Camargue wetlands and over the years it had educated a small coterie of top biologists. These days there are more than eighty full-time staff working on a wide range of pan-Mediterranean conservation projects. But when we were invited to brief the Tour du Valat team in June 1977 it consisted of just a handful of scientists who focused on core research within the Camargue itself. I thought they would make good allies in the fight to save the Ebro Delta and the person I was most excited to meet was Dr Alan Johnson. I liked him as soon as we shook hands. He was a sandy-haired, quiet-mannered Englishman, about ten years older than me and quite diffidently he offered to show us what he had achieved with the Camargue's flamingos. He took us in his Land-Rover down the sun-dried mud tracks of the marshes to the edge of the Etang de Fangassier, the heart of his flamingo kingdom. The wide brackish lake was inflorescent with birds. There were thousands upon thousands of flamingos, adults sweeping their shoe-like bills through the lake surface, and chicks huddled on mud piles out in the middle.

Fringed on one side by green, salt-resistant tamarisk bushes, the water, clotted with birds, spread out southwards, gradually choking with scattered reedbeds and fingers of marsh and then opening out again behind the glinting Mediterranean. Alan explained that what we were looking at was partly a human construct. Salt water was pumped every spring and summer by the salt company, Salin de Giraud, from the Mediterranean through the lake systems to the great salinas on the Eastern edge, behind us. There the water evaporated, leaving vast encrustations of salt for the company to harvest, mainly for industrial use. The company was probably the largest of its kind in Europe, with production reaching nearly fourteen hundred metric tonnes in some years. During the winter, parts of Fangassier and the other lakes were left to slowly dry out, before being reflooded the following spring.

Although flamingos had bred here since the 1600s, success had only ever been sporadic. When Alan arrived at Tour du Valat in the early 1960s there had been almost no nests at all. Then he teamed up with Salin de Giraud. In the winter of 1969-70 he had helped oversee the building of a substantial, flattish, artificial island in Fangassier to provide a spacious nest-site, safe from flooding and predators. They waited excitedly the following spring as the flamingos returned and the lake was flooded as usual but only a few birds bred and none on his new beautiful island. What could be wrong? Perhaps they just needed to get used to it, but when it was ignored again the following year, Alan realised that a more daring approach was needed. Perhaps the flamingos required a nudge to persuade them that his stretch of mud was in fact prime flamingo real estate. In the winter of 1973, he constructed a smart new housing project with all mod-cons for homeless flamingos. This would have made any town-planner of the era proud and indeed the designs were pretty similar to the new buildings adorning my home-town of Oxford at the time. They were basically mud pies. Lots of them, dotted all over the island in lines. Could it really be that the birds would arrive, see that other folks were already settling and they'd better jump on the housing ladder themselves before it was too late? Well, not quite. But in 1974 some of his mud pies had tenants. And now, three years later?

Alan, in his gentle, modest way, told us that there were now nearly 12,000 pairs breeding there. Of course, there was a downside. He now had the job of ringing the chicks – a real labour of love providing you enjoy the broiling summer heat and being drenched in salt water and covered in flamingo poo. It was staggering to me that such a turn-around could have occurred so fast and I thought again of the small resident flock we'd just left on the Ebro Delta. Could they too, be inspired to reproduce? Alan explained that much depended on the management of the salt company. The date each year that the lake was flooded seemed to influence quite precisely the birds' breeding diary, with the first eggs being laid about three weeks later. Probably the birds needed to feel confident that their island home would last the season before they ventured to nest. No good plopping out your eggs and having them eaten by foxes because your protective moat had vanished.

Alan's charm, the status of Tour du Valat and the admirable good-will of Salins de Giraud ensured forty years of flamingo success, during which more than one hundred and fifty thousand flamingo chicks were raised on Fangassier's adobe housing project. But in 2007 no flamingos bred. The company had been forced by wider economic pressures to reduce its salt production by two thirds and so didn't flood the lake until August by which time it was too late for any breeding success. Subsequently, the area was absorbed into the Parc naturel regional de Camargue which now protects around six thousand three hundred hectares of key habitat but the crisis prompted an interesting footnote. At an international workshop promoted by IUCN's Species Survival Commission and held in Spain in November 2007, Alan and his Tour du Valat colleagues suggested that over-management of the flamingos' habitat might not always be entirely beneficial to the species. Flamingos have evolved a transitory habit of moving around their breeding range en masse so they can take advantage of good conditions where and when they arise. Was it possible that by creating too great a reliance on a single site, there was a risk of reducing the birds' flexibility? Such a question presupposes the existence of alternative breeding habitats. When Alan built his island there were very few left around the Mediterranean but forty years later regional flamingo numbers had increased to around a hundred thousand and, as we shall see, the Camargue was no longer their only major home.

It was uplifting, that day with Alan, out on the saltpans, seeing his pride in all his grey fluffy flamingo chicks, surrounded by that excitingly pungent odour of drying mud and guano. To sensible people it smells like something you don't want on your clothes but to bird-lovers it means you've hit the jackpot. And the jackpot that day was twenty thousand stately pink birds all around us. In the evening, we returned to Tour du Valat where I told Alan and his friends about what we'd seen at the Ebro Delta. In those days, the Camargue, the Danube Delta and the Coto Donana were internationally known but the Ebro was not. I described the lakes and reed beds, the long, long sandy beaches and the huge tern colonies. I mentioned the flamingos and the Audouin's gulls and what I believed to be the immense potential of the place. And I told them about the unimaginative but very real plan to cover it with concrete. For me, an important player would be their "boss" Luc Hoffmann. He wasn't there but I knew I'd piqued their interest and that they would help brief him. Luc Hoffmann, a scion of the famous Swiss-based Hoffmann-La Roche business interests, was the founder of the Tour du Valat Station. Although he was on the board of the great company his real passion lay with nature and especially birds. He was a founder member of WWF, had been involved in the purchase of the Coto Donana and back in 1947 he had bought Tour du Valat with the plan to make it a nature reserve. A word from him to the IUCN in Geneva would not go amiss.

A great day in the field, a mutual cause, both give a feeling of camaraderie. I still remember the pleasure of those couple of days at the station, even though I've never been back. We ended up all singing songs and playing guitars. I sang Vaughan Williams's Turtle Dove. It's a sad lament, probably sadder the way I sang it, but it was somehow not inappropriate.

Back home I waited anxiously for my slides to find their way back to me from the depths of the Kodak and Agfa laboratories. I wrote a lengthy, detailed report for FPS and IUCN and my article for Oryx. When the films finally turned up, I was pleased with them and I felt I now had a package that justified the grants I'd had and I went to see David Helton at London Zoo. He had a visitor with him, his friend John Burton. I'd never met John but I knew he was already an established contributor to New Scientist magazine, which I saw as a bit above my reach. He was quite a bit older than me but he listened along with David to my account of the Ebro and they both seemed genuinely keen to act. David promised to publish my piece in Oryx and then John said I should definitely write a major piece about the Delta for New Scientist. I was slightly overawed but, with what I later found was characteristic generosity, he offered to recommend me to the features editor and to guide me through the process. He was true to his word. A week later I took my draft back to him and David. John read it through quietly and then with a pencil he ringed a paragraph in the middle of the first page and arrowed it up to the top. With one stroke he'd taken the plod out of the piece and made it sprint. I was very pleased by this elegant little lesson. It taught me that the words you use are less important than the order in which you use them.

The New Scientist piece was published as a full feature a few weeks later. Of course, this was a small victory, but an important one. New Scientist was a respected journal with a worldwide readership. It was not a niche organ preaching to the converted – not that there were many of them in those days. It was read by scientists and decision makers. For the Delta to be bandstanded over four or five pages would, I believed, give the place added status. Richard Fitter had agreed to present my report to the IUCN and Rob Hume, the excellent editor of Birds, the RSPB magazine, had commissioned me to write a portrait of the Delta for him as well.

So there it was. Toni had set me on an impossibly Quixotic quest. I had saddled my horse and tilted at the windmills and lo and behold, the windmills were vanquished. I don't think for a moment that it was the sight of my steed alone that frightened them off but, nevertheless, the forces of darkness retreated and plans for a tourist urbanisation on the Ebro Delta were abandoned. In 1983, an increasingly empowered conservation movement in Catalunya, inspired among others by my friend Xavier Ferrer, ensured that the Ebro delta was declared a Natural Park. It included seven thousand eight hundred hectares of the key habitats. It has since been declared in addition, a Ramsar site, a Natura 2000 site and a Special Protected Area. At the last count there were five thousand nine hundred breeding pairs of flamingos in and around the salinas where I originally photographed them and on the sandy point where Susan and I camped with Brutus there is now a colony of fifteen thousand Audouin's gulls, nearly seventy percent of the world population.

6

AMERICA

Three wildlife films made an indelible impression on my early childhood. Heinz Seilmann's 1955 woodpecker film, Zimmerleute des Waldes, (Carpenters of the Forest) used one-way glass to provide windows into the secret world within the trunks of trees. Suddenly, inside our living-room we could watch woodpeckers hollowing out nest cavities, laying their eggs and feeding chicks. At home, we had three of the four film stars on our bird tables but I had never seen anything as intimate or revelatory as this. Seilmann also created a memorable sound-scape including a carpentry competition in which the little, middle-sized, large and humongous woodpeckers seem to take it in turns to show-off their tree-whacking skills, like jazz players tossing the rhythm back and forth amongst themselves, each trying to outdo the other in ever more extreme and intricate syncopations. The second film I fell in love with was White Wilderness, made in 1958 by Walt Disney. I loved snow and clean empty landscapes and this was the world of White Wilderness, a portrait of Arctic wildlife. It contained the never-to-be-forgotten scene of lemmings apparently committing suicide, rushing across the tundra in their hundreds to throw themselves off a cliff. It was mad, it was bad science and it was subsequently much criticised but to my eight year-old eyes it was magic. And of course, it had the scene of baby polar bears popping out through the white ice-crust of their birth chamber and tumbling about on the snowy slopes just the way we liked to do. My favourite film, however, was The Living Desert. Made in 1953, this too was a Disney production and it won the 1954 Oscar for Best Documentary Feature. I loved it because it was about small folk, trapdoor spiders and tarantulas and lizards, the whole populous world of the Sonoma Desert which we assumed, wrongly, that we would never see for ourselves. There was a wonderful scene inside a bat cave when forty million bats, awoken when the filming lights were snapped on, rippled in a kind of massive Mexican wave before they all peed on the cameraman. But best of all was the notorious love-dance of the scorpions. I later learned that this was not a love dance but a brief fight. The sequence was then printed in reverse so that for every step forwards there seemed to be a step back and for every shuffle sideways there was a shimmy the other way. The whole combination was then edited to fit the music of a jaunty little waltz. It was outrageous, it was complete nonsense but I thought it was utterly delightful. I went straight out and bought the book, Song of Wild Laughter by one of the Disney cameramen, Jack Couffer and that along with David Attenborough's Zoo Quest to Madagascar, became the founding tomes of my wildlife and film-book collection. I still have them both.

I had always known that one day, I too, would make films. But I was like a tortoise thinking that somehow, I would learn to fly. My family inclined towards technophobia. My father did once change a wheel – on the car of my first, seventeen-year-old, sort-of-girlfriend in fact – but it fell off an hour later in the middle of Oxford. The thrust of our upbringing and education had been firmly aimed at books and matters of the mind. After the inspiration and excitement of the Ebro Delta adventure, however, I realised that my little life had reached a crossroads.

I had finished my Shakespeare thesis. At least I thought I had but I now had a new supervisor. John Bayley had taken a sabbatical to write his next book and John Wilders had taken me on. He seemed

genuinely appreciative of my insights but he pointed out that interpretation and scholarship were two different things. He could see that
I had planned an expeditionary life among the literary high peaks,
blown here and there by the winds of inspiration. Scholarship,
however, mostly involved years of digging and delving down in the
nettle patches and brambles, hoping to spot some small factual
seedling that others had neglected. I didn't want to dig and delve. I
wanted to change the way people thought – not what they thought
about Shakespeare, but what they thought about the natural world.
The way to do this, I was convinced, was to make films.

But how do you make a tortoise fly? Of course, I'd already made
three television films but Lone had done much of the photography
and anyway I needed to move beyond a clockwork Bolex, black and
white daylight spools and a toy tape recorder. I needed to get my
hands on a whole range of real professional equipment and play with
it until I was no more intimidated by it than by an electric tooth-
brush. I needed to go to film school.

I reckoned I had two choices. I could either try to gain entry to the
London Film School, or maybe Paris and work to pay my fees or I
could go to America, where I might be eligible for a scholarship. I sat
for days in the library, exercising my recently abandoned digging and
delving skills, and I discovered that Los Angeles alone had three
excellent schools. I was less interested in aesthetic theory, I wanted
practical experience, so I compared the pupil to camera ratio at each
school. The one that stood out was CalArts - the California Institute
of the Arts. It seemed to be quite a new, avant-garde set-up, established partly with money from Walt Disney who wanted a supply of
well-trained animators. I liked the idea of learning along-side Donald
Duck and, more seriously, it chimed with my memories of those early
wildlife films. It also had lots of gear and if I could get onto the
Masters programme I would be issued with my own camera package.
But even if I got in, how on earth would I pay for it?

There were two alluring post-graduate scholarships that could
fund a British graduate to study in the USA, though both appeared to
be intimidatingly competitive. One was a Fulbright Award. The

advantage of the Fulbright was that there seemed to be quite a few of them, the disadvantage was that they didn't cover living expenses and their remit was highly academic. The Harkness Fellowships offered more money and, though they did occasionally go to practicing artists and journalists, there were always around a thousand applicants and they only offered a maximum of twenty a year. Worse still, for me, the selectors seemed increasingly – and wisely – to be focusing on new cutting-edge science, particularly modern genetics, gene manipulation and potential medical developments. Indeed, one of my Merton friends, John Rosamund, had won a Harkness a few years earlier to pursue post-doctoral work in an abstruse area of chemistry at Stanford. Needless to say, neither scheme, Fulbright or Harkness, had ever given a scholarship to someone who wanted to make wildlife films, or films of any sort. I decided to apply for both.

The application forms were demanding. I had to face the fact that I didn't have a lot to offer. I had my list of adventures. Yes, I wanted to change the world and I regarded that as a big plus in my favour. But I was not high-powered in the sense that they would understand it. I was never going to be an Einstein or a Stephen Hawking. I was just a boy who loved animals and wanted other people to love them too. I did, however, have a secret weapon – or two to be precise. John Jones and Bruce Campbell. John Jones was my tutor at Oxford and I'd loved him from the moment I met him. I still remember the day of my interview, a scared schoolboy standing outside his big oak door. I was already entranced by the beauty of the college quads I'd just walked through – Merton was founded in 1264 and is one of the most ancient and lovely of Oxford's colleges. I listened at the keyhole to the candidate before me, talking about Keats and Shelley with an erudition far beyond me and I knew I had next to no chance of a place. And then it was my turn and John was all smiles. He sat me in an armchair so deep that, though I was over 6 feet tall, I disappeared. My knees were above my chin, making it hard to hold forth about anything. He then stuck an enormous sherry in my hand and astonished me by telling me I'd written excellent entrance papers and he'd like to give me an award. I still have his letter offering me an Open Exhibition. He later made it a full Postmastership after I'd won a couple of University prizes. We had an hour together every week for two years. How I cherished those times. John was very interesting. Bruce Campbell was my other guru. He had been the very first director of the BBC Natural History Unit, when it was mainly a radio operation, he had written the famous Oxford Book of Birds and he'd been on the committee of the Oxford Ornithological Society with me when I was a boy. Although he was a very well-known naturalist, Bruce was extremely generous with his time and especially encouraging and helpful towards young people. And like John, he was a man worth listening to. His profound knowledge, especially of British wildlife, was truly inspiring. So, John and Bruce would be my referees, as they had so often been in the past. I had never seen what they wrote about me but I had also never seen any glint of malice each time they agreed to vouch for me so I guessed they were on my side.

There was plenty of leeway for completing the Fulbright application but the Harkness was very tight. The application had to be delivered by 4 pm on 18th October and I ran out of time. I had to jump on a train and gallop through London, arriving breathless and sweaty at the Harkness office precisely ten minutes before the deadline. The expression of absolute disdain on the face of the Fellowship secretary as she took my proffered envelope between extended finger and thumb reminded me that my appearance was probably not quite Savile Row. "Well," she said, with icy disapproval "you've left it rather late haven't you?". I suppose I had, though I pointed out cheerfully that there were still ten minutes to go before the deadline. "There are indeed," she agreed. "But all the other applications have been in for weeks."

I didn't get a Fulbright but I was called for a Harkness interview. The secretary's shock alone, when she saw that I, of all people, had been short-listed, made my trip to London worthwhile. But, for her, worse was to come. I blame Freddy. Freddy Dainton, Sir Frederick, later Lord Dainton, was a nuclear chemist and Fellow of the Royal Society. He'd worked on the Los Alamos atom bomb project and had been nearly blinded by radiation. He was an iconoclastic Yorkshireman, a brilliant scientist and he was not a big fan of smart clothes. He was also Chairman of the Harkness selection committee. I'm really not sure what happened in my interview. I made Freddy laugh. He made me laugh. The other committee members all laughed. For 45 minutes. It was a bit of a riot. When I emerged, my friend the secretary was as white as a sheet. She looked as if someone had stuck a knife in her. She stared at me with fixed feverish eyes and kept muttering "What did you do to them? What did you do to them?"

I honestly believe that Freddy Dainton was the only person in the entire history of the Harkness Foundation who would have ever considered awarding me a Harkness Fellowship. It would be disingenuous for me to say I was not a good candidate. But so, I'm sure, were all the other applicants. In any competition there will be outstanding participants, who will always win. The rest of us, however, need a stroke of luck. I think I was extremely lucky that Freddy understood what I meant by "changing the world", that he believed it was feasible and that he was the sort of person who would flout tradition and offer an award in a previously unrecognised discipline.

When I received the letter confirming my Fellowship, I was stunned, not only that I'd won the award but by the generosity of the financial package. The Harkness Fellowship would pay all my fees, my airfares and my health insurance. It would give me money towards a second-hand car, a special vacation supplement to help me travel and see the States during holidays and it would pay me a monthly salary.

CalArts sits on a graceful rise just above Highway Five on the way north out of Los Angeles. On my first morning, in early September 1978, I sat in the big glass-fronted cafeteria looking out on what were the first vestiges of the new town of Valencia. These were tucked away Eastwards of our hill, and they ended in two smart, white boulevards that in those days represented the last fingers of the great city of Los Angeles, reaching out to the still-empty lands beyond. I needed a place to live. My eyes rested, not on the nascent estates of Valencia but on the rolling tree-clad hills and ridges of the Los Angeles

National Forest extending far to the north-east horizon. Somewhere up there among the manzanitas and scrub oaks there must be a cabin or a garage apartment where I could seclude myself at the end of each study day.

"Well," said the lady at the student accommodation office, " we just got this place come on the books". She handed me a picture of a funny little red, wooden A-Frame house. "It's miles up in the forest in a little place called Green Valley. I'm not sure it's habitable mind you," she said. "Another student looked at it yesterday and said the toilet wasn't plumbed in and it was lying in the middle of the sitting-room." I dialled the number.

To his dying day, the man who answered the phone swore I said "money is no object." He claimed he had covered the receiver and turned to his friends and family who happened to be visiting and said "Boy have I got a fish here. He's just off the boat and he says money is no object." Well, that's not what I said. What I said was that I didn't have a problem with his rent, I just couldn't pay it right away. I tried to explain that I had just arrived in California, I knew nobody, I had no bank account, no car and though I had a cheque in my hand for three thousand dollars, until I solved the administrative riddle, I couldn't actually hand him any money. I did not say "money is no object." The man, however, said he was driving down the mountain straight away to meet me.

Jim Hoag was the second youngest of four children. His father had abandoned the family when he was very young and Jim's mother, Cleo, had raised them alone, on a shoestring, working as a lab-technician. His mother's cheerful courage set against the struggle to survive made a deep impression on Jim. He turned out to be pretty bright. He won scholarships, he became a successful pharmacist and he seemed to have decided that no-one for whom he cared should ever have to worry again. He bought a house for Cleo, he bought a house for his aunt, he helped his brothers and sister when he was needed and he decided he would look after me a bit too. Those first days, he drove me to The Pacific Security Bank where I set up my account and received a beautiful cheque book, every cheque showing a different

Californian bird or animal. He helped me buy a car – an orange Datsun pick-up truck with a small camper shell on the back, lined with a built-in mattress, even more cosy than Brutus. He showed me round the whole area and helped me get installed in the A-frame, equipping it with useful, if unadorned furniture that I dubbed "Green Valley Modern." Jim loved debating. We would sit up late into the night under the oak trees talking about our lives and experiences and about politics and governance. Jim was quietly patriotic and we had fun goading each other into unreasonable stances. I remember one triumphant occasion when in absolute exasperation he said "I don't believe it. You've even got me defending Nixon." He was a wonderful friend.

The A-frame was not a sturdy building. If you looked carefully, you could see pinholes of sunlight through the wooden walls. It was too cold in winter and too hot in late summer. It was mainly one room with a sleeping platform upstairs at the back. But the whole front wall was a picture window leading out to a wooden stoop and opening to a view across the wooded valley to the mountains beyond. I could sit on my stoop and watch the sharp-shinned hawks hunting brown towhees in my bushes or the acorn woodpeckers, hacking holes in the telegraph poles. Into the holes they would post acorns. These were lined up all over the poles, like bullets, wedged into place so the woodpeckers could come back and open them when they felt peckish. Little families of California quails, with smart plumes wagging on their heads, crept about under the fragrant, resinous manzanita shrubs, turkey buzzards floated across the valley and sometimes at night the coyotes would shriek and howl. I loved my A-frame.

Cleo was to be my nearest neighbour. Her cabin was about a hundred metres away, down the crumbling dirt track called, grandiosely, Calle Rosalito. Jim explained that he had bought the A-frame, not for its non-existent investment potential but because it had attracted hippy types whom his mum had found a bit scary. Now she could have more say about who lived there. Cleo was an educated lady. She had gone to a fine university and her great love was literature. She was very happy to have a real live Oxford man living next door. And I was very happy to have a real live Cleo. Cleo was a terrible cook, completely disorganised, very eccentric and a master – or mistress – of the non-consequential remark. And probably the most delightfully teasable person I have ever met. I adored her.

The most important class for me at CalArts was the equipment workshop. This was a hands-on course in which you learned how all the cameras, tape recorders, microphones and lights worked. It was taught by TAs, Teaching Assistants drawn from the most competent senior students who had already excelled the previous year. They were a helpful bunch, led by Clyde Smith, a dead ringer for Clint Eastwood, especially his voice, who was destined for a long, successful career as a cameraman. I found the trickiest thing to learn was loading film into the camera magazine. There was no messing about here with the easy little daylight spools that Lone and I had used in our Bolex. Now I had to handle 400-foot rolls that were extremely sensitive to light. You had to zip the unopened film tin and the magazine into a light-proof black cloth bag. Then you inserted your hands into the one-way sleeves until you could locate the film tin. You opened it, removed the film from its black casing, opened the magazine, placed the film the correct way round on the central spool of the feed side, pulled out a length of leader which had to be fed into the exterior slot, engaging the sprockets so the film would roll out smoothly. Then you closed the feed door of the magazine and only then was it safe to unzip the bag and complete the job in the light. The last part was the most sensitive. You had to create a small loop, feed the starter end into the sprocket holes of the take up side, so the loop remained exactly the right size as the exposed film was wound up there. The loop would be flattened when the magazine was snapped home onto the camera and as the film flowed through during shooting, each frame would have to line up precisely at the small rectangular gateway where the lens was placed and each frame was exposed. For a beginner, this job was a nightmare. CalArts had a fleet of French Éclaire NPR cameras – Noiseless Portable Reflex as I remember. They were indeed silent when they were working properly. But they were very temperamental and every now and then, especially if you had been cavalier with your loop, they would tear your film up into confetti. They weren't noiseless then.

The other perennial danger was "hair in the gate". You had to keep your black bag clean. Any dirt, even a hair from your arm, could get caught up in the film as you loaded it. It would then travel through the camera with the unfurling film until it reached the film gate behind the lens. There it would probably sit, waggling its horrible little finger in front of every single frame you shot. The only way to avoid this disaster was to turn your bag inside out and shake it fiercely between every load and remove the magazine between shots to "check the gate" – making sure it was always clean. One of our favourite games when we watched films was "hunt the hair". It's amazing how many pre-digital films contain a scene marred by a pesky little thread living its own pesky little life around the edge of the picture. All because someone didn't check the gate! It was a very simple lesson to learn – and one of the most useful. In the miles of footage I shot in my subsequent career, I don't think I ever suffered from an illicit hair.

CalArts's considerable fleet of equipment was stored in an Ocean's Eleven-proof lock-up compound called "The Cage". The Cage was guarded by an enormous African American called Brian who despised students. He was not susceptible to cookies, muffins or doughnuts and there was no way you could get unsupervised access to gear until you'd passed your camera-driving-test. Those who had, were busy making their own films and during my first year I volunteered to crew for some of them. I remember Bob Levy's film, in particular. Bob had dark, curly hair and looked exactly like a young Greek god. He didn't behave like one though. He was sweet-natured and gentle. He was Jewish and like many of the Jewish-American youngsters I met at CalArts, he was just discovering his own history. He wanted to tell a Jewish story that wasn't about being a victim, so he decided to re-enact the Jewish uprising in the Warsaw ghetto during the Second World War. It was an ambitious enterprise. The studio filled with smoke from all the fake Molotov cocktails that had to be consumed. I was the magazine loader and it was hard to keep everything clean with all those bombs going off. It was surprising, however, how almost realistic it looked when the footage was printed and the action compressed into that magic little rectangle that frames the make-believe world of film.

The Dean of the film-school was Alexander (Sandy) Mackendrick. Sandy was a heavyweight. He had directed one of my all-time favourite films, The Lady Killers, with Alec Guinness. In those great days of the "Ealing Comedies" he'd also directed Whisky Galore and The Man in The White Suit, before heading for Hollywood. There, his best film had been "Sweet Smell of Success" about an overweening, tyrannical society columnist played by Burt Lancaster and his sycophantic, sleazebag of a stringer played quite brilliantly by Tony Curtis. At the Box Office the film did not live up to its title, it was too sour and people were not used to seeing their screen heroes playing such realistically unpleasant characters. I have no doubt, however, that it is an absolute masterpiece. Disillusioned by Hollywood, Sandy had accepted the challenge of leading a new film-school. He was a master of film grammar and his course notes, adorned with dozens of his own line drawings depicting and explaining key scenes from great films, were an art-work in their own right. I have kept them all, as I suspect most of his old students have.

Another heavyweight was Terry Sanders. A double Oscar winner, he ran an excellent documentary course. We all had to make a two-and-a-half-minute film and I chose as my subject a Salvation Army Shop out in the desert town of Lancaster. I'd bought all my pots and pans and camping stuff there and had got to know the manager. She called herself Sno Jo. That's what her car called her too, as it was on her number plate. I think the car was a Cadillac. She was hilarious. Definitely worth more than two and a half minutes. It was very funny when we all arrived in Lancaster to film. Terry was a fastidious man and he could barely stand the smell of the old clothes and the slightly less than clean feel of all the items for sale. His wrinkled nose was a picture. He did pick up on Sno Jo's insane star quality though.

Don Levy, another star teacher, was much admired by the

younger students who found him cool and mysterious. He had made one significant film, called Herostratus, about a young man who plans to make his own suicide a media event. There was always excitement when Don was going to show the film at the college, but sometimes he cancelled at the last minute if he felt the vibes were wrong. I understand that he had gone on tinkering with the film for years, which I took as a warning. I began to see that while perfectionism is a valuable quality in the production of any artwork, it mustn't hinder its release. There comes a point where a piece must be left to stand or fall on its own, in order to free the creator to get on with the next project. Perhaps this is why I have always been reluctant to look at my own films or reread my own writing.

Sound engineering was taught by Don Worthen, a retired industry pro who could coil forty metres of electrical lead with a few deft flicks of his wrist. It was a beautiful thing to behold how he could subdue an unruly length of flex into a perfect circle. Even now, whenever I coil up the garden hose, I try to practice the Worthen flick, but I have never mastered it.

CalArts was not just a film-school. There were also painters and print-makers, animators, musicians, dancers and a drama department. We were all supposed to inspire each other and where possible work with each other. My own filming became increasingly solitary, as it had to, but I enjoyed the contact with musicians and dancers. I made friends with a violinist who was good enough to have a job on the side playing for the Ventura symphony orchestra. As she had no car, I used to drive her the thirty-odd miles to rehearsals and as a reward I got to hear the concerts for free. I think that was probably where I first heard Samuel Barber's emotive Adagio for Strings. One of the dancers was an exuberant African American, very camp, presumably very gay, who was overbrimming with kinetic, musical energy that was quite infectious. He founded his own dance troop called, alluringly Rodeo Ex Machina and he used to invite me to watch their rehearsals. I never tired of their rhythmic defiance of gravity.

I was friendly with many of the students at CalArts. I respected their often tongue-tied talent and their otherness – very much not "Oxford". But I only made one life-long friendship and that was with a teacher. Kris Malkiewicz had written an excellent book on basic film technique which was one of our main learning aids. He was in charge of the equipment workshop, which he hired me to run in my second year when he took-over as acting Dean, and he gave a course on film lighting. He was now working on a new book, which involved him interviewing many of the major cameramen in Hollywood. He was a big asset to the school because he invited star speakers like Haskell Wexler and Sven Nyquist. He also had contacts in Eastern Europe so we enjoyed amazing visits from seriously inspiring film-makers like Kristof Zanussi and Ivan Passer. As a "trusty" I was always on the welcoming committee so I heard some brilliant anecdotes. Kris was Polish, living in exile. Although he was very handsome and popular, he was lonely. He was oppressed by what I think he saw as a barbarous philistinism in California, even in CalArts and he missed the thousand-year footprints in the stones of old Europe. He'd been married to the daughter of the Irish writer, Monk Gibbon. He'd worked for Irish television and perhaps he saw in me a young, but nevertheless acceptable, ally.

At weekends Kris would occasionally drive up to Green Valley and we'd sit in the evening round my wood-burning stove while he told me about his early life in Krakow in Poland. His was an old land-owning family which had not been well-served by communism. His uncle had been executed for sedition and his mother had been imprisoned for seven years and so badly treated that she would never walk properly again. His father and older brother had managed to escape from Poland but he had been left there to bring himself up more or less as a semi-orphan. He was obviously clever and he had not been blocked from going to film school where he'd made friends with Zanussi and Roman Polanski but there was no life for him in Poland. The story had left a sadness in Kris which, I suspect, only lifted years later when he married again, very happily, and was able to return to Krakow and regain his old home. Kris was a nervous man. He was afraid of illness and he was very afraid of earthquakes.

We all lived on the San Andreas Fault which at any time, now or a hundred years from now, was expected to convulse and wreak havoc. Kris kept his earthquake-survival-kit to hand at all times and he would cram the essentials into a little rucksack which he'd always carry even if we were just walking in the hills above the A-Frame. Of course, I used to tease him unmercifully about his very unmacho little bag but one day we were high up on one of the top ridges when I began to develop a very insistent head-ache and I said we might have to turn back. "No" he said "we don't have to do that. In my rucksack I am carrying, as I always do, a box of head-ache pills. And you can have some. But on one condition. From now on you have to show nothing but respect for my foresight and my little bag." It was a heavy price to pay, but I took the pills.

Apart from being my friend, Kris showed me many acts of kindness. The most important concerned a camera. CalArts staff were allowed to borrow equipment for long-term use and Kris trusted me enough to sign out a complete package on my behalf. This was incredibly helpful because I was, obviously, going to make a nature film and would need a camera at all seasons, especially during the long vacations when the cage was closed. There was a piquant footnote to this arrangement. The camera that Kris took for me was a 25 year-old Arriflex ST. It had come from the Disney bequest and had been used for the making of The Living Desert.

At the end of my first term at CalArts, I didn't film. I went home for a two-week break to the UK. It was a Christmas holiday, and it was something else. After Susan had drifted back to America the year before, I had commuted for a while, flying back and forth several times. But I'd had a thesis to complete and that had nailed me for many hours onto a seat in the Bodleian Library in Oxford. There, I began to notice a strange-looking girl. She was older than me, slim and quite tall, with the face of Isabel Adjani. But her hair was pure, platinum white. She was amazing. Apparently, she'd noticed me too. She'd observed my dirty gym shoes, my shirt half tucked in, my books carried in a plastic butcher's bag from the covered market and the fact that I always ran up the hallowed library stairs whistling loudly. She thought I was very irritating. After a week or two, I plucked up courage to speak to her. I told her that I was about to go to America, but that I had a Land-Rover and before I went, I could show her all the best places in the area to bird-watch. It was a pretty weird invitation. I had never actually met a girl who was really interested in birds and I can't for the life of me think why I thought she might be. But, quite astonishingly, she was. Her love of nature was, in its way, as profound as my own. She told me later that nothing else I could have said or done would ever, under any circumstances, have induced her to go out with me. But this was an offer she couldn't refuse.

Her name was Patricia. Over the next few weeks, we grew very close. It was an odd relationship in that, although we talked all the time, we always seemed to know exactly what the other was thinking. One night I took her badger watching. We were staying for a few days with my parents and we walked over the fields at dusk to the copse where I'd been studying the badgers since I was seven years of age. On the way, I lectured her severely about how she must keep still and make no noise at all. At the copse, we swung ourselves up onto the long low branch of the old beech tree which overhung the setts and settled down to wait. On cue, just before dark, one by one, badger cubs began to appear and they played and trundled about beneath us. Everything was going gloriously to plan until, suddenly, I needed to sneeze. This had never, ever happened before. It welled up inside like an express train, gathering speed until it burst out of the tunnel with a truly appalling ATCHOOO. The terrified badger cubs piled, as one, down their escape hatch. But they weren't one, they were four and they got stuck in the hole. Badgery legs and bottoms and stripy heads were wriggling and writhing in panic just below us and the whole ridiculousness of it overwhelmed me. I laughed and laughed and laughed so much that I fell out of the tree almost on top of them. I only mention this comedy because of what happened next. We walked home in the dark in a state of high gaiety. It's not often that I made such a complete ass of myself so the moment had to be enjoyed. When, finally we walked past my parents' big stone loggia, I saw something very peculiar. It was an old man, wearing a slightly crumpled grey suit. He was sitting in a deckchair, his hands were folded on his lap and he was looking down at them with a vague, friendly smile. The strange thing was, I didn't stop. I guess I knew in my heart that he wasn't there. As we reached the front door I turned to Patricia and asked her if she'd seen it. "Yes" she said. "What did you see?" "I saw an old man sitting in the chair. He was wearing a grey suit and smiling down at his hands, folded in his lap." We were neither of us surprised. By now we were already used to this other-worldly confluence of thought.

So, in December 1978, I wasn't going home for Christmas, I was going home to get married. Patricia looked Swedish, she spoke Swedish fluently, her English accent sounded like the Queen's cousin but she was in fact Irish. Not just Irish. Patricia was from South Armagh, bandit country, the home of the IRA. Her own cousin had been Moira Drumm, a notorious IRA leader murdered in her hospital bed after a previous assassination attempt had failed. The little family farm lay at the foot of Slieve Gullion, the famous whale-backed mountain where the hero Fionn mac Cumhail had dived into the lake to fight a potent witch and emerged days later, victorious but with his hair turned pure white, like Patricia's. Patricia had been the first person from her school to go to university. Her schoolbooks were still preserved as local wonders. Her immediate family were not IRA supporters and that was respected by the neighbours, many of whom were. Before the wedding we received an anonymous tip-off not to book my family into the Ardmore Hotel, which we had planned to do. The night before the wedding someone put a bomb in it. The damage was minimal but I suppose it was just a rehearsal. Six months later the Ardmore was blown to smithereens.

The wedding took place on 21st December in Drumintee Church, just round the corner from the infamous Three Steps pub. We were very idealistic. We didn't want anything commercial to sully our day. We asked for no presents. The ceremony was private. My brother Terry was my best man, Chris played the music, and David took the photographs. In the absence of Patricia's father, her brother John gave her away and her mother and two friends cooked all the food. Three of Patricia's old university friends heard there was a wedding and they turned up anyway. One was the first Catholic Lady Mayoress of Belfast and she came with her husband the Mayor in the mayorial Daimler, which looked delightfully out of place parked by the farm gate. We all ate our pies and cold meats perched round the farm table, while the postman handed reams of telegrams through the window. The nicest was from Green Valley, from Jim and Cleo. Although no specific invitations were issued, Patricia's mother, a very popular lady, had let it be known that the doors that evening would be open to everyone. And everyone came. They came with pipes and drums and flutes and huge cheerfulness. They talked and drank and sang until six o'clock in the morning. And, although they had been forbidden to bring presents, they were Irish, who go nowhere empty-handed, so they came with little envelopes of money and they paid for our entire wedding.

By early March 1979, I was back in Green Valley. My little monastic, bachelor A-Frame now had a new inhabitant. Jim, Cleo and Kris all agreed that I was greatly improved by the addition of a wife. Patricia was much nicer to look at and she was a much better cook. Without doubt, our friendships deepened over the next two years.

Patricia had a fellowship of her own, from the University of Uppsala, in Sweden, to write a doctoral thesis about eighteenth century theories of originality. The Bodleian had been a prime source of period material but she had discovered that the Huntington Library in Pasadena also had a significant eighteenth-century collection so now, several times a week we would make the journey down the mountain together. She'd drop me at CalArts and then continue to the Huntington to carry on with her literary excavations. It was a blissful and industrious period. I loved the drive home at night, leaving the lights and the buzz of the city below and winding up the lonely mountain road above San Francisquito Canyon to the scattered log cabins of Green Valley. There was always something to see in the darkness: often a big, black, hairy tarantula laboriously crossing the road, or coyotes melting away into the undergrowth, or, very occasionally, a bobcat, its spotted coat and tufted ears caught for a moment in the headlights. One night, I was alone and I stopped when I saw a huge owl lying in the gutter. It was a horned owl, the biggest American species, as big as an eagle. I wrapped it in my coat and put it gingerly on the seat beside me, hoping it didn't wake up and decide I was a giant mouse. Patricia was intrigued when I crept into the A-frame nursing my new patient. We put it in a big cardboard box with a lid and left it alone close to the fire. This is the full extent of the patented Stephen Mills hospital treatment for sick birds. You keep them warm, so they don't lose body heat and you keep them completely in the dark so they don't use up their last bit of energy fretting about the future. You check on them a few hours later. If their feet are still tightly clenched, they will die. If, however, they are standing properly, and if they have no obvious broken wing, they will almost always survive and can be released immediately. The next morning, we peeped under the owl's lid. It was standing four-square on its huge, feathery feet and it was spitting nails and clapping its beak with unspeakable fury. We carried the box outside, tipped it gently on its side and the great owl stepped out, opened its huge soft wings and glided silently away into the waiting woods.

In the middle of February, just when spring should have been massaging the buds and tweaking the volume on the bird song, we woke to absolute silence and the amazing sight of a thick blanket of snow. A few minutes later, we saw Jim, wallowing towards us up to his knees in the snow drifts. He was dressed uncharacteristically in his much-despised old national service battle fatigues and shouting "Gooood training!!" and "bizarre and unusual" at the top of his voice. These were two of his staple phrases. The other two were "noooo problem" which he said whenever there was a problem and "Kids and dogs" which was a marker he laid down whenever you did something stupid. It was short for "anyone who hates kids and dogs can't be all bad", a saying attributable to WC Fields of whom Jim was a staunch admirer. I still say "kids and dogs" most days, in Jim's memory though no-one knows what I'm talking about. Now, however, Jim was stumbling about in the snow, laughing madly, clasping a big brown paper parcel in one hand and falling flat on his face in the snow every twenty yards or so. Eventually he reached our stoop and flopped up the steps like a human snowball, bursting through the door with the inevitable and triumphant shout of "nooo problem". The parcel contained a huge joint of delicious Santa Marie Tip Steak, the best you could get, because he was afraid we might have run out of food. Of course, there was a problem. Two actually: one little one and one big one. The little one was that his car was stuck in his drive and he wanted me to help him dig it out so he could go to work. The big problem was that Jim had Multiple Sclerosis and very, very slowly, it was killing him.

The four of us, Jim. Cleo, Patricia and I, ate together probably twice a week. Each of us, in our own way, needed looking after and so we looked after each other. It felt effortless, like family. Cleo was very funny. She would tell mystified stories about her run-ins with the police. She drove a very old, turquoise, Ford Rambler, which had no working speedometer. One day she was pulled over on the Pacific coast road for speeding and she explained in her quavering voice "You see officer, I usually judge my speed by what the other cars are doing, but there weren't any other cars." "That" lady, he said, with deep sarcasm "is because you passed them all." Cleo was worried about Patricia. She was convinced that Patricia's habitual attire of a light blue denim jacket and jeans was a uniform that I forced her to wear and that I was discouraging her from having "nice clothes". "He should let you wear something more feminine" she would say. We neither of us knew why she attributed such powers of veto to me but it obviously nagged at her because one day she left a package labelled for Patricia at our door. Inside was quite the most hideous dress either of us had ever seen. Strike one: it was made entirely of nylon. Strike two: it was brown, patterned with yellow and black stripes like a giant hornet. Strike 3: it was cut in empire line, which is only flattering to people shaped like pyramids and anyway it would have been a loose fit on a hippopotamus. Patricia was dismayed at the prospect of an ongoing flow of impossible gifts so I told her I had an idea. I put on the dress, covered my head with a scarf, walked over to Cleo's house and knocked on the door. When she answered I said "Hello

Cleo. I've just come to say thank you for the dress." Her eyes widened with horror and she stammered "Oh Steve". That was it. We none of us mentioned it again. But there were no more dresses.

A few weeks later, I had to alter my appearance in earnest. My old friend Jules, she who had helped release me from the Dungeons of Agadir, came to visit us on her way home from Australia. We had a happy few days camping in the Mohave Desert and in Joshua Tree National Park but after I'd taken her to the airport for her onward flight to the UK, I got into trouble with the police. Apparently, driving in the middle of Los Angeles, I was inexact in my selection of a lane from which to turn left. When the police pulled me over, I got out of my pick-up to show how friendly I was. Don't ever do this. You're liable to be shot. Both policemen sprang from their vehicle with pistols pointed at me, shouting "Freeze". I did definitely freeze. One of them wrote me out a ticket while the other kept me covered in his gun sights. But by the time I'd explained that I was a foreigner and had been confused by the myriad maze of traffic lanes they began to relent. They said they couldn't rescind the ticket but if I turned up at court and told my story, they wouldn't challenge it and I might get away without a fine. When the summons arrived a few weeks later, I cut my hair, shaved off my moustache, put on clean clothes and headed down town. A court official told the large gathering of woebe-gone felons that when we faced the judge, we had three choices: plead guilty and hope to get a reduced fine for appearing in person; plead not guilty and come back with supporting evidence; or plead guilty-with-extenuating-circumstances – i.e. tell your story and hope the judge sympathised. The judge, when he appeared, had obviously not shaved nor cut his hair. He was a snappy mover and I watched, dismayed, as he demolished the frightened folk ahead of me in the queue. It was clear that none of them had understood the third option. When it was my turn, I was the only one to say "guilty with extenuating circumstances" and the judge visibly perked up. "As you can probably tell," I said, "I'm a stranger in Los Angeles and I was lost." As quick as a flash he quipped "Boy, I've been living in Los Angeles for 48 years an' I'm still lost." Well, I had to laugh. Good move. I continued "Apparently when I wanted to turn left, I used the penultimate left lane rather than the far left one." "Penultimate?" he said "Did the court hear Penultimate? Case dismissed!" I think it was the first time in my life that my Oxford education had really paid off. It saved me at least a hundred dollars.

For the Master of Fine Arts Degree at CalArts, the key requirement was to make a film. Most people had dramatic ambitions. Some had really good story ideas, some were heading for the avant-garde, some wanted to hear themselves calling "roll sound, roll camera, cut". I, of course, wanted to make a nature film.

7

REFUGE

I have always had mixed feelings about the use of music in nature films. In a film about people and their emotions, music is a vital underscore, as important in its way as the dialogue, acting and photography. I would argue that Enrico Morricone's soaring orchestrations and those tunes that alternate between the deeply menacing and sometimes downright cheeky lift a film like Sergei Leone's Once Upon A Time In The West to a level of greatness that it might not have otherwise achieved. So closely did composer and director work together, that apparently some key scenes were cut to the music rather than the other way round – and to fine effect. In High Noon the simple theme song carries a pulsing rhythm which invades the film, etching lines of anxiety on the face of Gary Cooper's beleaguered marshal as the minutes tick away towards the fatal shootout. For his 2001 Space Odyssey, Stanley Kubrik commissioned an original score which he jettisoned in the cutting-room, using instead what could have been the corniest music – The Blue Danube Waltz as the earth appears in space and Also Sprach Zarathustra for the eureka moment when early man discovers tools – but which instead proved to be a stroke of genius. Schindler's List, Dr Zhivago,

Lawrence of Arabia, The Godfather, Star Wars and even Jaws are all enhanced and made more profound, by their music.

The same is not true, however, of nature films. The reason is very simple. They are not about humans. They are about a different world, a world of birds and animals, insects and landscapes, which have their own harmonies. Of course, the audience is human, so if a film-maker wants to emphasise an emotional passage, he would be foolish to deny himself the powerful tool that music provides. But too much music obscures the sense of being in the wild and detracts from the feeling of "other" that a good nature film can offer. This is why I decided that for my Master's Degree, I would make a wildlife film without either music or commentary. I would try to distil the essence of a place, to give a sensation of being there through intense sounds and pictures with only the intervention of the lens and the microphone. I chose for my location, the Salton Sea.

The Salton Sea is a huge, salty, inland lake in the far south of California, close to the Mexican border. It sits in a wide, low-lying basin that was once part of the prehistoric delta of the Colorado River. The lake covers around three hundred and forty square miles and it derived most of its modern water from a spillage from the Colorado Dam project in the early twentieth century. The surface of the water lies far below sea level, at minus two hundred and thirty six feet and at its deepest point it is only a few feet higher than Bad Basin, the nastiest, hottest, lowest point of the notorious Death Valley. As soon as I heard about it, I thought this was just the place for me and my borrowed Living Desert Arriflex camera. These days it wouldn't be. Apparently, the water has receded, and a toxic dust now blows across the scant human communities there but in the 1970s it was, in its way, a haunting, beautiful place. In the spring and summer, elegant stilts, handsome avocets and strange-beaked skimmers nested in colonies on the open sands. The reed beds were full of rails and bitterns and herons and in winter the shoreline filled with resonant snow-geese. It was also home to significant numbers of brown and white pelicans. All these, along with the cacophonic yellow-headed blackbirds, would star in my film, where they would have to speak for themselves.

The southern sector of the Salton Sea, around thirty seven thousand six hundred acres, was declared as a Federal National Wildlife Refuge in 1930. I decided to focus on that area and I would call the film "Refuge". So, in the spring of 1979 we packed our orange Datsun truck with cooker and water carriers and extra fuel tank and all the filming gear and headed south. Our first stop was the refuge headquarters on the far southern tip of the lake. The manager, Larry Dean, had the look of a man born in the saddle. He was strong, sturdy and frank, a good man to have on your side. He listened to our film plans and I guess he liked the look of us because he gave us carte blanche to do what we wanted and go where we liked. He would ensure we had water and advise us on safe places to camp and good spots to work in. He was a huge help and over the next year we became good friends. He had a young family and we were often included in family meals and companionship.

On and off, we spent many months on the Salton Sea, visiting for a week or so at a time, filming round the seasons. By June, the sulphureous smell of the dry mud and the sea-salt crystals was so intense that I realised my film could never give a complete sense of place with only sounds and pictures. But I let the camera dwell on the landscape as if it might convey a little of its magical essence. The growing heat was easier to portray, with the shimmering light off the water, but even that couldn't tell you the real temperature. Larry had an assistant manager called Jose. He was Mexican, always gentle and smiling and liked to visit us. One day he drove up, got out of his truck laconically and watched us for a while sweating over the camera and then he said, in his singing, Mexican tones "It's gonna be a hunded twenny in the shade today." Adding, after a suitably dramatic pause "An' there ain't no shade."

In one way, the heat was a bonus. In my late teens, I was diagnosed with Ankyllosing Spondilytis, an inflammatory condition which attacked the bones in my neck, spine and sacro-iliac joints. I had been given a slightly alarming prognosis by the Nuffield Orthopedic Hospital in Oxford which warned that I could end up in a wheel-chair. The initial treatment entailed exercises to keep my posture straight even as the bones were eroded. Later, I started taking Diclofenac, the anti-inflammatory drug that has wiped out many of Asia's vultures. Fortunately, I'm not a vulture it seems, because I still take the pills and they have kept me largely pain-free for decades. I kept the condition more or less secret throughout my career, partly because I didn't want to give myself an excuse for failures, but mainly because a cameraman with a bad back is unemployable. But in those early years I was still suffering a lot of discomfort. Not in the deep dry heat of the Salton Sea, however. There, I found the woolly sponge bed that filled the back of our pick-up, perfectly comfortable. I loved our warm nights, parked by the water, lulled by the soft lapping of the waves and the night calls of our film stars and during the hot days I was loose and easy, coiled over my camera as I tried to perfect the silky-smooth pans and the invisible shifts in focus that allow you to follow birds in flight.

My beloved Disney Arriflex was in truth a bit of a beast. It whirred and clanked like a kitchen appliance so I often had to work with a very long lens to avoid chasing everything away with the racket I was making. The longest lens I could get hold of was a very old five hundred millimetre. I don't even remember what make it was, only that it was as long as a rifle barrel, shook in the faintest breeze and was thoroughly unwieldy. It had a very narrow field of view which meant it was almost impossible to find anything when you looked through it. But it was sharp. Gradually I learned to work with its limitations – and reduce my own. I had all the time in the world. I loved sitting out in the hot marshes practising and I had only myself to answer to – myself, that is, and my bank balance. Every 400-foot roll of film cost a quarter of my monthly stipend to purchase, develop and print. So I couldn't actually afford to make many mistakes. Harkness Fellows who married before their assignment commenced received a married allowance which was fifty percent higher than a single person's. I was married but I hadn't wanted the date of my wedding to be influenced by these considerations so I was treated as a single Fellow. Consequently, money for film stock was a bit tight.

In the early summer, in the middle of filming, we received important visitors. One of the perks of being Chair of the Harkness Selection Committee was a trip round America visiting your protégés. So it was that one lovely June day Freddy Dainton and his wife Barbara, an Oxford Zoology don, turned up at the door of the A-Frame in Green Valley. We had a wonderful day together. Patricia cooked a meat loaf for lunch. We bird-watched and showed them the esoteric delights of the cluster of huts that made up our village and we talked. We talked about films and wildlife and about academics and politics. Freddy would emerge as a keen supporter of the soon-to-be-founded Social Democrat Party in the UK, and one of its leaders, Shirley Williams, in particular, so their take on Britain was especially interesting. They were clearly captivated by the simplicity of our life in Green Valley but as an afterthought, Freddy asked us if we had any problems and I did just mention the cost of film stock. Two weeks later we received a letter from Freddy, entitled "For the Love-Nest". Apparently, there was an additional fund available, mainly to help scientists with the cost of lab materials. My film and lab development costs were deemed to fall into this category – sort of – and the letter contained a sizeable cheque, which meant that from now on I could press the button on the camera without hearing the terrible whoosh of our dinner money rattling through the film-gate. A few years later, Freddy was made a Life Peer. We duly wrote to "Lord Dainton" congratulating him on his elevation and mentioning that we'd quite like to become lords too. He wrote back addressing us as "Dear Villeins". Freddy was a good sport.

The following March we had a rather different visit. There was a new Chairman of Selectors and I was summoned to Los Angeles to meet him. I never went to Los Angeles, except to Deluxe Film Labs in Hollywood so this was already a traumatic idea. Sir Douglas Wass was the Permanent Under-Secretary at the UK Treasury, the country's most senior financial Civil Servant. He appeared to be an extremely sober man and his Hungarian–born wife, Lady Melissa was conspicuously elegant. When we arrived, somewhat wild-eyed and unkempt at their hotel, Sir Douglas was dismayed to find I was not wearing a suit. He had intended, he explained, to take us to a rather special restaurant. But it imposed a dress code. We could either go, instead, to Macdonald's or I could borrow a jackets and tie from him. Definitely jacket and tie I said. So, we repaired together to his suite for a fitting. This rather broke the ice and, during a delicious dinner, it became obvious that our hosts were very charming people. As the evening wore ever more cheerfully on, they told us that the Harkness Fellow they were due to meet the next day was suffering some sort of crisis and refused to see them. They had pushed tactfully but in the end they couldn't insist. This meant they had an empty day ahead. Would we like to join them? Well, of course we would, but I explained that we really didn't do cities so, instead of a cultural tour of LA, I suggested a walk in the Mohave Desert to see the California poppies at the height of their brief but blazing spring bloom. We returned the next morning to pick them up and then I remembered the limitations of our vehicle. It only had two front seats and a bed behind. So Patricia drove, with Lady Wass in the front and Douglas and I lay full stretch in the back where he chatted amiably all the way up to Green Valley, for lunch, and then on over the mountains to the desert beyond. Lady Wass was perhaps a little out of her comfort-zone, picking her way on high heels amongst the flowers, puffing on her cigarettes. But I could see Douglas was entranced. It was a bumper year, with millions of flowers, deep yellow and orange, hugging the ground and stretching in all directions as far as the eye could see. And on every tenth or twentieth telegraph pole along the straight, empty desert road sat a golden eagle, as if they too, had gathered to view the magical inflorescence of that bare landscape. Like Freddy, Douglas also wrote me a letter after his visit. He said he'd decided to give up his job and live in a cabin in the woods. I think he was only half joking.

In the summer of 1979, after classes had finished at CalArts, we took a break from filming to travel. There was a generous provision made in the Harkness funding to encourage this and I decided to go right round America. I wanted to see every mainland State, with a focus, where possible, on conservation management. I discussed this with Larry Dean at the Salton Sea and he pulled out a map and a list of the National Wildlife Refuges, with the names, addresses and phone numbers of all the managers, which he gave me. That was Gold Dust. Then he put a mark next to the people he knew, scattered across the States, and said he'd phone them to let us know we were coming. So, in effect, we planned our route according to the location of the friends of Larry Dean. It was a brilliant idea.

Our journey took us up the coast of California watching migrating grey whales and sea otters. We halted for a week above Mendocino because we fell in love with a little deserted beach and headland where there was an osprey's nest to watch and we just couldn't bring ourselves to leave. Then across into the wilds of Eastern Oregon, and the amazing bird life of Lake Malheur, up into Canada to visit my Godfather on Vancouver Island, back down to Idaho and Wyoming, across the Dakotas and Minnesota ending up on the East coast and the beautiful forests of New England. We watched bluebirds nesting in the Great Dismal Swamp West of New York, found bald eagles and thousands of horseshoe crabs in the DelMarVa Penninsula and canoed for four days amongst alligators through the Okefenokee Swamp on the border between Georgia and Florida. We camped by beaver dams in the Rocky Mountains, by quiet streams, in forests and in deserts, in vast sage scrub and on empty beaches. We saw bears and badgers and marmots and moose and antelopes and armadillos. And wading round a desert island off South Carolina I got hit by a shark.

This was actually one of the high points of the trip, in that we'd been invited by one of Larry's many friends to help release thousands of baby loggerhead turtles. In an experiment to try to protect them from racoon predation, the nests had been dug up and reburied in a coon-proof enclosure on the island's beach. The problem was that the relocation seemed to have upset their time clock so many of the eggs were hatching during the day and the hatchlings didn't seem to distinguish land from sea in the bright light. We had to help them down the beach to start a sea journey that might last thirty years before the females amongst them would come home – now six hundred times bigger – to lay eggs of their own. If they survived. Many did not make it past the first line of gulls. It was heart-breaking to see the tiny clockwork toys waddling furiously into the sea only to be snapped up by marauding herring gulls. But previous to the enclosure experiment, mortality rates had been nearly a hundred percent so this was a big improvement. Now, I believe, nests are left in place and individually protected with mesh coverings. And any releases are made at night. Conservation is not always an exact science and we had joined the learning process. At one point I paddled out to my waste to take some photographs from the sea. Suddenly I felt an almighty bash on my thigh and turned to glimpse a suggestion of a fin arcing away from me. Or did I? I decided I had enough seascape pictures. It was probably a wise decision. I read later that that was one of the few areas on the US East coast where fatal shark attacks occurred. Sharks like to test you out with a bang before they come back and eat you.

We travelled for more than two months and I gathered material for a number of articles – on bighorns and burros in Death Valley and on the California Condor breeding programme – for New Scientist; and on the turtles and Okefenokee Swamp for Wildlife Magazine, among others. It was the journey of a lifetime and I'd already done some of it twice, so I felt pretty lucky.

By mid-September, we were back in Green Valley. Term had started again at CalArts and I was kept busy teaching the equipment workshop, learning a lot myself in the process. It was exactly what I'd come to CalArts to do. I now looked on cameras, and tape recorders, film tins and microphones as my best friends. Even fearsome Brian, ruler of the equipment cage, was tame and amiable now. I had one big scene left to film at the Salton Sea, which gave us a chance to see Larry Dean and share some of our summer's adventures with him. In the late autumn and early winter, tens of thousands of lesser snow geese follow the Pacific flyway down from their breeding grounds in North-West Canada and Alaska to settle in the fields around the Salton Sea. There, Larry and his team had ensured that the refuge fields had been harvested in a goose friendly way so the birds would stay on the reserve rather than scatter to other farmlands where they might be shot. I wanted to capture the massive sound of their arrival and the kaleidoscopic pixilation of their thousands upon thousands of black and white wings. I still remember the first successful shot I got, filmed in slight slow motion so that the myriad flashing wings seemed to hang forever on the screen.

The process of editing was especially laborious in those days of manual cutting and sticky tape but even on the shimmering screen of the flatbed, and despite its many imperfections, I could see that my film was beautiful. Word got out and staff members would pop their heads round the editing room door for a peep. Terry Sanders was particularly encouraging. Here was a man who knew how to win Oscars. The film needed a commentary. He was right, of course. But I had to disappoint him. This was my baby. No commentary. No music. And indeed, certainly no Oscar nomination. But it was chosen by the school as an example of "best work" to show Stephen Spielberg when he visited. God knows what he made of it. Ironically, a few years later I received a sweetly-worded request from a CalArts music student who'd watched the film in the library. Could he please set it to music? Yes, of course he could. I called the film "Refuge". I sold it subsequently to PBS, Norwegian TV, Irish TV and the BBC. Most importantly it earned me my Master of Fine Arts degree.

The CalArts degree ceremony of 1980 was one of the most bizarre events I've ever attended. My friend B R Ramkumar, who was to import the first ever optical printer to India for his film business in Chennai, arrived in his best suit. A girl I didn't know, but who would have been beautiful whatever she wore, wore nothing at all and took her certificate completely naked, leading a live leopard on a leash. I'd invited Jim to the event and he was, uncharacteristically, speechless with fear and awe. The worst insults were reserved for Bobby Fitzpatrick, the President of the College. He was a handsome energetic man and a canny political operator who brought in solid financing for CalArts and was an outstanding and sympathetic administrator. But these very real qualities were not always appreciated by the rebellious students of the late seventies. One of my sillier film-school colleagues went up to the podium with a fake arm attached. This he cut off after receiving his degree, spraying fake blood all over Bobby's fine linen suit. For a spectacular finale to the award ceremony, Bobby was supposed to float off in a hot air balloon but somehow this couldn't be controlled. It did float up but it didn't come down again. It disappeared far over the horizon, long after Bobby had stopped waving, continuing out of sight towards the Mohave Desert from where he had to be rescued hours after our revels were ended.

8

NATURE IN ITS PLACE

When I look admiringly at successful people, I discern three defining characteristics. The first is energy. When the rest of us get tired, drift off to the pub or steal that extra hour in bed, they are like the Duracell rabbit, they keep going. Energy is only partly a physical phenomenon. Of course, it's hard to be energetic if you're ill but when you think of someone like the physicist Stephen Hawking who achieved so much even though he could neither move nor speak naturally, there seems to be more to energy than mere oxygen supply. My friend John MacAuslan was the cleverest person I knew at Oxford. He got a Double-First in Greats – Latin, Greek, ancient History and Philosophy – and took a post in the Treasury, where Sir Douglas Wass was his boss. Then, just after I left for America, John broke his back in a hang-gliding accident and spent the rest of his life in a wheel-chair. Yet he became the Financial Director of the National Gallery, a Civil Service Commissioner and, in his spare time he ran the finances of the charity War Child. When he retired, he completed a doctorate in music and wrote a book on Schumann. He also had a wonderful wife and a family and my point is that energy, therefore, also stems from some quality of inner joy. John never knew it but he was a great inspiration to me, and probably to his many other friends. Watching him haul himself glowingly through his long, exhausting days reminded me that I had no excuse for being as lazy as I often was.

The second key to success is simple perseverance. This entails self-belief and a deep sense of the value of one's craft, qualities that are especially important in the creative arts, where rewards often come too late or not at all, or to the least deserving. Take Vincent Van Gogh, for instance, or John Keats. Both were richly productive throughout their short lives and neither had much success. Indeed, it's said that Van Gogh only managed to sell one painting. Yet he is currently the most highly valued artist in the world and Keats is regarded by many as second only to Shakespeare among England's lyric poets. What inner drive kept them at the easel and the desk? The answer, I think, can be found in their astonishingly profound letters, Vincent's to his brother Theo and John's to, among others, his fiancé, Fanny. In them, they lay out highly intellectual, artistic manifestos of a complexity and completeness that has rarely been equalled. Those uplifting letters persuade me that Van Gogh and Keats, despite doubts and disappointments, never lost belief in the worthwhile cause at the centre of their lives nor in their own powers to discern artistic truth. And this is why – though my own abilities are of course at a laughably different level – those two artists are my heroes.

The third factor common to most successes is one that, by contrast has little to do with the abilities of the individual. It lies for the most part outside their control. It is luck, sheer luck. It is a cliché to say it is important to be in the right place at the right time, but like most clichés it is true. Timing is often critical. I once reviewed a book on how to be a Green Consumer. It was the early 1980s, the ideas were original and interesting but the market for such work was dormant and the book went nowhere. A few years later I reviewed an almost identical work, perhaps a little better packaged and more user-friendly in its design. By now the readership was ready for such a work and, I believe this second book sold a million copies.

I was extremely lucky to come out of film-school in 1980, just after

Life on Earth had taken the television world by storm. Life on Earth, which was released to awed audiences all over the world in 1979, was the first definitive televisual essay on the natural history of our planet's ecosystem. It was modelled to some extent on Kenneth Clarke's Civilisation which had done something similar for the cultural history of man. It was devised and written predominantly by David Attenborough and the work of a single, subtle hand gave it the coherence and profundity of a thesis, something which subsequent BBC series have increasingly lacked. Its production method was also to a large extent new for wildlife on TV. Previously, most nature films had relied on what I call the "Hairy Man Syndrome": Hairy Man, maybe with Attractive Companion, is sent off into the "wilderness" where only hairy men dare go. There he films what he can and Survival Anglia or whoever the TV company may be, hammers out some sort of a story and that's your TV programme. Life on Earth, however, was coordinated like an industrial process. The essential sequences were farmed out to a whole range of specialist camera teams who worked separately but simultaneously in locations all over the globe, with David Attenborough then flown in to complete the short, connecting pieces to camera thereby providing the narrative continuity that gave the impression he'd been there throughout. This has been the model for all the big BBC nature series since.

The well-deserved success of Life on Earth changed the world of television for people like me. It professionalised wildlife film-making and it opened the eyes of programme commissioners to the potential attractions of well-constructed concepts in natural history broadcasting. They began to see that wildlife films didn't have to consist of bothersome one-offs that were hard to place but could instead comprise six-part or eight-part series, that would occupy a useful space in the schedule and tell a coherent, definitive story that audiences apparently responded to. The world of television is very fashion-driven. After Life on Earth, wildlife became "Flavour of the Month" indeed, of the decade. TV New Zealand, German TV, NHK Japan, Discovery and the new Channel 4 all emerged as competitors or co-funders with the BBC and National Geographic in pursuit of decent natural history material. This spawned a brave new world of small, independent producers. Quality companies like Partridge Films, London Scientific Films, and Cicada joined the already outstanding Oxford Scientific Films and, along with individual film-makers like myself, were all able to do good work and ride a commis-sioning wave that lasted for the next twenty years. It was a bit like the great days of TV Western series in the 1950s and 1960s. Who now remembers The Virginian, The Man from Laramie, Cheyenne, Bronco, Wagon Train, Wyatt Earp, The Sisco Kid, the Lone Ranger, Gunsmoke and the like? Well, probably lots of us old fogies but they're all gone now, yet for fifteen years they were as ubiquitous in the very limited schedules as CSI has been. And that's a little how it was for natural history in the 1980s and 90s.

The film "Refuge" provided me with a calling-card that allowed me to visit commissioners and it was just about good enough to give me the confidence to try to interest them in future projects. When we took it to Dublin, to the headquarters of Raidió Teilifís Éireann, Ireland's national broadcaster, we had an additional stroke of luck. RTÉ's Controller of Programmes turned out to be John Kelleher, whom Patricia had known during her student days at University College Dublin. Fortunately, Patricia had been highly regarded at UCD so John was pleased to see her and consequently, was willing to listen to any programme ideas I might have.

In the remit for my Harkness Fellowship, I had pledged myself to Public Service Broadcasting, arguing that quality television was a perfect medium for alerting the public to the significance of nature and the threats to it. This was not so self-evident at the time. Environ-mentalism was not generally fashionable but I was convinced that, as the printing press had unleashed an interest in things spiritual in the 15th Century, so television would spearhead concern for the earth in ours. My initial plan had been to work, not for the BBC, but to campaign somewhere new, perhaps in the Middle East, where these ideas were much less familiar. It now occurred to me, however, that I could start much closer to home. Ireland did have some home-grown nature films, mainly by Eamon de Buitlear, but these were more culturally based, often in Irish and laid no claims to scientific profundity. I now began to conceive a project that would be quite different. It would be a sort of "Life on Earth in Ireland", telling the story of Ireland's main ecosystems, of the influence of soil, climate and altitude on the accrual of species and of how those species interact with each other. Most importantly, it would take into account the relevant work of Irish scientists.

I've had lots of good advice during my career but two pieces stand out, one from Terry Sanders and the other from Richard Brock, one of the producers of Life on Earth. Terry said that, while a film should be coherent and well-planned, there's always a place for a really great shot even if at first it doesn't seem to fit. I've been trying to get "a great shot" ever since just to see if I can squeeze it in. More relevantly, however, at this juncture, was Richard's advice. He stressed to me the importance of a good title. Good titles sell ideas. He told me how, in the gent's toilet at the BBC's Broadcasting House he stood next to the Director-General and recognising an exceedingly brief window of opportunity he said "What about Around the World in Eighty Minutes?". Jules Vernes had allowed eighty days for such a venture but modern cameras could paint a round-the-world portrait much more quickly. He got the commission.

I planned to begin my Irish series in the City of Dublin, where a fifth of the human population of the country lives. I would show how this landscape of streets and squares and walls and wastegrounds, so familiar to the audience, is deeply hostile to wildlife and must be adapted to step by step. These strategies of invasion, survival and colonisation, however, apply equally to natural habitats so the series would go on to reveal them at work in the sand dunes and forests, the mountains and bogs and islands and rivers where Irish nature flourishes beyond the suburbs. Very few films had been made about the wildlife of cities at that time, so the idea for the first film felt quite original. The title would have an echo of Ireland's favourite author. It would be called "The Other Dubliners".

The series was commissioned on a single sheet of paper. It would consist of eight half-hour programmes, one for each representative habitat, to be shot on colour negative and the series title would be Nature In Its Place. At this point, only the first film would be funded, as an official pilot for the series. But the promise was clear. If the pilot was acceptable, RTÉ would then commit to the whole of the rest of the series.

To work out the budgeting details, John Kelleher passed us over to RTÉ's Finance Director, John Baragwanath, who turned out to be something of a character. That first meeting, we sat in his office while he was on the phone to someone in German television. John had quite a strong accent. He was trying to explain to the unfortunate German on the end of the line who he was but his way of saying radioteleviseaireann, was clearly not being understood. So he tried simplifying it to RTÉ but instead of AR T E he said OARTEE. And then OAR, OAR (louder) and finally OAR for RUMINEGGER. At which point we fell about laughing and so did he and we became firm friends forthwith. John's first friendly act was a surprising one. He looked at my draft budget and increased it by forty percent. "We want these films to be made," he said. "We don't want to be paying for your funerals because you've starved to death." It was true, I had imagined eating baked beans and living in a tent but John could see this was naive and wouldn't help to get the job done. A few years later I was given similar advice by Hugh Miles, undoubtedly one of the best wildlife cameramen of our generation. He told me always to make myself as comfortable as possible, to stay in the best available hotel or, if camping was essential, make it luxurious camping. Only sleep on a bare board if a bare board is the only thing you've got. Filming for weeks or months is exhausting enough. It's thoroughly unprofessional to be too tired to do it.

The next job was to buy a camera. My ambitions had moved beyond a clockwork Bolex, and anyway, Lone had kept the one we'd bought for our NRK films. But where to look? I knew no-one in the industry. My contacts were all far away in California and there was, of course, no internet to facilitate the search. But there were a couple of trade magazines and eventually I fixed on an old Arriflex BL that I bought as a package, with tripod, lenses, magazines, batteries and chargers. It was an ugly beast. It lived in a huge metal case the size of a coffin; it was awkward to use and heavy to carry. It did, however, have the ever-reliable Arriflex motor and registration pin.

The BL was, theoretically, a "silent" camera but to keep it quiet you had to use a "lens blimp". This was a tailor-made sound-proof cylinder in which the lens sat. Because it was impractical to blimp all your lenses, it was usual to use a single, all-purpose variable focus lens for work where silence was required. Mine came with an elderly French Angenieux 12:120 lens designed originally to pair with the flimsy Éclair cameras I'd learned on at CalArts. It was light and serviceable, though not as sharp as the Zeiss lenses to which I aspired but could not yet afford. The package also included a prehistoric macro lens for super close-up work – something I would need for the flowers and insects that were part of my story. The macro was exceedingly "slow", meaning that its optics were not very good and its diaphragm could not open wide enough to allow you to film in low light. To achieve even a half-decent depth of focus with artificial lighting, which gets very hot, you would probably incinerate your unfortunate subject before you could actually film it. I soon discovered that the macro was only usable in good natural sunlight, quite a rare commodity in Ireland. I had a third lens. That was the four hundred millimetre Novoflex, that had been kindly donated by its German manufacturers before the eagle expedition. It was a good lens but it had one drawback. Its pistol-shaped design, which had landed me in prison in Morocco, included a spring-loaded, follow-focus system. This was excellent for still photography, allowing swift refocusing for single shots of a moving subject. But it could get tiring on the fingers to hold the spring steady on a long cine shot, with the risk that a beautiful scene might drift out of focus. Nevertheless, with these somewhat inadequate tools, I set out to make my first television series.

Filming in the heart of Dublin was the most difficult work I had ever done. The busy townscape was as alien to me as it was to the plants and animals whose stories I was trying to tell. It wasn't Dublin itself, which is a city of many subtle charms. It was simply the whoosh of traffic and the rush of people that I struggled with. But that, of course, was the point. City life is a challenge for sensitive organisms. I had heard that there were red squirrels in St Anne's Park so I decided to start there, but I soon found there was another native species in the park, one I didn't want to film. The "gooriah" is endemic and ubiquitous in Dublin. It is much smaller than its cousin, the gorilla, and is invariably armed with a stick. As soon as I set up the camera, I was surrounded by a gang of small boys, typically armed, the boldest of whom stepped forward and said "Hoi Mishter, watcha doin?" I explained that I was trying to film squirrels. "Well, mishter" he replied "Oi could hit that camera with moi stick." This gave us all pause for thought. I could be a bit like a grizzly bear when threatened, only marginally more dangerous. But the idea of a scattering of mangled, mauled or moribund children did not seem like a good start to my project. Indeed, I reasoned that they were actually my intended audience, so, I suggested they all come and look through the camera. The offer was instantly approved and one by one they squinted through the eyepiece, marvelling at how bins and park benches suddenly crept up on them when I zoomed in and how menacing a little ichneumon fly loomed through the macro lens. Then we saw a real live squirrel. This proved the ultimate diversion. They immediately grabbed their sticks and set off after it in a pack yelling "squiddel, squiddel" and that was the last I saw of them. It took me three hours to find another squirrel.

Patricia and I were very modest botanists. By which I mean we didn't know very much. We had spent ten July days camping out on Fareidh Head, in the far North of Scotland, before we were married. There our main pastime had been crawling on our hands and knees in search of the tiny, very rare *Primula scotica* and we had learned all the submaritime heath species with which it associated. Now, however, we were making a series predicated partly on the ecological role of plants and we needed help. One of our main aims was to reflect the work of Irish scientists, but we were finding it hard to find any. I had hoped that one of our star witnesses would be Dr James Fairley, at University College, Galway, who was Ireland's leading mammologist. I had written to him immediately but his reply had been slightly discouraging. Yes, we could use his published material but under no circumstances were we ever to refer to him or credit him in any of our films. It seemed he had an extremely low opinion of RTÉ's nature output to date and did not want to be associated with it. I'm proud to say that I think we later helped to modify that opinion. The fifth film in the series focused on the famous old oak woods of Killarney, a particular interest of Dr Fairley's. After its transmission, he wrote us a very different letter, kindly asking us if he could use the film as a teaching aid, which we took as a seal of approval.

Our search for experts had led us to helpful meetings with Julian Reynolds at An Taisce, the Irish National Trust and Dr Alan Craig at the Ministry of Public Works. Alan was to prove a great friend to us. He facilitated our access to Ireland's nature reserves and ten years later, would collaborate with us on our last Irish series, The People's Landscape, portraits of the country's five National Parks. We made friends with Vincent Sheridan, chairman of the Irish Bird Society and with Oscar Merne, a leading seabird specialist and Ian Herbert who had published on wetland birds. Oscar and Ian were later hugely helpful in our second RTÉ series, Natural Causes. But help on the ground was still hard to find. It was a meeting with Dr Peter Wyse Jackson at the National Botanic Gardens that provided the breakthrough. He put us in touch with Declan Doogue, an "amateur" botanist of considerable repute in Dublin. "Declan" he assured us "was a gasman". Gasman is a special term of endearment which implies, above all "good fun". One of the many wonderful things about Declan was that he understood precisely what we needed: lucid ecological stories that connected plants and animals and illustrated the processes of colonisation. For example, Oxford ragwort (*Senecio squalida*) is an exotic plant with a penchant for railway lines. It is native to Sicily where it grows on dry volcanic ash. In the early 18th century, it probably "escaped" from Oxford's Botanical Gardens and found refuge in the stony cracks of college walls. When the railways were built it took a liking to these new, arid, ashy corridors and threaded its way across the country. Eventually, it arrived in the port

city of Cork, probably in a load of British ballast, and from there it
followed the railway line northwards to Dublin, where it was first
spotted around 1960. Declan now showed us the pavements and walls
and wasteground edges where it had settled. But this was only part of
the story. Ragwort – any member of the Senecio family – is the main
foodplant of the larvae of the cinnabar moth, a conspicuous day-
flying moth with brightly coloured red and black wings. Unfortunately for the moth, Ireland's native field ragwort (*Senecio jacobaea*)
can be poisonous to cattle so farmers often grub it up. But the urban
habits of the Oxford ragwort have offered an alternative food source,
luring the cinnabars into the heart of the city. In the summer it's not
hard to find the startling orange and black-striped caterpillars
roaming the streets and thronging the narrow leaves of the hardy
visitors from Sicily.

There's no doubt that botanising with Declan Doogue kick-
started my deeper interest in plants. We had no budget for consul-
tants, we could only pay his expenses but he worked with us anyway,
out of sheer enthusiasm and good will. His brilliant on the spot seminars about salt-resistant seashore plants, drought-resistant mosses or
the orchids of limestone clints and grykes, provided me with the tools
and the inspiration to start learning for myself.

About half way through our somewhat haphazard shooting
schedule, we got an anxious call from John Baragwanath at RTÉ.
John Kelleher had suddenly moved on and there was a new
Controller of Programmes who wanted to see what we were up to. I
was to make a rough-cut of what I'd shot so far, show it to the new
boss and talk him through it. I had two days. What a panic. I didn't
even have editing facilities, but managed to find a news-room I could
use for a few hours at RTÉ. When we arrived for the meeting, John
was very nervous. The new b-b-boss, Muiris Mac Conghail, he
explained, didn't take p-p-p-prisoners. When John was on edge, his
stutter appeared. As he introduced us, he kept assuring Muiris that
we were very ch-ch-ch-ch-cheap. Our little assemblage of "Other
Dubliners" was certainly esoteric. We had a colony of Artic terns at
the docks, blithely incubating their eggs and feeding their chicks on

top of a pile of gravel which was being continuously eroded by bull-dozers. Would the birds or the diggers finish first? We had our squir-rels, clinging to their bit of greenery in the park and all manner of creepy crawlies, like our cinnabar moth caterpillars riding their ragwort into town and the larvae of ladybirds living in the railings beside busy streets. Muiris listened, quite intently I thought, to my off-the-cuff narration and when I finished, he stood up, shook us both by the hand, nodded to John and that was it. We had the green light to complete the whole series.

Muiris Mac Conghail was, himself, a respected documentary film-maker of the old-school. He liked films to tell a story, he knew how they were constructed, he understood the tribulations of production and he could see whether a concept had the legs to last the distance. In those days, a commercial half-hour consisted of 26 and a half minutes, maximum 27 minutes including titles and closing credits. The extra minutes provided space for adverts after the end which, of course, partly paid for the work. If you strayed into adver-tising time your credits would be chopped off, which meant you lost your few seconds of glory and failed to thank people who had contributed to the production. Not a good idea.

I think it was the Oxford-based film-maker, James Gray, who introduced me to the useful rule-of-thumb that a half-hour film needed a back-bone of thirteen sequences, mini tales that should connect with each other and form a coherent and larger story when presented as a whole. James had just completed a brilliant "Wildlife on 1" for the BBC about the natural history of a compost heap and he was one of the first people I turned to for advice. James and his wife Caroline lived on meagre funds with their two young daughters in an ancient cottage in the Oxford village of Cote. They'd bought the cottage at an auction in a pub where they'd been amazed to find themselves the only bidders. Apparently, the competition had all gone to the wrong pub so they secured an astonishing bargain. With just three acres, they set out to be pioneering organic small-farmers. The first day I met them they'd just sold their goat. It had assaulted their pride and joy, an apricot tree that had, finally, produced three apricots, of which the goat had eaten two. As they were loading it into the trailer, James told me, the goat escaped again and, leaping over the wall managed to stretch up and pluck the final apricot as a parting shot. From our first meeting, James was generous with his help, time and advice and we became friends.

Ours could be a lonely path but James introduced me to a small circle of like-minded film-makers which included people like Hugh Miles, Mike Richards and Sean Morris, a founder of Oxford Scientific Films. These were undoubtedly some of the best cameramen of our generation and they'd recently banded together to form what became the International Association of Wildlife Film-Makers – the IAWF. Their aim was deeply altruistic. It was to share technical information and field experience, to help each other with contracts and to develop a clear ethical stance on the treatment of wildlife in film. And not least to get together and have some fun. As the membership grew, we organised annual family weekends, with lectures and activities and that chance to dissolve some of the isolation intrinsic to our work and life-style was, at least to me, a godsend. I started, appropriately, as a lucky mouse in the corner, but eventually I joined the committee. This was frankly pure fun because Sean Morris, for example could make me laugh until I cried. He still can. Most meetings were in Bristol so Sean, James and I often shared the drive, which meant a lot of crying. Ten years later, in the 1990s I was to take over from Mike Richards as Chairman, by which time our membership read like a Who's Who of the world's wildlife film-makers. I felt a little awed to make friends with legends like Diete Plague, Martin Saunders and Alan Root and grow close to tough operators like Richard Kemp and Tony Bomford – all names I'd admired from afar. As Chairman I managed to rope in Arriflex as our sponsors and, since many of us were using their gear, it was helpful to keep everyone abreast of the latest technical advances. And the exchange of information went both ways. We could lobby them for adjustments that were required. For example, when the SR3 first appeared it had a rim around the drive plate at the bottom, on which the magazine would rest. This could gather a film of water, most unwelcome on an electronic device.

Subsequently, Arri inserted a little soak-away to stop this happening. It's worth noting too, that much of the specialist, cutting edge technology, especially in the development of macro lenses, was driven by extremely inventive film-makers, like Peter Parks at Oxford Scientific Films and Martin Dohrn.

In the early days of Nature In Its Place, however, I was still rather alone so, apart from James, one of the only other people I could think of to ask for advice was Ron Eastman. Approaching Ron required some courage, which I was not entirely sure I had. Ron was something of a genius with the reputation for being able to solve almost any technical problem. He had been director of photography on feature films as well as filming extensively for the BBC. I knew him for his magical kingfisher film which was a miracle for its time and, as far as I know, the first to show life inside a kingfisher's sandy burrow and the first to go underwater to show the bird's fishing technique. Broadcast in 1967, it had also been the first BBC natural history programme to be shown in colour. But Ron had recently had a bust-up with the BBC and had become notoriously misanthropic, especially towards anyone connected with film, the BBC or even possibly with wildlife. All this was reiterated to me by his wife Rosemary, as she explained that there was no way he would even come to the phone to speak to me. But both Ron and Rosemary were fundamentally extremely kind and a few days later I was on my way to Hampshire to meet them. They lived in an old Mill house in Whitchurch, whose large sitting-room straddled the beautiful River Test, which ran right under the house. The Test is a chalk stream. With the Itchen and the Kennet, it is one of the most famous trout rivers in England. Indeed, a few miles downstream my father had a regular beat, where he had taught me to cast a dry fly. But the wonder of the river was dwarfed by the astonishing contents of the room. For, leaning against the pristine white sofas, and taking up most of the living space was a large segment of the enormous wing of a World War Two Lancaster Bomber.

Ron explained that he was rebuilding the bomber, one of the last of its kind, as a show-piece for the RAF. It was a labour of love.

Indeed, he was taking no fee but the fact that the RAF were happy to under-write any expense he deemed necessary, made him feel appreciated. I am not especially interested in planes. Model kits and Meccano sets were not part of my childhood. But I am always enthralled by other people's enthusiasms and having a guided tour from Ron around the complexities of a bomber's wing and the unfathomable mysteries of a famous old engine was quite beguiling. As he relaxed, our talk turned to film. One of the less scurrilous stories he told me about working for the BBC concerned a film he'd been asked to make about hedgehogs. There is an old wives' tale – well, I've always assumed it was something of a myth – that hedgehogs regularly suckle the milk from sleeping cows. It was supposed to be the cause of a degree of traditional enmity between hedgehogs and farmers. According to Ron, the producer was obsessed with filming this behaviour, regardless of its dubious scientific basis. Consequently, an agreeable local dairy farm was selected and in due course two hedgehogs arrived in a limousine, courtesy of the BBC. Of course, the cattle were not interested in lying down to be milked by a pair of prickly hedgehogs and the hedgehogs mainly curled up in embarrassment. Eventually, a vet had to be called in to sedate the cows and the folded-up hedgehogs were stuck onto the udders, so Ron could film their snouts as soon as they unrolled. And we all know the camera never lies.

I found Ron so entertaining that I nearly forgot to ask him the question I'd come for. I wanted to know how he would put lights into, for example, a puffin's tunnel so he could film the birds. It was probably a simple question for him but I didn't know much at all so anything he could tell me was helpful. The answer involved low-wattage bulbs to minimise disturbance and a small, quiet generator, to ensure constant light levels and avoid amateurish flicker.

There was one more person I decided to contact. That was Colin Willock, the managing editor of Survival Anglia, the natural history output of ITV's Anglia Television based in Norwich. I sent him a copy of "Refuge" with a covering letter and looked forward to meeting him or perhaps chatting about film over the phone. I received a curt reply simply saying "we'd all like to make films without music and only using natural sound" and implying that only a fool would do it. I had to admit that he had on his books some of the best names in the business – Alan and Joan Root, Des and Jen Bartlett, Dieter Plage – so the thought of Stephen Mills might not be expected to brighten his morning. Nevertheless, I was disappointed by the brusqueness of his response and I felt it rather begged the question that if you want to do something why don't you try it? Perhaps for this reason, I was all the more determined to have pure, relevant and continuous natural sound tracks over all my Irish films, thereby breaking with the fine old local tradition of larding pan-pipes, half drums and general pub music over scenes of the natural world. Only with the final series did I relent, slightly. The People's Landscape, about the nature and the management of Ireland's National Parks, had people in the title and people and their conflicts and concerns in the films so a little human-orientated music seemed appropriate. Patricia and I liked the music of the blind 18th century Irish minstrel and composer, Turlough O'Carolan. Indeed, we had named our son Turlough after him. I also admired the work of modern composer Elizabeth Parker. She was highly inventive and had worked for the amazing BBC Radiophonic Workshop so I asked her to write a little one-minute overture in the mood of O'Carolan that we could use as an opening and closing theme tune for each film of the series. It was exciting to commission a piece of music from someone I deeply respected and the piece she produced was perfect. When I heard it over the dreamy wide-angle opening shot of Lough Veagh at the beginning of the Glenveagh film it brought tears to my eyes. But that was ten years later.

It took us four years to complete Nature in its Place. Looking back now, there are some incidents that still stand out. The first is a cautionary tale. We were botanising in the dunes of Murlough, a National Trust property on the coast of County Down which we had selected as the location of our second film in the series, The Green Sandcastle. It was late in the afternoon when we found a beautiful little colony of bee orchids, tucked, as they should be for our story, in the depression of a dune slack. The light was fading, we didn't have the camera with us and we were sorely tempted to leave filming the orchids till the morning. Something, however, prompted me not to delay. We trudged back across the dunes to our caravan, hauled out the gear and slogged our way back again to film a provisional sequence. The next morning was sunny so we returned to film the orchids in better light. Which we would have done, except that the orchids had disappeared. Not a single flower remained. Were we in the wrong place? No, definitely not. There was the marker we'd left the night before. We scoured the ground and eventually we found what was left of the basal leaves of several vanished flower heads. The leaves looked as if they'd been eaten by slugs. Had an army of slugs slithered along our trail eating our subjects or had a rabbit breakfasted on the lot? I'm going to pin it on the slugs. Either way, the subdued shots we'd obtained had to serve in the film because we never saw another bee orchid at Murlough that year.

The second incident concerns peregrine falcons. We were up in the nearby Mournes Mountains, filming our uplands story: "The High Road". James McEvoy, one of the assistant wardens there had found a peregrine's nest and he cheerfully offered to guide me up to the steep crag and help me erect my hide opposite the ledge and little cave where the birds had two tiny chicks. With my powerful lens I could see right into the nest site. But that's really all I could see and I dared not move or try to peer out down the dizzying precipice below in search of the parents for fear of disturbing them. So James, excellent man that he was, said he would place me in the hide and descend, concealing himself far below and as soon as he spotted a peregrine approaching the nest, he would let out a whistle to warn me to start the camera. That way, I'd be able to capture the all-important arrival at the ledge. I hunkered down to wait and, sure enough, after little more than half an hour I heard James's piercing signal and the next moment the infernal eyes of the falcon were burning right into my brain. I got a hell of a shock. I'd never seen anything so close. Of course, she wasn't that close, she was just big in the lens and I was an idiot. Such an idiot, in fact, that I gave a jump and the camera jolted, rendering the shot unusable. But what happened next was quite remarkable. The mother bird had arrived with the plucked corpse of a small pigeon, which she now carried to the back of the ledge before noticing that one of her minute, white fluffy chicks had crawled out to the very rim of the nest where it was teetering dangerously. She left the prey, walked carefully back to the edge and very gently took the chick by the back of the neck in her beak and carried it inside to safety. Then she set about ripping the carcass of the pigeon into bloody shreds, proffering them at the very tip of her beak to the hungry chicks. And this she did with all the delicacy of a Japanese geisha administering titbits with chopsticks to a revered guest. Finally, after breakfast, she settled down to incubate the chicks and from her squatting position she revealed one more use for her carrying, ripping, chop-stick beak. She used it very deliberately as a trowel, scraping up the earthy floor of the cave and building a parapet, several inches high, to keep the chicks safe from further errancy.

In his excellent book on seabird behaviour, Brian Nelson describes the limitations of the gannet's dagger-like bill. Its prime use is for skewering fish but it can also be used to pick up attractive pebbles that an amorous gannet will offer as love-tokens to a prospective mate. Gannets nest in crowded colonies where they are aggressively protective of their one square metre of space. A chick that wanders out of position may get killed, yet its parents, seeing it as neither fish nor stone, seem unable to pick it up in their beaks and bring it back to safety. My peregrine, however, was clearly a multitasker and, having regained my composure, I managed to film the entire episode. I later discussed this sequence with my friend, Derek Ratcliffe, a world expert on peregrines. He had never seen anything like it and, as far as I know, this was the first time such behaviour had been filmed in the wild.

One of the reasons why I had had so little experience of peregrines is that, during my childhood they had been nearly extinct. Derek Ratcliffe is credited with discovering the link between persistent pesticides like DDT and Dieldrin and egg-shell thinning in birds of prey. This discovery was popularised in Rachel Carson's influential masterpiece, Silent Spring, and led to the banning of such chemicals.

By the 1980s peregrines were recovering and many of their old nest-sites, recorded in falconer's notebooks as far back as the middle-ages, were being repopulated and I relished the chance to film them at last. I needed James's help to replace the arrival shot that I'd messed up the first time, because the female often came silently to the nest without warning. When the male was around, however, things were much noisier. During the egg-incubation period and the early days of the chicks, the male does most of the hunting. But he's a lot smaller than his mate so, probably to ensure he doesn't get clobbered himself by a hungry mum, he is very vocal when he comes to the nest. Indeed, they both are and their loud whickering calls of keekeekee-keekee are a give-away. The size difference between females and males is found in all owls and birds of prey but is particularly obvious in peregrines, goshawks and sparrowhawks – all raptors that engage in spectacularly dynamic hunting chases. Given that in most other birds, males are larger than females or size differences are minimal, this anomaly in raptors must have a survival significance. Presumably her larger framework allows the female to hunt effectively even when she's burdened with unhatched eggs.

One of the themes of "The High Road" was rain: how rain is precipitated in the mountains and helps to carve the landscape and create the bogs, how it feeds the streams and rivers and how even some plants, like bog asphodel, are pollenated by rain. So, I returned one rainy day in late June to film the peregrines again. Now, the chicks were almost full-grown, wearing proper peregrine clothes, only a little browner than the mature slate-blue plumage and with just a hint of tufty chick down on their heads. They stood on their ledge looking quite disconsolate in the pouring rain. I filmed the raindrops running off the stones above them, dripping onto their heads and down again off the ends of their beaks. Within a few days their parents would lure them off the nest-site for ever, with promises of fresh-killed prey that would only be available if they left home. By the end of the summer, they would be hunting for themselves. But for me, that last, sodden shot was just what I was looking for.

The Mountains of Mourne, however, hold one more special

memory for me. James McEvoy also showed me the location of a rare ring-ouzel's nest that he'd found, high up in the last sprigs of heather below the bare crown of the hill. Just after dawn the next morning, I toiled up to where I'd erected my hide, close to the nest, only to find the chicks had flown. Fortunately, the parents, like large blackbirds with white chests, were still feeding them where they were scattered in the nearby tussocks. But as soon as I began to film them, they disappeared, one by one, into a dense mist which all of a sudden rolled across the mountainside and swallowed them up. It swallowed me too. Soon the fog was so thick I could see nothing at all. I waited for hours, huddled against the damp, insinuating cold, hoping against hope that the mist would lift, the ring ouzels would still be there and I could carry on filming. Then from far below I heard the gentle bleating of sheep and the commanding whistle of a shepherd. Somewhere down on the lower slopes the sun must have peeped out again and a bucolic scene of rustic companionship, one man and his dog, was playing out on warmer pastures beneath me. And then the bleating turned to panic and the dog began to bark and the whistling became more and more frantic and the shepherd began to swear. Echoing up from the invisible valley came a great roar "aggh yer whore yer, yer whore, yerv run through the feckin lot of em". I've never forgotten how much it cheered me up.

Of course, there were many other high points. I remember commandeering a rowing boat in the harbour of Cape Clear so I could film a huge basking shark that had just appeared. The owner, who'd just got out, didn't seem at all concerned when I jumped in with my big movie camera, shouting "shark". I remember the swathes of aromatic wild garlic carpeting Killarney's ancient oak woods and the woolly green overcoat of mosses and ferns covering every tree, like some pre-historic forest. I remember filming Patricia's hardy uncle Ned as he cut the back field of their farm with a scythe, each stook of hay tumbling in perfect time to the effortless sway and sweep of his body. Only it wasn't effortless because when I had a go it didn't tumble like that for me. But one other little story pokes its head up above the others. The Burren, the great limestone pavement fringing the coast of County Clare in Western Ireland, became one of my favourite places on earth. Between April and early June its complex ecology of lime-rich soils and bare rock, of levelling winds and warm stone, produces an inflorescence that is unique in northern Europe – or indeed anywhere, giving rise to strange floral anomalies. It was, for instance, one of the delights of our Burren film, "Limestone Land" to film – at sea level –the inconspicuous spikes of dense-flowered orchid, a mainly Mediterranean plant, growing side by side with the open white crowns of mountain avens, normally found in the high alps. With its blue gentians, red-purple bloody cranesbill, tiny white saxifrages and golden rockroses, the Burren is the most beautiful wild rock garden I've ever seen. But best of all are the orchids. The Burren holds at least 22 out of the 27 species of orchid found in Ireland. None of them grows tall on the bare plateaux and some, like the tiny frog orchid are quite hard to spot. Some of my happiest weeks were spent crawling over the limestone trying to find them. This is what I was doing one day when I found myself being observed by a very puzzled-looking American lady. It was extremely rare, in those days, to meet anyone else in the field so I stopped to answer her questions. She'd heard about the Burren and its orchids, she told me, so she'd come to see them. But she couldn't find them. "Well, they're right here I said," pointing down to the cracked lattice of wild stone-work where we were standing, "but they're quite small. You have to crawl around a bit to sort them out." She looked at me with utter disbelief. "Aren't there any glasshouses here where they can grow properly?". "No," I explained' "they're tiny and wild and delicate but they're lovely when you get to see them." She shook her head, turned round and strode off over the invisible orchids to her car. It was a pity because I'd just found a little colony of exquisite fly orchids. I'd have loved to have shown her but I guess they would have been a disappointment to someone who was looking for something three feet tall that would bite your arm off.

My book, "Nature in its Place: The Habitats of Ireland" was published by Bodley Head in the spring of 1988. It had many delicate line-drawings, following some of my own rough designs but beautifully executed by a young artist called Chris Jones, who was chosen by the publisher. It also had 42 of my photographs. The famous botanist, David Bellamy, supplied a blurb for the cover. He and I had recently worked together making a BBC radio programme in Turkey on turtles. We'd had a lot of fun but he was a kind, generous-hearted man and would probably have written something anyway even if we hadn't become friends. The reviews were favourable, indeed enthusiastic, especially in Ireland where the book seemed to fill a distinct gap. For those of us who are bibliophiles, a handsome book is a wonderful artefact. But more importantly, I felt we had done what we had set out to do. We had completed the series and had nudged the public, ever so slightly, towards a deeper understanding of the intricacies and the value of their natural environment. I believed that this new appreciation might make the future conservation battles in Ireland just a little bit easier to win.

9

WOLF SAGA

I suspect that one of the most important factors separating people in the way they think is not race, or language or even education. It is whether or not they have children. Those of us who have children are forever vulnerable. Our happiness hangs not by the single thread of our own existence but also by the multiple threads, so fragile when they are young, that connect our children to life. I have come to understand that for a parent, the loss of a child is a shock from which there can be no complete recovery. A stillbirth, a miscarriage even, leaves parents with a feeling of somebody forever waiting in the wings who will never be permitted to come on stage. These are holes in the fabric of a parent's life that can never be filled, wounds that can never be truly healed. Perhaps I was unusually childish, but I never had thoughts like this until I became a parent.

Our son Turlough was born on 20th July 1981. Three months later he was rushed to hospital with a soaring temperature and in a highly fractious state. We'd just driven back in our rattling Land-Rover from Ireland where I myself had been hospitalised with similar but undiagnosed symptoms. All I know is that I'd never felt so ill, before or since. We waited, agonised, to hear what was wrong with our sweet little boy. The dreaded answer came the next day. It was Meningitis.

But was it bacterial – more dangerous but treatable with antibiotics if you catch it early enough – and had we? Or was it viral – less predictable but less likely to be fatal? By the time we knew it was viral, Patricia was ill too. She ended up in a room in Oxford's JR2 Hospital, occupying exactly the same position as Turlough's but one floor up. For the next few weeks our new little family was divided by hospital stairs and shaken by terrors of brain-damage or death.

I have enormous respect for the many, many parents who face these traumas daily, often with great courage, who deal with the aftermath uncomplainingly and who stare bravely into the abysses that surround us, abysses of whose existence I was blithely unaware until I became a father. Turlough recovered. Patricia recovered. But I'm not sure our relationship was ever quite the same again. A little of the carefree spirit was diminished – or perhaps we just grew up. Over the next few years our lives became more consolidated. Our daughter Kate was born on 27th August 1983. We bought the cottage at the bottom of my parents' long drive that we'd been renting from them and made it more habitable. This included changing the hungry medieval electricity meter that had constantly to be fed with coins for a proper adult one from the twentieth century. Patricia completed her doctorate which was conferred after a good-natured public defence in Uppsala in 1985. The doctorate was published as a book encouraging her to embark on a new research project on the history of women in science. Her contribution to our film-work became, inevitably, more sporadic. In the first years of filming in Ireland, she and her family had been the absolute rock on which the work was built. Her mother, Mary Kate, had looked after Turlough and then both children with absolute competence for long stints. Her brother John, a teacher in Rathcoole near Dublin, had welcomed us whenever we needed a base near RTÉ. He and his wife Mary put up with me boarding in my caravan at the end of their garden on and off for years. But gradually our life had to settle into a more traditional groove, with Patricia playing the anchoring roll at home while I spent weeks, even months away.

I didn't mind being away for filming. I loved the solitude behind the camera and I loved coming home to my quiet caravan in the evening, with little to worry about other than cooking a steak and having a glass of wine. Most of my locations were in nature reserves or national parks where the staff were interested in my work and happy to find me somewhere beautiful to set up camp. But the long weeks of editing, always in Dublin, became increasingly tedious. I was lucky in one respect. It's not easy to find a good editor, someone who is compatible, sympathetic to what you are trying to achieve and good company. Peter Gahan was all of these. He had worked with David Shaw-Smith, one of Ireland's leading arts and crafts documentary film-makers and had taken on The Other Dubliners right at the beginning when the structure of the film was in some disarray. Peter had an excellent eye; he knew how to put pictures together. The only thing he struggled with was my natural sound tracks. "We need a raven croaking here over that mountain shot... and now the wheatear." Crackle crackle crackle splat. He didn't always seem to hear the difference between a crackle, a splat and a croak. But to be fair, some of the sound effects I gave him were awful. Peter, however, was entirely patient. He would quietly dismember the offending tracks and we would painstakingly rebuild them until they were usable. And slowly I accrued a bigger library of much better recordings. I also discovered useful repositories of material I didn't have myself and our sound tracks became more profound. Peter soon learned that a close-up of a flower, with the sound of a fly buzzing somewhere not far away becomes three-dimensional and comes alive. "Ah, the beautiful flies, " he would say.

I didn't want to lose Peter, but he was based in Dublin. Everything changed, however, when he said he could come to Oxford. Peter was something of an ascetic, extremely self-contained, with a deep love of opera and an intellectual interest in George Bernard Shaw, about whom he was later to publish a book. He decided that, during an editing period, he could use our home as a temporary base from which to explore the theatres of London. Consequently, we bought a six-plate Steenbeck editing table and set up our own cutting-room in one of the many little bedrooms at Church Cottages. I never had to go away for editing again.

Without discipline, film-making and editing in particular, has a habit of expanding to fill all time available and indeed time not available. Peter was totally reliable in doing what he promised to do, but he was equally scrupulous in defence of his spare time. Weekends were sacrosanct, as they should be, and I learned not to try to solve an editing problem at quarter to five on a Friday evening. It was a good lesson. I suspect Peter found me exasperating but he never actually told me so. We ultimately edited 27 films together and I don't remember sharing a cross word.

There were two other developments that transformed my working conditions and helped us eventually to compete at the highest level. The first was that we invested in a new camera. I say "invested" because this was a top of the range, high-speed Arriflex SR II. It was the best sixteen millimetre camera in the world, albeit still employing the original claw-system registration pin that had kept the old 1950s Disney CalArts ST so steady when I'd used it at the Salton Sea. And in the mid 1980s the SRII was the price of a small house. It was the most expensive thing I'd ever bought at the time and it paid for itself within nine months. Hence an "investment". I was already friendly with the staff at Arriflex's London office near Perivale, mainly because I'd been a bit of a nuisance there for years. Our old, cumbersome BL, had developed a light leak – a one-second flash of reddish frames that occasionally spoiled a take – and I went to Arri cap in hand to ask for help to diagnose the problem. The workshop couldn't find an obvious fault but a couple of senior men, Alan Piper and Ron Harris, decided to keep the whole kit for weeks one winter, when I wasn't filming, to try and puzzle it out. In their spare time they stood the loaded camera in different positions, alternating the different magazines and developing each separate bit of film from each experiment to see where the leak showed up. After much effort they found a pinhole leak in one of the magazines. It wasn't really a problem if I taped the throat of that magazine after loading it and it was useful information for the new owner when I sold the BL package. I was delighted to get rid of the BL because it was so heavy and unwieldy, though as solid as a rock. The man I sold it to, Roger Wood, later told me it had been hit by a train. I don't know what happened to the train but apparently the camera survived.

I think the whole Arriflex team had been dragged into solving the BL problem so when I decided to buy a new camera there was general rejoicing. It was always fun visiting the workshop there. I loved chatting with the knowledgeable technicians, asking them which lenses gave problems, which cameras were most reliable. They also enjoyed tales from the bush. Descriptions of how cameras behaved in the wild seemed to bring their work to life. But the story of mine that they liked best concerned Turlough. Just after he turned five, he had discovered the blower that I used to clean lenses. It was a large, beautiful blue pear-shaped rubber ball with a long narrowing nozzle. The ball was naturally full of air and when you squeezed it firmly the air shot out from the end of the nozzle like a dart. Turlough, however, being an inventive character, thought that this might be the perfect implement for picking up marmalade to spread on his toast. Unfortunately, I wasn't aware of his discovery. When I described the sickening "thwapp" of the unexpected marmalade hitting the pristine glass of my brand-new Zeiss 10:100 zoom lens, the lads at Arri laughed till they cried. I still have the official plaque they sent me that Christmas as "Most Important Person" of 1986.

During its first year, when I was filming in Connemara, the new camera developed a dodgy-sounding grind in the motor. Arri immediately shipped a technician out to help me. We had to meet in a room in the bonded warehouse section of Shannon Airport to avoid payment of duty. I don't quite know whether this was kosher but it worked and they put in a new motor. When I got home, they called me in for a couple of free seminars, teaching me how to keep my camera going in the unlikely event of future breakdown and all the things I could do without special calibrating equipment. The most crucial lesson was probably how to remove the motor board and isolate it in the event of the camera falling into the sea. Of course, it's much better not to drop it in the water but wise to be prepared. In fact, the only trouble I ever had later was with the drive belt for the shutter swelling with damp. In Ireland, the rain, though it may not be torrential, is often horizontal which can be difficult to fend off. I think maybe twice, in fifteen years, this caused me brief delays. It never happened in India, even at the height of the monsoon, only Ireland. My friend Stephen de Vere, however, had a much worse problem in Antarctica with his drive belt. Two days after the last plane flew out, his belt snapped. He faced an entire Antarctic winter with nothing to do. So he scoured the research station for a dormant computer, took it to pieces, dug out the tiny rubber belt for its disc drive and somehow making precise measurements he managed to glue it into his shutter system as a replacement. He told me he filmed the whole emperor penguin sequence for Life in the Freezer with this bit of making-do. Brave man. I expect if it had happened to me, I'd have just asked a passing leopard seal to eat me.

The other development that transformed my working life was that we bought a second home in Ireland. This was a complete accident. In the summer of 1986, we needed a little holiday so we hired a cottage on the coast of West Cork. I'd noticed on the map a small peninsula sticking out into the sea close to Cape Clear and the famous lighthouse of Fastnet. It looked like a good place for migrant birds. It was called Toe Head. Only in Ireland, I thought, would you find such a delightfully paradoxical name. The Irish have always had a flare for paradox. I seem to recall an advert for the wonderful Fortnight magazine which read "from now on Fortnight will be published monthly and there will be ten issues a year." Anyway, Toe Head had to be visited. It was a rare sunny day when we toiled up the steep lane to the ruined watch tower that overlooks the headland. The views of wide sea, scalloped cliffs and tiny, wind-sculpted fields was breathtaking. Below the tower was a tumble-down white cottage which made me think that if I ever bought a spare house it would have to be something like this. But this one was inhabited and not for sale and in any case, there was no way we would saddle ourselves with an unaffordable domicile. There were chough nesting in the crumbling tower. They kept us enthralled with their curved red beaks and red feet, their piercing metallic cries and the synchronised dance of their flight and by the time we arrived in the local market town of Skibbereen it was too late for lunch. The only thing I'd heard about Skibbereen was the famous headline trumpeted on the front page of the town newspaper before the First World War, which had read, splendidly, "The Skibbereen Eagle is keeping an eye on the Kaiser." Apparently, the local estate agent, Charley McCarthy, was keeping an eye on us too, because as soon as we stopped, aimlessly, in front of his shop window, he popped out and asked us what sort of house we were looking for. "Absolutely no house," I assured him hastily. "Absolutely not." "Ah, but if you were," he said, "what class of a house would that be?" Charley was clearly a playful character so, in the same spirit I began to describe the little cottage I'd seen as "a class of house" I could fall for. "But haven't I exactly a house like that for sale," he said. "What are you doin' now? I've nothin' to do myself, sure I could show it yer." He didn't seem to mind us wasting his time so, God help us, we agreed to let him show us a house "exactly like that". Charley wasn't exaggerating. With the accuracy of a homing pigeon, he drove us straight back to Toe Head, to the little white cottage under the tower. It was so remote no-one had bothered to put up a For Sale notice.

On closer inspection, the house only seemed to have two drawbacks. The first was that it really was tumbling down. The back wall seemed to me to stand at a most ungainly angle. The second, more serious problem was that the cottage stood on a stiflingly tiny patch of ground. You wouldn't actually be able to walk right round it on the land you owned. We agreed to buy it but only if the local farmer could be persuaded to sell us sufficient land to allow the house to breathe. Irish farmers hate to part with their land. I can only imagine the Byzantine process by which Jeremiah Sheehy was brought to the negotiating table. There must have been powerful inducements but sure enough, one day he turned up, armed with wooden pegs to mark out the meagre strip of gorse and furze he could imagine living without. Jeremiah was a small, solid man with a bald head fringed with bunches of white hair that blew tuftily in the wind. He had been born in the house, which was known locally as Mary Dearg's (pronounced jarad) or Red Mary's. I was advised not to mention this to Jeremiah because the epithet apparently referred less to her colouring than her language. Jeremiah must have inherited her linguistic traits because, even though he turned out to be in every other way the gentlest, politest man, he nevertheless swore vociferously and continuously as we worked our way round the new plot. He would poke a marker in the ground and swear. Mightily. I would move it out a yard. He would swear again and put it back where it had been. This battle of oaths and pegs was fought for hours in a blinding gale but at last we both retired happy. He knew he had been vastly overpaid and I knew we would henceforth be able to walk round our house.

We had to hire an architect to oversee the very basic works on the house: a damp course for the floor and new, raised windows at the front, upstairs. We needed these because the only way you could look out of the existing windows was to lie on the floor. One day when we were back in Oxford, I got a call from the architect. He asked would I like a window in the West wall as well. "No thank you, Donal," I said, "I can't afford an extra window". "Ah well," he replied "it won't cost you anything". "How's that?" I asked. "Well, the wall's fallen down anyway so it would be cheaper to put a window in now." So, we got a lovely new window from where we could sometimes see the far away glow of Fastnet lighthouse.

It is customary for writers who move into the remote countryside to make fun of the ignorance and naivety of the people they encounter. I'm going, more or less, to resist this temptation. I've always found people in general, and especially in Ireland, to be pretty clever. It may be that the English have cultivated a traditional contempt for education – perhaps because the upper classes didn't feel they needed it to ride around catching foxes and the lower classes, however hard they worked, had no hope of improving their lot. But in Ireland education has always been held in great respect. It was a way out that would help them become presidents and Nobel prize winners. Toe Head, however, did have some peculiarities that took a while to get used to. For one thing, it was part of the "Gaeltacht", the Westerly fringe of Ireland where Irish is spoken as the native tongue. I'm no linguist but I understand that there are no formal words in Irish for yes and no. Instead, statements have to be affirmed or denied in full, which can considerably elongate conversation. Hence: "may I buy your land?" answer "you may buy my land" or "may I move the peg?" answer "you may not move the frigging peg". Furthermore, rather than saying "I have moved the frigging peg anyway" you might translate direct from the Irish and say "I am after moving the frigging peg anyway." And if the fence post falls over you might say "the fence post has fallen out of its standing."

Accents and idioms could make it hard to understand people. I found the Buckleys particularly opaque. They were three brothers who lived in a little farm house on the other end of the headland. They were a bit like the three Billygoats Gruff. The oldest, Big Buckley drove a car, Middle Buckley had a motor bike and Little Buckley rode a bicycle. Little Buckley may not have been the full shilling. He had apparently been hung up on a peg by an exasperated teacher as a schoolboy and he was definitely inconsistent as to what side of the road he cycled on, which could be problematic at night because he had no lights. At one point his bike was confiscated by the Gardai but I think it was restored after a communal protest. The Collins's were also hard to decipher. Their farm was about half a mile away, on a sharp bend on the lane that wound down from our house. They always wore Wellingtons and so did we when we stopped to talk with them because their dogs mistook us for sheep and bit our heels if we stood still for too long. John and Eileen were nearly always together and always very happy to see us when we arrived on the headland but one day when I stopped, John was missing. "He's gaarn naaart," was Eileen's reply to my asking after him. Eileen had quite a high, shrieky voice and it was quite painful to have to ask her to repeat herself. "He's GAARN NAART" she said again, higher and louder. Quite rightly, she thought I was a bit stupid but was too kind to say it. Eventually I realised she was saying John had gone North. This surprised me. I couldn't really imagine John all the way up in Belfast, in his Wellingtons, doing any sort of shady business. It took me some months to discover that "gaarn Naart" simply meant gone off the headland. Everywhere off the headland required an initial northerly journey. John had actually been in Skibbereen. A couple of years later I was more alarmed when I stopped and found John on his own. "How is Eileen?" I asked. "She's gaarn West," he replied. And indeed she had. She'd gone West to Bantry Hospital. Fortunately, she recovered from whatever ailed her but it taught me to listen carefully.

Toe Head became our haven. For as long as we were allowed to, we took the children out of school from March to October. In those days, state schools were not supposed to have a formal curriculum. We could get no clear instructions as to what to teach them so we took their school books and gave them lessons for fifteen minutes a day, mainly in Maths. In addition, I forced them to endure my dramatic renderings of my favourite children's books: The Wind in the Willows, The Hobbit and later, The Lord of the Rings, Emma and Pride and Prejudice. For the rest, they amused themselves. They made friends among the adults all over the headland. They built miniature rafts down on the deserted beaches and played games out over the fields and up at the tower. When it rained, they, like their mother, could disappear into their books for days, even weeks. Turlough had read all of Jane Austen by the time he was twelve and in due course, he took over the dramatic readings, giving us deeply wistful performances of the Moomintroll cycle and The Mouse and His Child. Of course, we had visitors. Over the years, many friends came, either staying with us or renting one of the few available cottages elsewhere on Toe Head. But the children were self-contained and kind to each other. When they were quite small, they devised a game called Troll Village which endured for years. They built houses and sewed clothes for the trolls and they wrote dozens of miniature books for the Troll Village library. Troll Village was a profoundly bourgeois establishment. It had a bank and a building society but there were no arty film-makers permitted to live there. When Turlough eventually went off to boarding school – which is another story – Katie wrote in her diary "my brother has gone off to school and now I must learn to amuse myself."

Perhaps life at Toe Head gave the children freedom and autonomy. I hope so. For me it was an invaluable hearth to return to during the filming season and, increasingly, a peaceful retreat where I could write and develop new ideas.

Our second RTÉ series was settled with a handshake in a pub on the border between Northern Ireland and the Republic. "Natural Causes" was originally planned as ten half hour films, that would focus on aspects of animal and plant behaviour using, of course, only Irish examples. It would explore the uses of colour and shape, the existence and role of wildlife colonies and the causes of extinction. But it would also allow us to tackle some important Irish stories that we'd rather skated over in the first series. In particular, we could devote a whole programme to the fascinating theories of how Ireland acquired its flora and fauna after the near clean-sweep of the last Ice-Age. We could also do an in-depth portrait of the wonderful life in the bogs – very Irish, after all, and a subject that David Bellamy had inspired me to take seriously. We sketched all this out over a pint of Guinness and a light pub lunch with Muiris McConghail and John Baragwanath. It was an extremely affable meeting but I must admit I was a little anxious about the informality of the proceedings and I asked John if he would draw up an immediate memorandum of agreement, prior to the formal contract. He laughed and, as we parted, he said "Don't worry, Stephen. What dyer think we are? A Banana Republic?"

Was I right to worry? On the one hand, no. Over the course of fifteen years, we made 21 films for RTÉ and I would say that they were, overall, the most honest people and the easiest to deal with that I have met during my career. On the other hand, two major glitches emerged. The first was a change in personnel. We had barely started the new series when Muiris was replaced as controller of programmes by Bob Collins and John by Mike Kelly as the new Finance Director. We were called in for a meeting with Mr Collins who bluntly informed us that he had a mind to cancel the whole series. It seemed we were not cheap anymore and he could not see the value in allocating so much funding to a sideshow like natural history. I didn't agree with him. I pointed out that RTÉ had, by statute, a duty to supply "Public Service" content and that our series would fulfil that purpose on its own, freeing him up to fill the rest of the schedule with whatever he wanted. We argued for an hour. To his credit, he didn't just throw us out, he listened. He even postponed the firing squad, saying that we'd meet again in a week, after he had made some inquiries about the impact of our first series. Precisely a week later we were back in his office and his demeanour had changed. He'd taken the trouble to sound out a range of people for their opinions of Nature in its Place and he'd been impressed by the comments. Consequently, he would reverse his decision and confirm the contract for Natural Causes, only, in the interests of economy, it would be eight not ten films. In truth, I had not done my homework on Bob Collins. If I had, I would have discovered that he was, himself a believer in public service broadcasting, of which he would become a distinguished defender. I understand that after his retirement he was asked of which achievements during his tenure he had been most proud. He had singled out the promotion of RTÉ's public service remit, for example, with the commissioning of series like... you've guessed it: Natural Causes.

The second glitch occurred when Mike Kelly called us to say there wasn't any actual money to pay us. RTÉ was in conflict with the government over its annual budget and the cash flow had dried up. To me, this sounded like a nightmare, a catastrophe, definitely not a good thing. Mike, however, seemed very relaxed about it. "Don't worry," he said, "it will get sorted out. Probably. In the meantime, what you have to do is borrow the money from the Allied Irish Bank and RTÉ will underwrite the loan. Start with a hundred thousand. It'll be fine." I'm not a gambler and I'm not a business man. Interest rates were running at ten percent. At best it felt like a waste of RTÉ's money at worst I might be swimming with the fishes. I nearly died of fright. I needn't have. Mike was right, of course. It was all sorted out and RTÉ fulfilled their obligations to the letter. As they always did.

For me, the Irish programmes fulfilled a general purpose of presenting nature in a new depth to a fresh audience, but beyond that, they were not campaigning films. So, while I enjoyed myself filming around Ireland, I was trying, at the same time, to develop a parallel career as an investigative environmental journalist. It was a route that would eventually lead me back to the BBC and to the making of perhaps the two most important films of my life. This sort of journalism was not mainstream in the 1980s. Concern for the environment was still lamentably low as a political priority and, in a modest way, I felt like a pioneer. I had two crucial contacts who helped me. The first was Roz Kidman Cox. She became the editor of Wildlife Magazine after Nigel Sitwell sold it and I'd written several pieces for her from America. While still based in London she had met my friend David Helton at Oryx and when the BBC took over her magazine, she and David moved to Bristol together and became life-long partners. There, David wrote clever scripts for the BBC and Roz continued as editor of what was now BBC Wildlife. She commissioned me to write the first ever cover story for the launch issue in November 1983. It was a soft story about pandas but in the years that followed, I was encouraged to introduce more hard-hitting subjects. One of my interests was in highlighting the disgraceful management of wild predators, especially in Norway where – curiously because I was a foreigner and writing for the BBC – I was listened to. Roz was a brilliant editor, with an acute sense of the potential role of the magazine in raising public awareness. With only a very limited budget, she managed to charm and cajole frequent contributions from the very best natural historians in the country, outstanding writers, thinkers or scientists like Richard Mabey, Chris Baines, David Macdonald, Charlie Pye-Smith and Mark Cawardine and she was kind enough to include me in this core group. Over the next 20 years, she gathered an unpaid panel of advisers around her. We would meet for occasional, amazing brainstorming lunches where she amassed the ammunition which allowed her to ring-fence sufficient space in the magazine for serious stories despite the commercial pressure from her bosses for more advertising, more photo features and more stories that said nothing or at least nothing controversial.

My other crucial contact was Colin Tudge, the Features Editor for New Scientist. I did write occasional pieces for John Vidal's new Environment page in the Guardian, for Rob Hume, who edited Birds, the RSPB Magazine and my friend Redmond O'Hanlon kept me supplied with books to review for the Times Literary Supplement. This last gave me some enjoyable kudos but it was only occasionally a campaigning opportunity. So, it was undoubtedly New Scientist that gave me my most important writing platform in the 1980s. Colin Tudge showed the sensibilities of a fine writer. He grasped the significance of environmental stories effortlessly and was always interested in new ideas and hitherto unexplored territory. We developed a very friendly working relationship. He would encourage me to come up with anything that interested me that wasn't being addressed elsewhere. He would give me a minute development budget and a generous deadline and I would strive to produce a completely original full-length feature that, ideally, could serve as the week's cover story and would be picked up by BBC radio in their weekly magazines review and by flagship outputs like The World at One. These articles had to be very carefully researched. They were often about subjects beyond my own limited expertise and sometimes, almost every line required background reading. There was no internet and no instant access to easy knowledge. I was lucky to live in Oxford, where, for each feature, I spent days in the Bodleian Library, the University Science Library or the Edward Grey Institute, often poring over micro-films of unpublished doctoral theses and what, for me, was fairly esoteric science. In the July 1981 cover story, Graveyard of the Puffin, I described a decade of disaster on the Norwegian island of Røst where the entire puffin production of half a million chicks had starved to death almost every year since 1970. It was a catastrophe of epic proportions yet it had gone almost entirely unreported. I linked it to the steep upturn in commercial catches of sprats and sand eels, prime puffin food, to which the fishing industry had turned after decimating the North Atlantic herring population. In Demise of the Landlord's Fish, another cover story, I described the unsustainable destruction of Ireland's salmon stocks at sea by illegal fishing boats using banned monofilament nets. I attributed the lack of public concern for this priceless natural resource to a hangover from colonial times when poaching a salmon had been regarded as a blow for freedom. I believe this post-colonial malaise, which I call "the landlord's fish syndrome" afflicted many countries as they got to grips with independence. It takes several generations for people fully to understand that their nation's natural assets are also their own birthright for which they can take responsibility. In "Rabbits Breed a Growing Controversy", which was illustrated by a gorgeous cover painting of a giant rabbit looming over a hobbit-like landscape, I described the Agricultural Ministry's detailed studies of myxomatosis, tracing the ying and yang fluctuations by which a virus and its host come to terms with each other. Rabbits had been all but wiped out when the disease first surfaced in the 1950s but now they were back. My story looked at the pros and cons of that return, reminding people, for instance, that rabbits, agricultural pests though they may be, could still mow a meadow massively to the benefit of wild flowers and that their recovery had seen the consequent recovery of wild predators, like polecats, that had all but vanished, and the spread of buzzards to landscapes where they hadn't been seen for decades. In another, more philosophical, cover story, Shades of Reasons for Protecting Wildlife, I examined the wide spectrum of views that were driving the growing conservation movement. I interviewed writers, scientists, politicians and philosophers but there was one glaring absence: religion. I approached both the Church of England, and the Catholic Church but apparently neither institution had a coherent policy on conservation and the environment and they had formulated no position at all on the preservation of God's Earth. I very much doubt this would be true today. We've come a long way in 35 years.

I loved writing those features for New Scientist. I loved the chance to influence the agenda, to write in some depth about whatever I thought was important on such a respected platform. Colin rarely changed a word and the articles were increasingly well produced. Colour photography was introduced in the early 1980s and my articles – often with my own photographs - were usually well-suited for colour treatment. I went to France, where I discovered that the

French interpretation of the European Common Agricultural Policy, much criticised in the UK press, was actually much more beneficial to wildlife than our own. In the UK, grants were geared towards the largest, most intensive farms. In France they favoured small-holdings which meant, for instance, lots of boundary hedges and consequently lots of wildlife habitat. I wrote extensively about UK forestry policies, highlighting the nascent movement to foster native hardwood species – much better for plants and animals – and how, with the right husbandry, they could be as economically viable as the stifling conifer plantations notoriously promoted by government. The germ of one of my favourite pieces, "Britain's Native Trout is Floundering" actually came to me when I was out fishing with my father on the River Test. The kind and enthusiastic river keeper showed us the new American brook trout that he had introduced into the river, along with the various hybrids of American rainbow trout, brook trout and brown trout with which he and other keepers were experimenting in order to supply flyfishers like ourselves with the perfect treat. I was shocked to realise that the management of our wild rivers was being driven by the interests of anglers not ecology and that the fundamentals of conservation policy – like never introducing alien species – were being completely ignored. Theoretically, rivers are sealed systems and fish species that do not go to sea gradually diverge into genetically distinct subgroups. If you mess with that, which we have done almost everywhere, you probably lose those subgroups and hence biodiversity, forever. These were apparently new ideas in the 1980s but during my researches I discovered that my worries were shared by several far-sighted government scientists. Their views, however, had in some cases been silenced or the money for research had been attracted towards commercial interests. I know my article was circulated at the ministry and I believe it helped, in a small way, to change views. These days, the introduction of alien fish in the UK is discouraged by anglers themselves and in most places is illegal.

Inevitably, many of my articles were critical of government policies, not because I was particularly bolshy but because I was questioning the status quo, and governments were usually responsible for that. I'll mention just one more piece. I'd begun to notice that during the road-building boom of the 1980s, new routes seemed to have an uncanny habit of damaging nature reserves and Sites of Special Scientific Interest. It really looked as if someone important at the Department of Transport hated plants and animals. I examined a representative tranche of new projects and there was no doubt that wildlife sites were disproportionately affected. It turned out there really was someone important deliberately making these choices. It was the Department's computer. Nature reserves, although they might be ecologically priceless, had little commercial value precisely because they were supposed to be unavailable for development or agriculture. So, when the computer was asked to plot the cheapest route for a new motorway it was actively selecting protected land-scapes and the new road plans were wiggling their way through the countryside not to avoid nature reserves but deliberately to cross them.

If you try to do good, worthwhile work, people help you. I built up a contact list of knowledgeable informants who would often give me a new slant on an idea or point me towards data that I might other-wise have missed. Derek Ratcliffe, who was chief scientist at the Nature Conservancy Council, was perhaps my most brilliant agitator. I suppose he trusted me not to reveal my sources but he was anyway pretty fearless in revealing the conservation failings of officialdom. He was, of course a serious naturalist which was unusual in govern-ment circles, so he acted from the heart. Other reliable guides included Charles Secret at Friends of the Earth and David Bowles and Debbie Banks at The Environmental Investigation Agency. But my best informant and spur to action was my old friend from Norway, Viggo Ree. It was he who had tipped me off about the seabird studies of Gunnar Lid, the ornithologist who had recorded the puffin deaths on Røst. He also introduced me to Odd Lindberg, whose epic battle with the Norwegian authorities over illegal seal-hunting methods I covered. The most important story that Viggo prompted me to explore, however, was Norway's ongoing war against its own wild predators.

Norway, as we all know, is a very rich country. It is more than one and a half times the size of the UK, with a population of just five million people. By any standards one would assume there was space there for a healthy population of bears, wolves, lynxes and wolverines. One would be wrong. The Norwegian authorities wage a systematic campaign of slaughter against their big predators. The government predator research programme is mostly concerned with ways of killing not conserving the animals. Wolverines, for instance, are one of the rarest, most endangered mammals in Europe. In Norway, it is government scientists, not poachers or angry farmers, who dig them out of their dens and inject them with poison. So ruthless is the culling of lynxes, that Viggo, who has lived in suitable lynx terrain almost all his life, has only ever seen one in the wild in Norway. Over in neighbouring Sweden, which has a human density almost double that of Norway, there are more than three thousand bears. In Norway there are perhaps a hundred. All the rest have been shot. This pogrom is carried out in the name of sustaining viable remote human populations. The root of all evil is sheep. In Sweden, farmers look after their sheep but in Norway, they have been traditionally subsidised to put them out on the hillsides in spring and to go and look for them again in autumn. Predators would be a threat to this indolent life style so they are not tolerated. I love Norway. Some of my dearest friends live there. But a visit is often tinged with sadness as I travel through wilderness landscapes that are still resonant with their lost fauna. You can camp out on the lip of a lonely valley. You can wake at dawn and watch the mist creep back among the trees and imagine a bear or a wolf edging along the treeline. But you know, in your heart, you will see nothing and this robs the wild beauty of some of its meaning. When the Taliban blew up the monumental Buddhas of the Bamiyan Valley in 2001, the world was justifiably horrified. I believe Norway's treatment of its great predators is likewise a crime against culture. Imagine if you visited the National Gallery to find all the pictures had been destroyed and only the hooks and the bare patches on the wall marked where they had once so inspiringly hung. That is how a naturalist feels in Norway. One day, I suspect the vast majority of Norwegians will come to understand that their birthright, their access to an intense wilderness experience, has been wilfully sacrificed for a handful of economically valueless sheep and they will be horrified. This is what I have been working towards but it certainly hasn't happened yet.

This perhaps puts into context the consternation that was caused in 1982 when the first confirmed wild wolf for nearly a hundred years appeared in southern Norway. It was seen near the village of Vegårshei, one hundred and sixty kilometres southwest of Oslo and its arrival fermented a truly biblical frenzy of fear and fury. The government promptly changed the law so it could be killed. The wolf had previously been protected under the Berne Convention on the basis that there weren't any. Wild West hunting parties descended on Vegårshei. One enthusiast even shot his own girlfriend who was moving lupus-like through the bushes and when the real wolf was finally cornered and dispatched in January 1983 the subsequent rejoicings echoed the end of the Second World War. The Monster's corpse was driven to Oslo and laid in grisly glory on the steps of the parliament building with its mouth propped open with a stick and its fur sticky with champagne. Meanwhile, another sub-Arctic Scandinavian wolf had appeared, in the county of Värmland in south central Sweden. It was a huge male and from the tracks in the snow it was clear that it was capable of bringing down an adult moose on its own – an animal nearly ten times its weight. Then a female turned up, also in Värmland and she, too was killing moose on her own. This prodigious solo hunting ability implied that both wolves had been on their own for a long time. Somehow, they must have made their way from deepest Finland or Karelian Russia, dodging the traps, bullets and poison paraded by the reindeer herders of the far north. These were, indeed, hero wolves.

Now that the wolf is creeping back across the domesticated landscapes of Europe, even breeding in countries as tame and orderly as the Netherlands, it is hard to remember how impossible this all seemed forty years ago. When I first visited Norway in 1971, the thought that there might ever be wolves again near Oslo seemed an impossibility. For us, then, the wolf was the ultimate symbol of wilderness, its howl a cry from our own pre-history. So far had we relegated it to the realms of fairy tale that we'd have as soon believed that there were trolls in the hills as wolves. Little did we know that the wolf was not a wilderness creature by preference but by necessity. We had driven it there. Now we understand better that wolves, like most animals, will live almost anywhere where there is enough food and not too much disturbance and persecution.

Värmland is not rugged wilderness. It is a rolling landscape of forest and lakes and hills, peaking at around five hundred metres. In the spring of 1983, the two Värmland wolves finally met up and mated. They dug a deep earthy den near the woodland village of Bjurberget where they produced six pups. It was the first time in living memory that wolves were proved to have bred in Scandinavia south of the Arctic Circle. In the summer of 1984, the pups dispersed and the parents produced two more litters. The ensuing extraordinary adventures of these wolves became the subject of a string of articles I wrote for Oryx, the Guardian, BBC Wildlife and, of course, New Scientist, as well as several radio broadcasts. One by one, the travelling wolf pups from the first litter cropped up all over Scandinavia. They were looking for other wolves to attach to but because there weren't any, they just kept on going. One walked six hundred kilometres to Trondheim in Norway. One scared a courting couple in their car outside Jonkoping. One was run over by a taxi on the outskirts of Stockholm and the most famous one walked all the way down to Malmö, in the populous southern tip of Sweden, killing sheep on the way. This wolf caused a particular stir. It was initially planned to capture it and put it in a zoo but because, in Sweden zoo animals naturally need a mate, which this one didn't have, an alternative was decided upon. It would be tranquilised, transported to a remote landscape and fitted with a radio-collar so its movements could be monitored. There's a wonderful newspaper photograph of a Swedish police car pursuing a terrified wolf through a field of ripe corn, but eventually the wolf was caught and released far to the north in the wilds of Darlarna. It promptly turned round, headed due south and started killing sheep again. It was eventually shot dead in a field in the county of Goteborg, not a hundred yards from where the very last wolf had been killed there a hundred years before.

Back in Värmland things also took an ugly turn. Even though Värmland has the highest density of moose anywhere in Europe, local hunters didn't like having competition for their prey. One young wolf was deliberately smashed by a snow scooter and in July 1985 an emigree from Estonia called Hugo Ekman, a man who incidentally had rowed himself across the Baltic to escape Soviet rule, shot the mother wolf in the belief that she might attack his neighbour's sheep. This little tragedy put a temporary stop to the wolf idyll. The male wolf howled for weeks in search of his mate and then disappeared. Only when a new male arrived, again probably from Finland, in the early 1990s did the revived wolf population begin to take root.

The death of the mother wolf polarised opinion. Hunters were happy, so were some farmers. Conservationists were deeply disappointed. The general public were divided. While many were excited by the thought of the wilderness at their gates, others were frightened. I remember attending a university dinner in Uppsala in 1985 when one of the professors admitted that she was very glad she lived on the third floor where she was safe from wolves.

One day I received a call from Richard Brock of the BBC Natural History Unit. As I've mentioned earlier, Richard had been a producer on Life on Earth and had been in charge of the beautiful sequel, The Living Planet. This was an exciting call. Richard explained that he had been reading all my wolf articles. He thought the story would make a brilliant film and he wanted me to write it. He was experimenting with some new ideas for a series he was calling Survivors, a series that would – unusually for the BBC – deal with conservation issues which would be presented partly from the animals' points of view. Consequently, this would not be a standard portrait of wolves. The natural history footage would be subordinate to the story. We would incorporate the fascinating press photos, we would reconstruct incidents, for example asking Hugo Ekman to fire his gun from the spot, now marked with a plaque, from where he killed the breeding female and occasionally, we would ask the camera to be the wolf, looking back at the response of humans to its presence.

A few weeks later we were off to Sweden and Norway, with Patricia, a fluent Swedish speaker to interpret on the rare occasions that was necessary, and meeting up with a local cameraman on the way. We interviewed all the key human actors in the story. The most interesting were probably the two trackers who had monitored the wolves every day for several years. They were polar opposites. Erik Isakson was a six-foot five ironman who thought anyone who didn't wipe his bottom with tree bark and sleep with a hand-hewn block of ice as a hot-water bottle was not worth talking to. Jan Witberg, on the other hand, was a gentle soul who had clearly fallen in love with the female wolf, had actually stumbled over her when she was in labour and who remembered her as "Amber Eyes".

Working with Richard was a revelation. He was extremely good company, a great talker and very funny and he maintained that relaxed demeanour when we were working. But more important, he turned out to be a very good listener. He, who had achieved so much and had filmed in sixty countries round the world, never tried to intimidate or impress others. He was infinitely curious, asked excellent questions and listened carefully to the answers. He put people at their ease. I've tried to learn from this. Not very successfully I'm afraid.

The film closed with a two-minute sequence, shot by an amateur on his home video camera. It shows his dog, a big German shepherd, jumping around in deep snow on the edge of a forest. Then from among the trees a huge wolf emerges. It has legs up to its armpits and a fluffy winter coat to die for. It utterly dwarfs the dog but they begin to play together, chasing around gleefully, throwing up the snow like puppies. Then the voice over tells you that, a few weeks later, the wolf was dead, chased down and crushed by a man on a snow scooter who didn't like wolves. Wolf Saga tells the whole story: the fiasco of Vegårshei, the first amazing breeding in decades, the loss one by one of the pups, the killing of the mother and the disappearance of the father. It was a sad film. It was nominated for the Prix Italia, won the Conservation Award at the Pacific Film Festival and helped to change the law, at least in Sweden, so that a female wolf would never be legally shot like that again.

When we'd finished our preliminary work on the film and Richard had headed home, Patricia and I wanted to celebrate with a meal. I've never really liked indoor restaurants. I often find them crowded, stuffy and distracting. We bought a roast chicken, some fresh bread and a bottle of white wine and we drove thirty kilometres into the Värmland forests to a beaver dam I'd found. We sat on the twined dry branches of the dam in the settling evening light, watching a black woodpecker dismantling a tree stump, excavating it for ants. And then the beavers came out, swimming beside us round and round their lake, checking their handiwork. It was a perfect moment, a perfect meal. You only get ten such days in a life time.

10

MAN-EATER: TO BE OR NOT TO BE

A few months after the successful broadcast of Wolf Saga, I was sitting on the back of an elephant, crunching into the jungle of Chitwan National Park in southern Nepal. It was early February in the foothills of the Himalayas, when dawn is cold and drenched in mist. At night, in my tent, from the early hours, I'd listened to the dew dripping like rain off the teak and sal leaves and now the chill spray caught me as the elephant ploughed on amongst the trees. Criss-crossed between the trunks hung the diamond-dewed, roped webs of huge yellow wood spiders, as big as my hand. The mahout, vigorously pedalling his feet back and forth behind the elephant's ears, would politely lift these away from my face with his stick as we passed. I'd read that the webs were so strong that tiny Pallas's leaf warblers could get caught in them and the spiders would hungrily devour an unofficial meal of bird. As the new sun fingered its way into the forest, drying teak leaves detached and drifted down like paper plates, clattering crisply on the forest floor and the morning calls began. I could hear the low whoops of langurs, the bandar-log, greeting each other, the high whickering of a white-throated kingfisher, coucals hooting secretly from somewhere in the undergrowth and the sharp, sudden cackle of a flameback woodpecker. But this regular morning chorus also included some strangely familiar notes: the crowing of jungle fowl, the cooing of collared doves and a peacock's wail. I closed my eyes and for a moment I could be back home in the garden of the Trout Inn, by the River Isis in Oxford. And then I dropped my pen. Immediately the mahout called to the elephant "Rocco, rocco" and then "Picha, picha picha", or so it sounded, and the elephant stopped and slowly walked backwards, reaching delicately down into the leaves at its feet with its trunk, sniffing out something that didn't seem to belong in the forest. The elephant found my pen and with the utmost grace he lifted it and swirled it back to me over his shoulder. From that moment, there began a love affair that has lasted for the rest of my life.

Admittedly, I was already well-groomed for this love of India and Nepal. Like most literate children of my generation, I had read Kipling and had known the Jungle Books almost by heart. So, when I arrived and discovered that Hathi and Balou and Bandar were simply the local names for elephant, bear and monkey, I experienced a secret, naïve delight. But there was more than Kipling. On my parents' bookshelves was a small collection of intriguing old hunting memoires. We'd inherited these, along with several cutlasses, a stuffed leopard head and a complete lion skin that lay in my bedroom, when they had bought Suntrap, the house that became our family home in 1957. Among the books were two that I treasure to this day. They were large red tomes by Frederick Champion, entitled "With a Camera in Tiger-land" and "The Jungle in Sunlight and Shadow." Champion was something of a hero for me because, at a time, in the late 1920s, when his colleagues were boisterously slaughtering the wildlife of India, Champion hunted only with a camera. His dream was to photograph a tiger in the wild and to this end he travelled by elephant-back through the jungles around Dudhwa in Uttar Pradesh, where he was a forest officer, armed with an enormous plate camera. He did, eventually, manage to photograph tigers in broad daylight. This is easy to do today, now that, thankfully, tigers haven't been systematically hunted in India and Nepal for more than fifty years. But in 1927 it was nearly impossible. My favourite of all his photographs, however, indeed my favourite of all tiger pictures, was one he took at night, with an early form of Heath-Robinson camera trap. He tethered a buffalo as bait along a regular path used by a big male tiger, with a trip wire to set off the camera if the tiger approached. I can still imagine his excitement, albeit tinged with shame, when he returns the next morning to find the buffalo has been killed and the camera has fired. I look over his shoulder in the darkroom, full of expectation, as the developing-liquid slowly reveals an image. But despair and misery. The emerging centre of the picture is empty. No tiger, only the path and bits of bushes and trees. And then...amazement and joy, as the chemicals cohere down in the bottom right-hand corner and the head of a huge tiger materialises, perfectly exposed, in sharp focus, staring into your heart forever.

But on this trip, I had no camera with me, only pen and paper. I was on a reconnaissance expedition looking for a story. The jungles of Chitwan lie in the Terai, an expanse of riverine forest and vast stands of elephant grass that once filled the borderlands between Nepal and India and beyond. Chitwan is famous for being one of the last strongholds of the greater one-horned rhinoceros, the largest and most aggressive of the five rhino species left on earth. Like many of the Subcontinent's National Parks, it was once a royal hunting reserve with such a surfeit of sambar, spotted deer, hog deer and wild boar, that it could support a huge tiger population. We know this from the old hunting records. For instance, during a single safari in 1932, hunters shot 120 tigers. They returned three years later and bagged another 77. By the time I was sitting on my elephant, however, tiger numbers had dwindled to, perhaps 250 in the whole of Nepal and they had become extremely difficult to see. Nevertheless, it was for a tiger film that I was researching.

For the previous decade or so, Dr David Smith, from the University of Minnesota, had been leading the Smithsonian-Nepal Tiger Ecology Project in Chitwan, a co-operation between American and Nepali scientists that had produced superb results. The Project had put the world's first ever radio collar on a wild tiger back in December 1973 and had collared dozens of tigers since then. Richard

Brock had met David at a conference and had been impressed by him and he saw, in David's current work with local people on problem tigers, the seeds of a possible film. So Richard had phoned me with the attractive offer of flying me out to Nepal so that I could spend time with David, and unearth a story, which I was to write and film the following year.

I liked David Smith from the moment I met him. I've always enjoyed being with people who are competent in the field. David was very comfortable in the jungle. He was interested and knowledgeable about all forms of life there. He was charming, he was an excellent story-teller and he spoke with that educated Mid-Western accent that has always appealed to me, full of emphasis and enthusiasm. He told me how one day he had found a curious tunnel in the high elephant grass and had crawled inside, following it into the warm darkness, where he'd found three tiny tiger cubs curled up. Tiny tiger cubs mean a mother very, very close by. How he got out of there unscathed, God alone knows. Another day, he was not so lucky. He was doing a study of small mammals round his camp and was out checking the live traps when a rhino charged him. She came from nowhere, hit him in the stomach at full tilt and knocked him up, over and into a dense tangle of huge thorns. Those thorns are like five-inch knives and they shred you. One ripped his scalp open. But they probably saved his life because the rhino kept charging them to get at him but couldn't get through the thicket and eventually gave up. More dead than alive, he was taken by helicopter to Kathmandu and then on to Bangkok where a surgeon opened and cleaned the great flap of his stomach wound every day until it was clear of infection and could be sewn up.

Needless to say, David had my attention. One of the most important revelations to emerge from the Tiger Ecology Project, he suggested, was the way the landscape was found to be shared out amongst related females. At one point the Project had no fewer than eleven tigresses marked with radio-collars, giving an unprecedented picture of their social structure. It had turned out that tigers were more like lions than most people had thought. The whole study area was occupied mainly by a single, very extended family of tigresses. They lived in a tiger version of a "pride", not socially together like lions but separate and dispersed, befitting the scattered distribution of prey and the nature of the landscape. This system of tenure is more about genes than social life and it has huge implications for males. If all the females in an area are related to each other, the all-important fresh genetic material has to come from males who, in the service of the species, will have to travel far away before they can breed. A female, settling close to home, can enjoy the benefit of hunting in a familiar landscape, a massive survival advantage for a predator and one that will help her when she has cubs to feed. Males have to surrender this asset which can put them under considerable stress. Not surprisingly, annual mortality rates among young males are three times as large as those for females.

Somewhere in this male struggle, lay the story I was looking for. Richard had been interested in what might make a tiger into a problem tiger – at worst, a man-eater. Clearly, having to leave home, face starvation, learn to grab food wherever you can, maybe fight for a mate and then perhaps even lose all in a title bid, could easily get a male tiger into trouble. It can be a high-intensity life being a male tiger. David told me that even tigers who made it to the top table rarely kept their seat for longer than 33 months. This places a very high value on breeding opportunities. It is why new males may promote their own genes to the potential disadvantage of the species by killing the young cubs of a competing male. This brings the bereft mother back into oestrus, something he would otherwise have to wait eighteenth months for, thereby "wasting" half his breeding life. It is also why males occasionally fight catastrophic battles.

While Richard was initially sparked by the question of why a tiger becomes a man-eater, I found myself increasingly absorbed by the opposite question. Why, in fact, are not all tigers man-eaters? I arrived in Chitwan just at the end of the grass cutting season. The seas of elephant grass that fringe the reserve were of enormous value. Their seed heads were fodder for animals and their sturdy stems formed the staple of rooves and daub-and-wattle walls for miles around.

Consequently, every January, a hundred thousand people were allowed into the park to harvest this flexible asset. Every misty morning, hundreds of unwieldy, flat-bottomed wooden boats teeming with colourful reapers crossed the Rapti River, and crossed back again in the afternoon, wobblingly crammed with twenty-foot stacks of grass. On the village side, the bank was lined with big scales to weigh each grass-cutter's contribution so they could be duly paid. And within metres of this whole melee there must have been tigers lurking. Sadly, every year a number of people were killed by rhinos, bursting out of the grass like furious trains. But accidents with tigers were very rare. I tried to think like a tiger and I decided that tigers were disconcerted by the upright human form. From one angle, head-on, it appeared to be very large but from the side it all-but disappeared, having no discernible back on which to leap. This moment of confusion might be just enough to dissuade a tiger from attacking. I reckoned, too, that tigers, because they live and hunt mostly alone, would be very cautious about attacking something peculiar that might injure them, as an injury could stop them hunting and that might be fatal. I compared this with lions, especially lionesses, who live and hunt in groups, are much less likely to die uncherished and alone and who do, quite frequently, attack people. In a modest way, my own experience has borne this out. I have, since those early days, had numerous extremely close encounters with tigers and have never felt threatened. I was, on the other hand, very, very nearly killed by a lioness...

The story that began to form in my head, following Richard's prompt, would reconstruct the life of a real male tiger, from its recorded birth to its death. It would focus on the stress of being male, dispersal and mortality rates, the pressure to reproduce, infanticide and the ultimate loss of a home range and physical condition that might eventually lead to killing a human. We would call it "Man-Eater: To Be or Not To Be" so now I needed David to come up with a known tiger from his records that might fit the bill.

Like Wolf Saga, this would be an entirely true story, led by the facts not the available footage. I would hope to film wild tigers to illustrate key moments in the story but it would be clear these would not be the actual individuals since they would necessarily already be dead. Furthermore, because I could use the camera to tell the tiger's "point of view", we could find ways of including all the known facts about our subject. I think David appreciated the priority we wished to give to scientific accuracy so we sat down together to go through his notes in search of a hero.

Those were happy weeks for me. David was hosting a small group of Earthwatch volunteers, mostly middle-aged or older folk from America. They were friendly and keen to help one of David's doctoral students, Anup Joshi, with his excellent research on sloth bears, so we all spent time camping in the jungle and on elephant-back, following radio signals from collared bears. In the evenings David and I would discuss tigers. I remember one of the visitors had a guitar and could play and sing beautifully. One evening he sang Waltzing Matilda. I'd never realised how sad and profound the song was – all a matter of tempo and tone. In the main camp on the edge of the forest, which was the rustic headquarters of the King Mahendra Trust for Nature Conservation, I used to play with the elephants. When not in use, they were parked in a line, chained to posts. This always made me a little sad but one of them had a cheerful temperament. Every evening after work, they were rewarded with super-size sandwiches, consisting of a corn cob beautifully wrapped in a banana leaf. I found if I threw one of these to the friendly female, she would catch it with her trunk and with twinkling eyes and a flick, she would toss it back for me to catch. This game could keep us mutually amused for half an hour. The young cook in the camp was looking after a baby sloth bear that had been found a week earlier, orphaned in the jungle. She was a tiny, black bundle of furry mischief with a tongue like sandpaper. He called her Kali, and carried her everywhere, her arms wrapped round his neck. She was a focus of delight, unlike the food which was diabolical and tummy-exploding.

There were three possible candidates for our hero. There was the monumental Tiger 105, who had been radio-collared in 1974 and was very well documented. He had weighed six hundred lbs and had ended up as the dominant male tiger in a home range of one hundred and thirty square kilometres. This had included the home ranges of six or seven females with whom he had sired a staggering number of cubs – at least 51, of which 27 had survived to disperse. But 105 was almost too much of a hero to be representative, and there was no man-eating in his story. The next was Bangi Bhale, (Bhale means male). He was a dominant male in Chitwan in the early 1980s one of whose mates lost her cubs to infanticide by a possible rival male and who himself lost his home range after being injured in a fight over a kill. David actually witnessed this fight, a roaring, bloody affair in March 1984, when he was canoeing down the Rapti River. Afterwards, Bangi Bhale began to hang around the fringes of the park. In May 1984, he killed two buffaloes and a man cutting grass. The following month he killed another man and in August he killed a woman. In December 1984, after another attack, he was finally darted and removed to Kathmandu Zoo, where he lived a depleted life for another six years. Bangi was also quite well documented and perhaps if he'd still been alive, I might have chosen him. The third candidate, however, ticked all our boxes. Bahadur Bhale was born on Bandajola Island in the Rapti River in May 1980. I would be able to wade across to the island, pretending to be him, with my camera. Bahadur Bhale was the other tiger in the fight David had witnessed. It was almost certainly Bahadur Bhale who had killed Bangi's cubs and, between September 1985 and January 1986 he fought a running battle over an oestrus female with a much more dominant tiger called Kancha Bhale. Eventually, Kancha was so badly injured that he limped off to the villages where he, too, became a man-eater and was shot dead a few weeks later. From 1964 to 1979 there were no known cases of man-eating in Chitwan. This coincided with a period of social stability in the tiger world, but during the ensuing six years there was a lot of conflict between males and thirteen people were killed in the cross-fire. Bahadur Bhale, though thankfully he never became a man-eater himself, was at the heart of these conflicts. Once he settled in, however, there were no more human deaths.

Warring tigers are bad for cubs as well as people. During the worst couple of years in the early to mid 1980s, no Chitwan cubs survived to disperse. With this in mind, I often wonder if the blood-curdling behaviour of tigers from the past was not actually exacerbated by the people who thought they were dealing with it. An incident would occur or someone would be frightened by a tiger and off would go the great white hunter to kill the culprit. But did he really always kill the right tiger? Isn't it much more likely that he killed the first tiger he saw, which would almost certainly have been the most curious and therefore the local dominant male? In which case he caused a power vacuum that greatly increased the danger for everyone, tigers and people alike.

Although Bahadur Bhale was dominant for four and a half years, an unusually long spell, and had six females in his home range, according to David's records, he only managed to mate with four of them and only sired ten cubs. Of those, only six survived to disperse. The reason why such an impressive tiger achieved such modest results was almost certainly instability. He had to deal with three other dominant males on his way up, all of whose ranges he took over. In comparison, the prolific Tiger 105 rarely had to bring out the tanks. Bahadur Bhale's death was not recorded. Nevertheless, what we know of his end was quite piquant. More of that later.

On 30th January 1992, I returned to Chitwan to film Bahadur Bhale's reconstructed story, accompanied by Richard Brock. This meant comfort. No hard bunks and prison food this time. We were booked into Tiger Tops, very posh by the standards of the day and the only lodge permitted inside the boundary of the national park. The drive from Katmandu had taken more than ten hours. The distance was less than two hundred kilometres but in those days the single lane road through the high foothills was washed away every monsoon and had to be rebuilt each winter by hand. All along the route backlogs of groaning trucks ahead of us crashed through the gears while colourful girls knelt in their hundreds at the side, breaking the stones to strew in our path and ease our passage. The next morning Richard was busy settling into our spacious, three-roomed bungalow which we'd hardly glimpsed in the light of the oil lamp the night before, and I decided to impress him by doing some filming. I walked down to a little wooden hide nearby that looked over a scruffy bit of swamp and waited to see if anything turned up. After an hour, I was delighted to see a small brown rail step suspiciously out of the reeds. Funny birds, rails. I love them. You very rarely see them and when you do, they never do much, they just creep about looking infinitely dodgy. We needed a wide cast of extras to give our story a little background atmosphere so I filmed away happily for another hour or so. When I got back to the lodge, I found Richard having lunch. As I told him about my rail, I noticed a funny look forming in his eye and then he started on a riff. "Yes, the brown rail." He said. "Small and brown, you say? And it doesn't do anything? Could this be the famous brown rail that is so boring that it has evolved boredom into a defence mechanism? Tigers have been known to die of boredom when trying to hunt a brown rail. Eagles have tumbled from their perches out of sheer lethargy and drowned in the ponds below. Indeed, when groups of brown rails move into an area they can cut a deep swathe through the local population of predators. And cameramen, just looking at one, have been known to fall asleep, their fingers on the button, running off miles of useless film. Amazing bird, the brown rail. I'm so glad you got one." Well, he didn't get through it quite so fluently as that because by the end we were both laughing too much to talk properly.

Richard was not only one of the funniest people I've worked with, he was also one of the hardiest and most travelled. Yet I see from my diary that, a couple of days later, even he succumbed to the sickness that used to blight every visitor to the Sub-Continent. The problem was the water. You never knew if you'd be better off if they did wash the dishes or if they didn't. Stomach trouble was one of those unmentionable, endemic, unavoidable problems that you just had to work around. Even a lodge as exclusive and well-run as Tiger Tops was not entirely immune. Incidentally, for the last 25 years I've been leading small, specialist wildlife tours to India and, whereas during the first decade these incidents would affect half the group, now they are almost unknown.

On 4th February we enjoyed our first really good filming day. The sun finally found a way through the winter mists around mid-morning and at last we felt warm sunshine on our faces. We boated across the Rapti River where a gang of women and children were washing in the fast stream. This was exactly what the young Bahadur Bhale, born on the adjacent island, must have seen so I asked our driver Vijay to check with the ladies if they minded us filming them. There was one particularly graceful girl who was washing her hair. She was very shy but another buxom lass threw herself into things with raucous abandon, eventually floating off with a flourish downstream among the stones. Then the pretty, shy one came back and, like a gazelle, she scampered in or out of frame entrancingly as courage or fear dictated. Round the next bend we filmed the women beating their laundry on the rocks while three ospreys looked on. Then we walked across the dry rice paddies to a little, isolated village – just the sort of place a curious tiger might come at night or where a man-eater might prowl. Buffalo carts were passing, loaded with bamboo canes and grass and we found a perfect little mud-built farm, with pigeons, ducks, chickens, buffaloes, bee hives and a roof garden bulbous with orange pumpkins. There were two beautiful little buffalo calves and just as I zoomed out from them, a brightly clad lady walked into picture, drawing the wire fence closed behind her. It was exactly what I would have asked her to do for my "shutting the buffaloes in at night shot" but much better that it just happened. I noted in my diary that "the people were all so nice – so dignified, friendly and quite calm about the invasion of an outlandish film crew."

Our main task while we were in Chitwan was to film David Smith working in the jungle, checking tiger markings, canoeing down the Rapti River and riding on elephants – all scenes which we could record him talking over as he told the story of his connection with Bahadur Bhale. David was staying, as usual, at the King Mahendra Trust, which was actually a two-hour jeep drive because of the lay out of the jungle tracks and the location of the river crossings. When we reached the camp, I saw that it had not changed much from the previous year. Khali the sloth bear was still there but she was now full-grown and when she stood up on her hind legs to greet me, I saw that she was as tall as I was. We all decided that she had to be in the film, so we took her into the woods where she wandered around and rose to attention most co-operatively. I filmed some lovely tiger-meets-sloth bear shots as if from the tiger's point of view. Khali was an affectionate and co-operative bear but her story had a sad post-script. Wild sloth bears are amongst the most feared animals in the jungle. They feed mainly on termites, digging deep into their cement-hard mounds with claws as sharp as steel. When termiting, they tend to be somewhat self-absorbed and may not notice a person approach-ing. If you accidentally creep up on one it can explode on you in a whirlwind of fury. I once disturbed one with my jeep in Assam. It dived into a dense bamboo covet which it proceeded to demolish like a turbo-charged garden shredder. Had I been on foot, I would have been turned into human spaghetti. There was a guide in Bandhav-garh Tiger Reserve in Madhya Pradesh who had lost his entire nose to a ballistic sloth bear. He wore a handkerchief across his face when he was working. For this reason, people began to worry that Khali, as she grew older, might not be a steady companion for people and she was exiled to Kathmandu Zoo. Years later, I was filming again in Nepal and went to the zoo to shoot some super close-ups of tiger eye-lashes and toe-nails, the sort of shots that give you vital split seconds of surprise when they are mixed with wild footage. I wondered about Khali so I walked to the bear enclosure. There I found a dishevelled and disconsolate bear huddled in the corner of a small, iron cage. Could it really be her? I tried calling her name and she suddenly came alive, turning somersaults round and round the cage, rolling through her own excrement that no-one had bothered to pick up. Her electric happiness was astonishing. I don't think she recognised me, but she definitely recognised someone who knew who she had been. I stayed with her for half an hour but there's not much you can say to comfort a catatonically lonely sloth bear.

Richard and I were a good team. David later told me he had been amazed how fast we worked. He had expected a long day of talk and planning. Instead, we simply took out the camera and ticked off the scenes. I think we shot a good quarter of our film that day. This was the advantage of having a carefully crafted storyline. Over the next days, as we roamed the landscape of Bahadur Bhale's recorded youth, filming it as he would have seen it, we had fun photographing the other animals that would have shared it with him. We filmed the lazy, long-nosed crocodiles, the gharials, lining the shingle shores of the river. We filmed the grey langur monkeys feeding on the first gaudy orange flowers of the cotton trees and giant hornbills, plucking succulent early fruits in comical slow-motion. But there was still one big gap of course, one that would be much harder to fill. We needed some real wild tiger shots. These, we knew, would be difficult to achieve. The great explosion in tiger sightings, which began in the late 1990s, was still some years off. There were, so far, very few genuine tiger films. Historically, most of the tigers that had been seen by previous visitors and had made Tiger Tops famous, had been attracted by bait. This old-fashioned practice had now been banned and tiger sightings in Chitwan had become increasingly infrequent. To give ourselves the best chance, we decided to move West, three hundred kilometres away, to a little-known paradise called Bardia.

We started the day-long drive at dawn on 11th February. Our journey took us first northwards, through fertile fields, to meet up with the great west road, much of it the inevitable dirt track. There the route became increasingly forested, especially on the north side of the road. Some of the woodland was impoverished and scrubby, but as we wound into the foothills of the Himalayas there were expanses where the great sal and teak trees stood out like lampposts above a bare understorey. Elsewhere, the trees had been freshly cleared, their stumps left like stepping-stones across the new paddy fields. Towards the end of the drive, closer to Bardia, we found several dead buffaloes and gangs of vultures jostling along the ditches beside the road.

The modest Tiger Tops camp in Bardia was beautiful in the evening light. It stood in a clearing between woods and fields, right on the edge of the National Park. The glade was dotted with fruit trees and edged with a stream and that night we heard the tigers roar deep in the forest. Pradeep Rana, the joyous, noisy manager of the lodge, was full of encouragement. A pair of tigers were mating, and would be together and perhaps visible over the next few days, so he had a perfect spot for me to put up my hide. In the early afternoon, we drove through the forest to the edge of the beautiful, quiet Karnali River. There, on a little island where the three arms of the river met, Pradeep's men helped me clear the brush and we erected the hide. "The tigers have been courting here," he said. "You might see something." Then they drove away. After half an hour, a large egret came strutting slowly past, intent on his fishing. A pair of spur-winged plovers came to dabble about on the stream's edge. Small hog deer emerged to lick salt from the sand, their deep red-brown fur glinting in the evening light. They came for me by elephant, just after dark. The quiet ride home, through the moon-dappled woods with only the creaking of the houdah was very beautiful.

In the little rustic dining hall, glimmering with oil lamps, I saw that other guests had arrived. Among them was the ornithologist John Gooders, who, in those days before the internet, had published several very useful books about where to find birds in Britain and Europe. He was a pleasant, cheerful fellow and was glowing with triumph because he'd just seen his first ibisbills – a bit of a red-letter bird for enthusiasts. He very kindly drew us an excellent map of the area where he'd found them. But that evening, my head only had room for tigers.

The next day, I was looking forward to spending the whole day in the hide. Unfortunately, the Bardia water got to me in the night and I spent most of my sleeping hours pattering back and forth, with ever-increasing desperation, to the toilet. By dawn, I was feeling very ill, in low spirits and too weak to carry my gear to the jeep. But this was an opportunity that I must not miss. The hide, which normally would have been alluring at 7.30 in the morning, felt cramped and uncomfortable. The morning was muggy, with a little rain, airless and humid and by 11 o'clock, very hot. I had to keep sneaking out the back of the hide every hour to relieve my stomach, which was depressing since each sally reduced my chances of seeing anything. By 12.30, I felt so sick I had to lie down – my head wedged under the tripod and my legs sticking out as tiger bait from the bottom of the hide. I wrote in my diary that "I slept for an hour. Woke with a head-ache. Beginning to feel sorry for myself!" Sorry? I was dying here. A couple of mongooses came out to hunt together along the far bank, beyond the beach of pebbles. Then another appeared and was chased off and I heard the peevish sound of bickering from the grasses. And then absolutely nothing happened until just before 3 o'clock, when I heard elephants trumpeting to the north. After about ten minutes, they appeared. It was our elephants from the lodge with the new visitors aboard. A couple surged ahead and it was clear they had a tiger between them. The elephants screamed and rumbled and I heard a single distinct tiger roar. Then the elephants came, strung out across the river and from the pointing hands of the mahouts I guessed the tiger was still ahead of them, keeping within the stand of covering grasses. I checked my tripod was level and my light readings were correct and then I noticed to my horror that I only had eighty feet left on my roll of film. Silly man! There was no time to change magazines. If anything happened, I would have to be thrifty in my shooting. And then the tiger broke cover and ran straight into picture. He galloped obliquely towards me, stretching his great limbs over the yellow sand, on and on he came, in glorious light, a tiger at full speed in my lens – oh God did I have enough film? And then he dived into the river and swam. I followed him and then let him swim out of picture. Cut. Perfect. Beyond perfect. Now all I had to hope was that there was no hair in the gate, that the focus was sharp, that there was no fogging, that no-one would try to X-ray the film at the airport and that the labs would not scratch it or chew it up. None of which I would know for at least a month.

I picked the tiger up again just as he emerged from the water on the far bank. He tripped slightly, pulled himself up and disappeared into the long grass. The mahouts were all very excited. Apparently, the tiger had turned on them before running. I felt guilty that he had been disturbed and hoped, a little disingenuously, that it hadn't been done entirely for me. By 3.30, I was alone again and the jungle began to settle back into its siesta. A black stork came to paddle in the pool in front of me and I filmed him in super close-up and the piebald spur-winged plovers were back, mating now. Two thoughts crowded in upon me. The first was that I was actually feeling extremely unwell, almost too ill to pack up my gear when the jeep came for me at sunset. The other was that, in those few hectic minutes, I had joined what at the time was a rather small, elite group of professional camerapeople who had actually filmed a tiger in the wild.

In the event, the shot turned out to be perfect: not too long to use but long enough to be unique. For us, it was the ideal shot to illustrate that climactic moment in our story when Bangi Bhale having lost the fight with Bahadur Bhale, runs away and crosses the river to become a man-eater. For others it became a seminal shot. It was used in numerous subsequent tiger films and for many years you could watch it on a loop of star footage that the BBC sold to keep passengers happy on the Heathrow Express Train. That evening, I celebrated by going straight to bed.

The next morning, my breakfast's journey from mouth to toilet took fifteen minutes so I decided to stay in camp. It was a beautiful, clear morning. High on a light breeze, vultures drifted patiently and in our clearing, blue-purple rollers blazed between the trees. Little lines of slender girls went to and fro in the fields, coming back with neat bundles of firewood balanced elegantly on their heads. Such graceful people. So as not to waste the day, I spent the afternoon in the hide. Several kingfishers came to the perch in front of me and I regretted not having gardened away the grass stems more ruthlessly. One of them nearly had a heart-attack when a silver bullet of a shikar, a small sparrowhawk, made a pass at it. They both wheeled over the water and the kingfisher shot off without its dignity.

One of the delights of working with Richard was that he knew when to take the foot off the pedal – something I was not so good at myself. So the following day, we decided to go and look for John Gooders's ibisbills. This meant a trip upstream to the stony shallows of the river. When we walked down into the wide river valley, I spotted a likely ibisbill habitat, which I thought corresponded well to John's map, and offered to scout it out. This meant heaving and pushing myself through dense long grass until eventually I popped out onto a boulder-strewn river bed where an ibisbill was standing within a few yards of me. It fed, a little shyly, twisting its curved beak delicately this way and that under the stones. From this angle, I realised I had approached by the hardest possible route. I strolled nonchalantly back to Richard and together we crept back with the camera and for extra brownie points and to outdo John Gooders, we filmed our first ibisbill! For the rest of the day, we had arranged a raft that would float us calmly back towards camp. It was a very happy day. I wrote in my diary "The raft trip was brilliant – simply wonderful. It was cold, but so quiet, the water so wide and beautiful and the bird life astonishing." We saw a rare white-tailed sea eagle catch a fish, we watched elegant Montague's harriers and we saw our first wall-creeper, a bird I'd wanted to find since seeing a picture in Witherby's Handbook when I was three. It fluttered over us like a pink-winged butterfly. We stopped the boat and watched as it landed and crept about on the raised sandbank, inspecting the deserted sand martin holes for insects.

The 16th February was booked in as Tiger Day. Not the day when we would see a tiger but when I would be one. We needed shots of the camera being a tiger hunting for deer. The plan was to cruise in our jeep through the meadows and jungle clearings in search of parties of chital, the pretty spotted deer that would be our easiest prey. We would get as close as possible to each group and then Tiger Mills would switch on the camera, spring athletically from the back of the jeep and sprint straight at the herd. There were two problems with this scheme. The first was that I had to use a wide-angle lens. Anything else would have rendered the scene a total blur. But wide-angle lenses make objects appear small and distant. This meant we had to get very close to our prey before I charged. The second problem was that, although I was, of course, a wall of muscle, in some respects I was not the perfect candidate for tigerdom. The truth is, I tended to run in slow-motion. At school, because I had been captain of the rightly-feared and ever-unbeaten 3rd rugby fifteen and had played at fly half, the opposition understandably had assumed I was fast. Consequently, on several occasions they dived in front of me to tackle me, anticipating a burst of speed that never came. It was a wicked and successful ploy because I was too strong to pull down, especially for someone who was already lying on the ground and about to be trampled. But it did not make me a good tiger. By four o'clock we had located a good herd of deer, grazing peacefully in an open grassy glade. My first run was actually quite successful until I put my foot in a rabbit hole and turned a complete somersault with the camera running. In fact, I have a feeling we may have used that shot. It certainly didn't look fake. I got quite close to the next bunch of deer by bursting though the bushes on top of them. Finally, I chased a wild boar. He looked extremely sceptical. Could this clumsy oaf really be coming after him? The good thing was that tigers miss their kill nineteen times out of 20 attempts, so I was not really expected to catch a deer. The bad thing was that my whole Buster Keaton performance had been witnessed by a Norwegian scientist called Stein Moe, who had been trying to count the deer for his research. I'd met him the year before in Chitwan and he seemed to have been quite impressed by me. Probably not so now.

It was getting dark as we headed back to camp, a little inebriated with all the hilarity. I was sitting in the back of the open jeep, still pretending to be a tiger when a huge silhouette loomed up and stretched itself across the road and was gone. We crept up to the spot where it had disappeared and switched off the engine. Nothing. I stared into the almost blackness, trying to find shapes in the bushes. And then I realised they weren't bushes. They were mostly tiger: an enormous male. He was standing stock still in the jungle not ten metres away, his facial stripes breaking up his entire melting outline. Eventually our eyes grew accustomed to the dense gloom and we could see him narrowing his eyes and ever-so-slowly pulling back his ears. For seven minutes he hardly moved. Perhaps because I had been masquerading in his role, I remember feeling a very strange sense that he regarded me as vermin.

That was an era of comparative innocence, before civil war ripped through the country and before Nepal's Royal Family tore itself apart. I'm not sure what is left of Tiger Tops now, but at that time they operated a lovely tented camp on the high bank above the Karnali River. We soon discovered what constituted the perfect day. Before dawn, you set off on elephants through the jungle, with just a chance of seeing a tiger or a leopard. At Tented Camp you boarded a raft, watching ospreys and otters fishing in the river and little knots of deer or bluebulls drinking on the shore as you floated along. Around 9 o'clock you pulled across to a wide, grassy bank where breakfast of hot chai and barjis and samosas was laid out. Then on downstream to a wide pool where, if you waited patiently for an hour or two you would always see the river dolphins – small, pale, secretive and very rare. We had great fun trying to film them. Wherever I pointed the camera, they were sure to pop up somewhere else. Then a picnic lunch by the river in the afternoon and a jeep ride home through the meadows and the darkening jungle in the evening.

Towards the end of February, we moved our base to Tented Camp and my wife Patricia flew out from England to join us. By now, we felt we had secured the bulk of the essential footage for the film so when the time came for Richard to leave, he and I came to a comfortable agreement. Patricia and I would stay on for several weeks with our board and lodging covered by the film budget. In exchange, I would not charge for filming days but I would keep the camera handy, spend a bit more time in my hide and try to film anything exciting that might turn up. On her first day out on an elephant, Patricia had quite a christening. Her elephant was right beside mine when it stepped into a bush where a tigress was sleeping. The tigress exploded, like an orange rocket, roaring right under the elephant's belly. The elephant screamed, shot up onto its hind legs, houdah and all, and there was Patricia, hanging by a rope, with a furious tigress fizzing at her feet. Just a normal day, I assured her. Sadly, though I had the camera with me, it all happened too quickly for me to film.

During this unofficial holiday, I did manage to get one crucial piece of footage. One afternoon we were descending by elephant towards a part of the river where it makes a wide loop, leaving a broad expanse of reeds and open sand in the hollow of the bend. From a considerable distance, I thought I spotted the spidery form of a tiger crossing the plain. By the time we reached the place, however, the tiger had disappeared. I guessed it must be in the reeds and when I saw a red-wattled lapwing wheeling and darting above them, reeling out its shrill "did you do it, did you do it" alarm call, I assumed the tiger was on the move. I estimated where the tiger might emerge and urged my mahout to manoeuvre the elephant accordingly. Unfortunately, he was a young, inexperienced driver and not as keen on tigers as I was. When we finally skirted the reeds, the tiger was already half way across the sand on its way to the river. I could see this wasn't going very well, so I jumped down from the elephant, grabbed the camera and the tripod and began to run towards the tiger. I wanted to film it as it entered the river but just as I stopped and levelled the tripod, the tiger dipped down below the bank. Now, with my feet sinking in the sand with my weight and the weight of the gear, I ran to the river's edge in the hope of catching the tiger as it climbed out. But again, just as I levelled the tripod and focused on it, the tiger slipped into the forest. It was very frustrating to be standing, all set-up, with a tiger just across the river from me, but one that was now hidden among the trees. There was only one thing I could think of to do. When I was a child, I had often called foxes up to my feet by sucking vigorously on the palm of my hand. This would produce a long, piercing squeal like the cry of a dying rabbit. Maybe it worked on tigers too. I began frantically sucking and squealing and then, to my amazement, the tiger stepped back out of the forest, straight into picture. I filmed him as he stared at me. Then he turned and melted again into the jungle, while I slowly zoomed out and the receding forest seemed to grow smaller and emptier. I knew that this was the final shot of our film. And I knew what the narrator would say. He would say that no-one knew what happened to Bahadur Bhale. He just disappeared into the forest. But a few days later, another tiger emerged, badly injured, as if from a fight. It was Bahadur Bhale's own brother.

11

TIGER CRISIS

In February 1993, I was back in Chitwan again. The comparative success of my first tiger film seemed to have earmarked me as someone who could be trusted in the Sub-Continent and, indeed, I was to make many filming trips back and forth, mainly to India, over the next seven years. This time I was supposed to film the first part of an Indian rhino story for David Attenborough's Private Life of Plants. Along the meandering banks of the Terai rivers there grows a tree that has evolved a rather specialised technique of seed dispersal. The tree is called *Trewia nudiflora* and its seeds have to pass through the gut of a particular large mammal in order to germinate properly. The erosive journey through the digestive system helps to remove the outer skin of the seed, which would otherwise remain dormant. Unfortunately for *Trewia nudiflora* it chose *Rhinocerus unicornis*, the one-horned Indian rhino, for this job. This must have seemed like a good idea when hundreds of thousands of rhinos plodded round the plains of Northern India and Southern Nepal. After all, they'd survived nearly sixty million years, and they had very few enemies, so they must have looked like a sure bet. But by now, the rhinos were very rare, their numbers down to hundreds, not hundreds of thousands, and the tree's future hung equally in the balance.

To make the seeds attractive to rhinos, the tree wraps them inside an apple-like fruit. These fall in the summer, so I would have to return later to film the rhino-eats-the-apple sequence. In the meantime, I was to focus on dung, dung piles, dung beetles, trees growing out of dung and, if possible, rhinos manufacturing and depositing it. This last proved rather difficult. Chitwan, with its unbroken expanses of high elephant grass, was not the ideal location. I later discovered Kaziranga, on the floodplains of the Brahmaputra in Assam. There, the vast open spaces of short grass are a poop-peepers paradise. I eventually spent nine months there, over a two-and-a-half-year period, filming our own rhino film, Rhino Journey, for Discovery and NHK Japan. It had poop shots a-plenty. In Chitwan, however, for the close-up, we had to resort to the zoo.

Indian rhinos use communal latrines. They are solitary, somewhat morose animals, given to fits of violent, earth-shaking temper which are best avoided if they keep away from each other. The communal latrine, invariably visited alone and in privacy of course, is the ideal village notice-board. On it, or rather in it, are written the movements of all the local rhinos, with times and dates. Faecal notices may also include supplementary information about females coming into oestrus and who therefore, and for a few days only, will encourage an approach which would normally be unwelcome. *Trewia nudiflora* may well have had its eye on these latrines when it chose the rhino to disperse its seeds. In an individual blob or even pile of dung, the tree's seed would have an uncertain future but planted firmly in a substantial mound of immobile manure, any seed worth its salt would be in fat city. I had fun scouring the grasslands for incipient forests of *Trewia* sprouting from little hillocks, like trees planted on a barrow.

To help me, Tiger Tops, where I was staying again, set me up with an assistant. His name was Dan Bahadur and he was undoubtedly the best part of the job. Dan Bahadur was something of an elephant whisperer. He knew all the domesticated elephants in and around

Tiger Tops and could read their moods and characters. So good was he, that he had been seconded to a private zoo in Cricket St Mary's in Devon where he taught their elephants to be calm and taught himself to speak excellent English. One day we were going out on a particular elephant and he told me that for many years she had waged war against another elephant. They shared some deep, immoveable grudge and hated each other. Eventually they were separated and her foe was transferred to Bardia. A year or so later, one of the mahouts went himself to Bardia and worked there for some months with the enemy. When he returned our elephant picked him up in her trunk and whacked him on the ground, shattering the poor man's spine. I told Dan Bahadur I'd been in Bardia the year before. He said, with his big grin, that he knew that. He just hoped I'd washed my clothes properly.

Dan was a lowland Nepali from a nearby village but he had a Sherpa feel to him. He was very humorous, independent and intelligent. He knew most of the birds and could imitate their calls. He could read tracks. And he could, somehow, make the enormous, scary chuffing snort of an angry rhino. This was a wonderful after dinner trick, when unsuspecting visitors at the tented camp where we were mostly staying went off to the bush-toilet. I learned a lot from Dan.

Dan Bahadur told me two anecdotes that meshed with my growing interest in tigers. The first concerned Kancha Bhale, one of the male tigers who had been displaced by the hero of my film and had subsequently become a man-eater. It seems that Dan Bahadur was nearly his first victim. One evening, he had been walking home through the forest after a day's tracking when he saw a big male tiger coming straight towards him. Dan swiftly decided to go aerial, shinning his way with some difficulty, up a sal tree that stood near the track. At this point, a well-adjusted tiger could be expected to disappear, or, if he were a confident, curious male, he might come and check out the big monkey, now perched up on a limb above him. But Dan's tiger didn't just come for a look, it came for a lunge. It sprang up at his dangling feet, forcing him further up the tree, and then tried to climb the trunk. Then it circled below him, loitering menacingly for half an hour before slipping away. Dan Bahadur didn't move and, sure enough, after an hour, the tiger returned and had another go at him. Dan stayed up that tree most of the night, long after the tiger really had gone. A few days later, Kancha Bhale killed a man. The prints of the killer matched those round Dan Bahadur's tree.

While this story seemed to match my own information about a rare man-eater, Dan's other anecdote supported my view that most tigers are nervous of treating humans as prey. One day, he was accompanying a visitor through the forest and in the sandy surface of the track, they came upon very fresh prints of a tigress with two cubs. There was a bend ahead so Dan asked the visitor to wait while he walked forwards to check that it was safe to proceed. It wasn't. Just round the bend he walked smack into the family party and the tigress, in panic, charged him. He dived headlong into a big tuft of elephant grass. The tigress landed on top of him. Between them was only a folded layer of grass stems. Dan lay dead still, arms akimbo, the bottom part of a lethal sandwich. After a few, very, very long seconds, the tiger must have been satisfied that she had neutralised the threat. She slipped off him, honked softly to her cubs and they disappeared into the jungle. Dan was unmarked. The tigress could easily have killed him but she didn't know that. He wasn't prey, he was no longer dangerous, she didn't need to kill him, so she didn't.

What I now began to discover, though, through rumours and phone calls and meeting others who were interested, was that people were killing tigers. Again. Tiger hunting had been banned as a sport in India in 1970 and subsequently in all tiger range states. The push to save the wild tiger in India, which was reckoned to have at least a third of the world population, had been inspired by Guy Mountfort, of Coto Donana fame, and the friendship of three key Indians, Prime Minister Indira Ghandi, Prince Karen Singh and Dr Kailash Sankhala, Director of Delhi Zoo. Together they had spearheaded Project Tiger which was, at the time, the most celebrated conservation initiative in history, financed in part by an IUCN fund-raising bonanza called "Operation Tiger" which raised over a million dollars in eighteen months. The acute need for action was underscored in

1972 by India's first national tiger census. This came up with the shocking estimate that there were only 1,827 animals left. In July 1973, Project Tiger was launched. The ceremony took place on the banks of the beautiful Ramganga River in Uttar Pradesh, in the new National Park which was to be named after the famous tiger-hunter-turned-conservationist, Jim Corbett. Project Tiger established nine special areas that would become Tiger Reserves and earmarked the budget to run them for their first five years.

There is no doubt that Project Tiger had been a success, at least in its early years. The Indian government ploughed money into tiger conservation, more reserves were added, tiger numbers steadied. But then, as can easily happen, people probably took their eye off the ball. The tiger was "saved". There were other things to think about. I first heard hints that things were going wrong from Pradheep Sankhala, a family friend who had helped my older brother Terry see his first tiger in the early eighties. Pradheep was the son of Project Tiger's founding director, Kailash Sankhala, and remained a good friend until his sad early death in May 2003. Pradheep told me tigers were vanishing. The first person to publish his concerns, however, was Valmik Thapar, an independent naturalist who had been watching tigers in Ranthambhore National Park in Rajasthan for some years. With his friend Fateh Sing Rathore, previously the inspiring Ranthambhore Director, Valmik had learned to recognise many of the tigers as individuals. The most remarkable of these, they had named Genghis. Genghis had developed a novel hunting technique. He had learned to crowd large sambar deer into the water of one of the famous Ranthambhore lakes. The water would slow them down and he would then shock and dismay them by charging in after them and strangling them. These spectacular feats had even been filmed. And he seemed to have "taught" his daughters the same trick. Then, one by one, these tigers disappeared. According to the official census, Ranthambhore was supposed to hold forty tigers but by 1991, Valmik and Fateh couldn't find any of them. Another independent observer, Billy Arjun Sing in Dudhwa also claimed tigers there were disappearing too.

When I arrived home from Nepal, I was visited by Mike Birkhead, a freelance producer also working with the BBC. He wanted to involve me in a project called The Peacock and the Tiger, which he was going to shoot with outstanding cameraman Mike Richards. But all I could think about was the disappearing tigers and the only film I wanted to make would be the one that told the world what was actually happening. The mystery of the disappearances was, I believed, close to being solved and it was an important story. I told Mike what I knew and I think he was stunned. We agreed that I would write the film and he would produce it. He went straight to Alistair Fothergill who had just taken over as head of the BBC Natural History Unit in Bristol and the budget for an hour-long special was raised in three days.

Tiger Crisis begins with a spectacular opening sequence of the amazing tigers of Ranthambhore hunting sambar in the sparkling lakes. It's a long scene accompanied only by a haunting Indian lament. Mike Birkhead had fallen in love with this sad piece of instrumental music and, despite my usual reservations about music in nature films, it was perfect here. We didn't bring the narration in until the entire sequence was played out. Only then did the voice-over say that Genghis, Noon and all the well-known tigers of Ranthambhore were dead. The rest of the film tells you why.

At midnight on 30th August, Vivek Menon went to a secret rendezvous in the winding, stifling back streets of Delhi's old Walled City. He was meeting a Tibetan refugee named Pema Thinley who was offering to sell him fresh tiger bones. What Thinley didn't know was that Menon was working for Traffic-India, an NGO investigating illegal wildlife trade, that he would have the police with him and that the whole story would appear on the BBC.

The photographs of that dingy little warehouse stacked to the ceiling with the skulls and skins of tigers were utterly shocking. The total haul was 220 kilos of tiger bone. Some of it still had strands of fresh meat attached. A few days later the police raided Delhi's Tibetan refugee camp. There they found a further 87 kilos of bone and, in a nearby stash, a new massive haul of 200 kilos of bones, the skins of six adult tigers and two cubs, 43 leopard skins and 128 otter skins. The tiger component of this hideous cargo amounted to between 35 and 40 tigers. It was, at the time, far and away the largest seizure of tiger parts ever made. Its street value was nearly $1 million.

According to Thinley and the men arrested with him, the tigers had all been poached during the previous monsoon. They had already claimed to Menon that they could supply another thousand kilos. From the evidence eventually gathered, Menon's boss, Ashok Kumar, calculated that at least 500 tigers had been poached in the past three years. Menon suspected the figure was closer to a thousand.

Claude Martin, Director General of WWF and Arun Ghosh, Director of Project Tiger were both interviewed in the film. They both said that tigers were doing just fine. But they were wrong. They had been guarding the wrong bank. The tigers that had survived the widespread loss of habitat in the twentieth century had previously been brought close to extinction by trophy hunting. This was a form of conspicuous consumption and it had been stopped. The new threat, however, was more clandestine and far more insidious. These poachers moved at night, lived in the forest, outside society. Their paymasters were not interested in showing off their booty or adorning their homes with ghoulish trophies. In fact, they were not especially interested in pelts at all. They wanted whiskers and claws and, above all, bone and their market lay far away, in China. In the early 1990s few westerners had heard much about Traditional Chinese Medicine. After Tiger Crisis, everyone would know that in the Far East, practitioners ascribed great potency to tiger parts. The fat is used against leprosy, whiskers can cure toothache, the tail assuages skin diseases, the eyeballs protect against convulsions and cataracts and the claws can be sedatives. But tiger bone is the most valuable commodity. A tonic made from freshly ground tiger bone is regarded as an all-powerful promoter of vigour and well-being and people, especially in China, will pay handsomely for it. In 1993 the street value of a dead tiger in China was between six and ten thousand dollars.

The sudden renewal of tiger poaching, which had taken us all by surprise, was probably fuelled by the emergence of a new wealthy class in China coupled with the exhaustion of stockpiles of tiger parts derived from the general slaughter of China's own wild tigers that had occurred in the 1960s. The task, for Tiger Crisis, was to ensure that, henceforth, no-one doubted how serious the situation had become. In the final cut of the film, we juxtaposed the denials made by Martin and Ghosh with the flat statement by Kamal Nath, India's Minister of Forests that tigers definitely were in trouble. Peter Jackson, Chairman of the IUCN Cats Specialist Group of the Species Survival Commission told us that, at the current rate of poaching, tigers might not last into the new century. In the film, we asked George Schaller, whom I admired enormously and who had been the first scientist to study tigers professionally, what he thought. He said he wouldn't want to live in a world without wild tigers. I feel the same.

Tiger Crisis was enlivened by its focus on the role of several individuals: Fateh Sing Rathore, who tried to save the tigers of Ranthambhore, Valmik Thapar who first brought their story to the public and Vivek Menon and Ashok Kumar with their investigations, while Dr Ullas Karanth, one of India's few tiger researchers, brought some scientific ballast to the programme. But I also wanted to include something about the wider history of the tiger's decline. I had discovered a piece of archive footage showing the British Queen and the Duke of Edinburgh, accompanied by various dignitaries, taking part in what was probably one of the last big, public tiger hunts in India. I think it was a Pathe News clip and it contained the immortal words, after you see two puffs of smoke from atop an elephant, and hear two loud bangs, "oh dear, the Foreign Secretary seems to have missed." I felt that, in a film that was so critical of other nationals, it was important to acknowledge that our own views of tigers had been less protective not so long before. The BBC producer assigned to our project, however, Keith Scholey, was not a man to rock the boat, specially not a boat with a queen in it. Mike Birkhead was more mischievous so, finally, it was agreed that the clip could be used, but only if I could make it fit into the story in a way that made it feel "right" – that it needed to be there. I sat up most of the night with the editor, the long-suffering Hugh Tasman, as we dismantled all his hard work on a near-complete first cut, to weave the tiger hunt into the story. After several hours, Hugh began to sweat. He said he hoped I knew what I was doing because he wouldn't be able to put the film back together again the way it had been. But, after all, I'd written the story. I did know how it would fit and I was glad Mike had trusted me to make it work. It was, anyway, only a small adjustment, fair and necessary, to an unfolding and very contemporary tragedy – the new, massive poaching of tigers for their bones.

Tiger Crisis was first broadcast in January 1994. At the time, it was probably the hardest-hitting, most revelatory and most important conservation film the BBC had ever produced. The audience response was immense. People were genuinely shocked and tiger conservation was put right back at the top of their list of wildlife priorities, a position it continues to occupy. The film marked a watershed in public perception. Never again would politicians and the public be ignorant of the potential malevolence of Traditional Chinese Medicine in creating an underground market for illegal animal products.

The film helped to escalate the political debate even before it was broadcast. The fact that the BBC were asking awkward questions at the very top and confronting senior politicians with irrefutable evidence of an impending wildlife catastrophe, caused a stir. The United States even threatened trade sanctions against China and Taiwan for apparently encouraging trade in endangered species. On 7th September 1993, US Secretary of the Interior, Bruce Babbit announced that he was considering invoking sanctions under what was called the Pelly Amendment. "The United States" he said "cannot stand by while the world's remaining tigers and rhinos slip into extinction as a result of illegal commercial trade in the world marketplace. Our action today will send the message that unlawful trade in these rare species will not be tolerated."

Another result of Tiger Crisis and pressure from its stars, especially Valmik Thapar, was that the Indian Government promised to fund a special anti-poaching task force. The distance between talk and action, however, is often measured in decades. In 2005, history repeated itself. Another tiger researcher, Dr Raghu Chundawat, in another reserve, Panna in Madhya Pradesh, realised tigers were being poached during a changeover of senior personnel. Chundawat had had excellent relations with the previous park director and together their management had seen tiger numbers increase from seven to 35 in ten years. The new director, however, did not listen to the warnings. Instead, he banned Chundawat from the park. Panna then lost all its tigers. So did Sariska, a reserve that had been cleaned out in the first crisis and had been repopulated with tigers introduced from other reserves, including Panna. It's to the credit of the authorities, however, that this time they did eventually recognise the symptoms that Tiger Crisis had diagnosed. Although the Task Force never entirely materialised, more of a Task Force mentality emerged.

The most important action that was taken was to start counting tigers properly. In fact, I would suggest that this decision can be seen as the most enduring legacy of Tiger Crisis. In the film, Dr Ullas Karanth completely demolished the official census method. Tigers were traditionally counted by paw print. Gangs of foresters crawled around the jungle making tracings of the pug marks they found. The tracings were marked with time, date, location and soil-type (because the same print can look different in sand or mud) and submitted to a committee of experts in each park, led by the park director. The experts would then calculate how many tigers they had. Karanth had tested this system by submitting tracings of a known number of tigers to three different sets of experts. None of them came up with the correct number and some were nearly five hundred percent out. After Tiger Crisis, no-one trusted the official statistics any more.

In the aftermath of the 2005 Panna-Sariska tragedy, the authorities would finally admit that it was impossible to manage a species if you had no real idea how many you had. Fifteen years after Tiger Crisis, they agreed to jettison the discredited counting method. From now on they would use sampling by transects, prey-density assessments, and, most important, thousands of camera traps. The paramount priority of the new census would be accuracy. This was actually quite a brave decision. It was clear to all of us who were familiar with India's tigers that official statistics no longer bore any relation to reality. The same annual inflation was built into the guestimates as would be built into a departmental budget and over the years the tiger inventory had become more and more fantastical. Most of us believed that, if the census was truly accurate, and that was a big if, it would conclude that there were only a third as many tigers as the government believed. The clue as to whether we could trust the new count lay in who would be chosen to lead it: a politician, an apparatchik or a scientist. In the event the job was given to Dr Jadvendra Jhala. I knew him as something of a friend. He had helped me filming wolves and Indian foxes, several years after Tiger Crisis, when I was working on Land of the Tiger. I had also encountered him in my wolf work. He was and is undoubtedly one of the few truly world class Indian wildlife scientists and he laid the foundations, in that first new census, for an entirely professional count. This has become a benchmark for international censuses of the kind and something of which India can be justly proud.

And how many tigers were there? The official figure up to 2006 had been three thousand six hundred. Jhala found just 1,411, fewer than when Project Tiger had been launched 34 years earlier. We all feared the headlines: "India Loses 60 percent of its Tigers", "New Tiger Census Shows Catastrophic Decline". But of course, that was nonsense. India had only lost the tigers that had been there. The rest had never been there in the first place and now the authorities were brave enough to acknowledge it. I wrote numerous articles, in BBC Wildlife, The Guardian and even in the Evening Standard, in the hope that they would be quoted or re-printed in India, as they were. I pointed out that, far from being a disaster, this new census was the best thing that had happened to India's tigers in thirty years. It provided a bedrock figure which everyone could trust. From now on, management really would know how many tigers were in each reserve, they would be more alert to poaching or other threats and any change in the population could be accurately monitored.

In 2018 India's National Tiger Conservation Authority, the nearest thing to a Task Force that we got, published the report of the fourth four-yearly national tiger census conducted in collaboration with the Wildlife Institute of India. The survey deployed 44,000 people. They checked 381,400 square kilometres of forest for tiger signs. They walked 522,996 kilometres of trails and sampled 317,958 habitat plots. Camera traps were employed at 26,838 different locations, in areas the survey suggested represented prime tiger country. The cameras amassed an astonishing inventory of animals. There were 34,858,623 wildlife photographs to analyse. These included 76,651 pictures of tigers and 51,777 pictures of leopards. In all, it emerged that they had photographed 2,461 different tigers and standard sampling techniques produced a total tiger population of 2,967. It was billed as the largest camera-trap exercise the world had ever seen and it showed an apparent increase from 2,226 in 2014 and 1,706 in 2010. The bad news for tigers was that the populations outside tiger reserves had declined. The good news was that there were now 51 tiger reserves, with at least four more in the pipeline.

It is always reasonable to challenge the precision of wildlife population statistics. The new census still relies on interpretative skills. Not everyone can read the results of a camera trap accurately. Nevertheless, it is clear that India is putting serious resources into counting, managing and conserving its tigers. Since India now probably has more than 80 percent of the wild tigers left in the world, it is important that they keep their eye on the ball and that conservationists and commentators remain alert. Apathy and mission drift are the bane of all great initiatives.

There is no doubt that Tiger Crisis put down a marker. It gave a voice to informed dissent over how to manage tigers and encouragement to a new breed of more professional conservationists in India. But as science becomes more influential in wildlife management in India – as it needs to – I hope it will be in a uniquely Indian way and not at the expense of more spiritual approaches. When I first arrived in India, I didn't find many people who had expertise in the field. Many of the forest guides in the reserves knew nothing. This has all changed now. There is a new generation of excellent young naturalists. But what I did notice in my early visits is something that I hope will be forever preserved. I'm talking about the Hindu reverence for life, that gives value to all living things. I trust this even more than I trust high-quality surveys. For how else would India, with its human population numbering over 1.3 billion, have managed to keep almost its entire megafauna? In amongst those bustling human lives, just about hanging on, are elephants and rhinoceroses, bears, lions, tigers, leopards and lynxes, and wild asses and bison. Africa, wonderful Africa, has just ten species of cat. India has fifteen. It's an admirable achievement and I do admire it. In fact, the only large mammal India has lost in modern times is the cheetah and they are now working to reintroduce a seed population back in Madhya Pradesh, the province where the last ones were killed in the 1950s.

Tiger Crisis won lots of awards. It won a coveted Golden Panda at Wildscreen – the nature film Oscars. It won best film at Missoula and best TV film at the International Film Festival. It was repeated, updated and then copied umpteen times. For me there was one small downside. Guy Mountfort, my Coto Donana guru, apparently decided I was persona no grata and not to be forgiven for criticising WWF and Project Tiger, in which he felt his own spirit was bound. But there was a lesson here. I hadn't criticised Project Tiger, only what it had become. The lesson was that in conservation, a job can never be signed off. Tigers cannot be saved. They can only be kept going.

12

THE PRIVATE LIFE OF PLANTS

In the late summer of 1994, I returned to Chitwan. I was greeted by the reassuring sight of Dan Bahadur's smiling, friendly face and we began work straight away. We were involved with two sequences for The Private Life of Plants. One was a small bit about elephant grass and the main task was to complete the rhino-*Trewia nudiflora* story we had started the year before. The first thing I noticed as we drove into the park was that this was a bumper year for the flowering of the elephant grass. The tall stems stood stately and proud, spreading as far as the eye could see, their silver flowerheads glowing and glinting in the morning sun. I remember thinking how lucky David Attenborough was. I'd never seen the grasslands looking so rich and perfect. This was a once in a decade flower show. I decided to film these shining meadows immediately. We took an elephant way out into the heart of the them, where I'd noticed a small thornbush peeping its head above the waves of grass. The mahout angled the elephant up to the trunk of the little tree so I could clamber across and wedge myself in its branches. An elephant is a wonderful cross-country vehicle but it is not a stable platform from which to film landscapes. In the absence of the specially adapted twelve-foot tripod that is the only real way to work from elephants, the tree was my next best solution. From my perch, with my crystal-clear wide-angle Zeiss lens, I filmed the oceans of giant, bottle-brush grassheads spreading away in all directions. As it turned out, it was rather lucky that I did this.

There wasn't much more to do on grasses until David Attenborough arrived to talk about them on camera. He and the rest of the film crew were not due for a week, so, in the meantime, we needed to concentrate on filming elusive rhinos eating equally elusive *Trewia* "apples". Dan agreed to scour the jungle for fruit, while I scouted for rhinos and a good filming location. I found a well frequented stand of *Trewia* about half an hour's elephant ride from camp. There, the staff hurriedly erected a bamboo machan, a slightly rickety twelve-foot platform where I could set up my camera. Dan spilled his harvest of *Trewia* fruit in a well-lit clearing below me and we sprinkled a little salt on the offering to make it irresistible. Grazing animals are always short of salt so we thought this condiment might give our pile of fruit an edge over more naturally distributed apples.

On the first morning up the machan, I did something rather stupid. Not long after Dan and the elephant had planted me and left, I must have fidgeted in an unruly and inappropriate manner. Somehow, I bumped one of the short tripod legs. It didn't take kindly to this and I swear it leapt out of the machan, taking the camera with it. My entire filming apparatus landed with a squishy thud head first in the squelchy ground twelve feet below me. There was one problem with my machan. It had no ladder. So, though I might well be able to scramble, swing and jump down to the ground, I would not be able to get back up again with the equipment. I pondered the situation for a while but in the end, I could see no other solution than to hoist my flag of surrender and hope that Dan or the mahout would eventually spot it. Meanwhile I just prayed that nothing came to eat our apples. I didn't want some clumsy, fidgety, two-and-a-half-ton rhino to step on my camera and I was also afraid, that after such a flop, Dan Bahadur would expect me to commit honourable hara-kiri.

After an hour or two, the elephant showed up and I was able to rescue my camera. Apart from a bit of mud in its eye, neither lens nor camera seemed damaged. Dan couldn't stop laughing but I had to put up with that. Half an hour later, I was alone again. The day grew hot. A crested serpent eagle swung high above me, calling plaintively. The metronomic tocking of distant coppersmith barbets hammered away the afternoon and for hours nothing much moved. Then, finally, I heard a heavy rustle in the high grass and a rhino plodded into view. A young female. Suddenly I had action. I filmed her walk into picture. She headed purposefully for our fruit basket, smelt around it for a while and then began to tuck in. I filmed her in close-up as she licked the surface of the apples and then scrunched them up, one after another, the pulpy juices running deliciously down her chin.

Over the next few days, I filmed several rhinos enjoying the *Trewia* fruits. I grew to love these great leathery brutes, now so rare, whose needs seemed so modest; just a handful of apples. The Indian rhino is the "original rhino", probably the first one to be known about in the West. It was introduced by the amazing woodcut made in 1515 by the German artist Albrecht Durer. The image he produced is remarkably accurate, considering he never actually saw the animal. Apparently, he based his picture on some brief notes and a drawing made anonymously of a live rhino that had been shipped to Lisbon in the same year. He showed the characteristic folds of skin that hang like reticulated armoured plates around the flanks and loins and the comparatively short single horn. Watching the rhinos come and go beneath me was cathartic. I knew I had been lucky. I'd filmed a tricky sequence which had never been filmed before and now, watching and filming them in a relaxed mood I decided that, one day, I would try to return and make a film just about the great Indian one-horned rhinoceros.

On the day David Attenborough arrived, it began to rain. It rained all day. And all the next day. And the next. We gathered in the main hall at Tiger Tops, Mike Salisbury the producer, Dicky Bird the highly experienced sound-man, David and I and watched helplessly as the distant river inexorably rose. Metre by precious metre our beautiful elephant grasses began to disappear, their lush, shiny flower heads dragged down into the brown muddy waters. By the fourth day, all we could see beyond the first strand of scrub and meadow, was water. We saw a rhino mother pacing the menacing edge with her small calf, looking for a place to swim across to the safety of the distant trees. She became more and more frantic until suddenly she plunged in and began to swim. Her calf desperately followed her and was instantly swallowed by the swirling floodwater. We never saw it again.

There was not much to do but talk. It's easy to be disappointed when you meet and work with a childhood hero. But I doubt if anyone has ever been seriously disappointed by David Attenborough. Over the next week, I was to witness many good aspects of his professionalism but, during the downpour, he took it on himself to keep us effortlessly entertained. Like all great raconteurs he told the best stories against himself. I remember a couple of them. The first concerned his early efforts in front of the camera. The BBC had been looking for a new onscreen presenter and a senior manager had written a report on his audition. Years later, when David was himself controller of the new BBC2 channel he had found the report and read it. It said something along the lines that "the young Attenborough is all very well, but he will never get far on television with those teeth." Hardly a mordant prediction. The other story was about filming in Antarctica, where the long cold days were suddenly and unexpected enlivened by the arrival of a stunning Nordic lady scientist. The next day, when she asked for volunteers to help her, David had shot to his feet and soon found himself snuggled up with her in a helicopter, as any red-blooded man would have wished. He didn't enjoy her company for long though. She quickly explained what she wanted him to do. She was studying snow and ice conditions. They would fly low over a chosen bank of snow, he would jump out, laden with meteorological equipment and she would return for him when the gear had automatically collected the necessary measurements. Seconds later, whoosh, he was flying through the air and swish, he was stuck, perfectly upright in a deep snow-drift, with only the narrow, six-foot high tube made by his impact to move in. There he remained, like a human piston wedged in an ice cylinder, until she eventually returned to pick him up.

David loved music, especially classical music. He told us he always travelled with dozens of CDs, stored in anonymous plastic bags to save space. At night when he wanted to listen to something he would select a piece randomly in the dark. If it didn't match his mood, he could try again. He made a rule for himself, however, that if he moved to a third choice, he had to stick with it, whatever it was. I always carried a tiny, high-powered short-wave radio on which I listened obsessively to the BBC World Service late into the dead hours. One night I had been surprised to hear an interview with myself. Another night, years later, I heard of the death of a friend, killed in a small plane not far from where I was working. It wasn't always easy to find comfort on long journeys, far from home.

On the seventh morning a dove flew into the hall with a leaf in its beak and we knew it had stopped raining. Well, that's not strictly true. We knew because we had all heard the depressing, monotonous patter of raindrops gradually subside to silence during the night and we gathered just after dawn, eager for action. Outside the whole world was steaming in the morning sun. It looked like the aftermath of a nuclear explosion. In the meadows around us, hardly a single stem of elephant grass was still standing. Our plan had been to film David in close-up, holding two grass heads, as he talked about various forms of grass around the world. Then I would slowly zoom out and as he said "and some of them grow exceedingly tall", the viewer would see that he was actually sitting on top of an elephant and that the two giant grasses in his hands reached all the way down to the ground. And all around him the vast grasses would stretch to the horizon. It was a beautiful idea. The only problem was that there was no grass left. Or was there? Maybe a little bit had survived the flood somewhere. Dan and I set off to look. Eventually, we found a patch about thirty metres square. I reckoned that if I zoomed out just as far as the very edge of Custer's Last Stand, as I called it, no-one would see that that was actually the end of the grass. We could then cut to the shots of the virgin grasslands I had filmed when I first arrived and the combination would still tell the story quite well. So that's what we did and it worked fine. There was only one other problem. David suffered from hay fever. The hot sun and the drying grasses brought him out in sudden red welts and his eyes began to swell. He filled himself with anti-histamines but in the minutes before the shoot he looked more like an elderly man in a hospital bed than the world-famous presenter we all know and love. And yet. As soon as Mike Salisbury called "shoot" and I began filming, his face came back to life, his eyes shone with the old enthusiasm and he delivered his lines perfectly. I think we only did one take. I must say, I was very impressed.

The other scene we had to film together was the one in which David talked to rhinos. Well, he wasn't supposed to talk to them, he was supposed to talk about them, but that isn't quite what happened. Dan and I had earmarked several females with calves which we thought might make ideal backdrops for the narration sequence but the storm had probably scattered them so we took our elephants and went off to see what we could find. We were soon to come on one of the less skittish females still frequenting her favourite meadow. It was a perfect location so we hurried back to fetch the rest of the crew. The mother rhino must have been very surprised when she saw us the next time. We looked like the vanguard of Hannibal's army. We had half a dozen elephants. These we arrayed in a fan to form a safety net in case the rhino charged. Dicky Bird fixed a radio mic onto David, did a quick sound check and then David and I crept forward on foot towards the rhino and her calf. The location was perfect because the rhino had long grass behind her into which she could feel she could retreat, but it was separated from her by a ditch. I hoped this might deter her from running off. Even better, there was a small tree with grabbable branches about twenty metres in front of where she stood eyeing us suspiciously. Mother rhinos with calves are seriously dangerous, which is why we had our elephantine bodyguard. I told David that if she charged, he was to forget about me, keep the tree between himself and the rhino and pull himself up into it. He replied gamely that if she charged, I could be certain that I would be the very last thing on his mind. Unfortunately, one of our elephants was a young male who had not completed his training. He was clearly terrified of the rhino and every time we tried to shoot a take he would start to cry. Mike would say, "Shoot" and the elephant would bawl like a baby. Eventually, we had to give him the sack and pack him off back to Tiger Tops. He cried most of the way home and we had to wait ten minutes for his racket to subside before we could try filming again. The rhino was now getting quite edgy. The script required David to explain that *Trewia nudiflora* had, as it were, put all its eggs in one basket, selecting just one animal to spread its seeds. But the tree was in trouble because its seed carrier, the greater one-horned Indian rhino was now exceedingly rare. The rhino was quite close. David was supposed to peer round the tree at it and then look back over his shoulder and deliver most of the lines at the camera, only turning again as he mentioned the rhino's rarity. But David wasn't going to take his eye off the rhino for more than a second. He said a couple of words to camera over his shoulder and the rest he delivered full-frontal to the increasingly agitated mega-tonnage of pachyderm that he really thought was about to trample on him. He was right, of course. If we hadn't had the elephants with us, it would have done. I still wonder if he'd have made it up that tree.

David was a trooper. You could not imagine a world-wide star who was less of a prima donna. He was very much a team player. If you needed a third pair of hands to move equipment, David was always there to help. He'd grab a heavy camera case, hand you the tripod up on the elephant and never stand around doing nothing when others were busy. It's no surprise that crews have loved working with him for nearly seventy years. And that wonderful voice, always with its hall-mark lift of curiosity, conveying unexaggerated wonder and enthusiasm. I doubt if his record will ever be equalled. During our unscheduled monsoon lay-off, however, we had time for some serious discussions and I did challenge him over one issue that bothered me. My main reason for wanting to make wildlife films had always been to change hearts and minds and, however modestly, to further the cause of conservation. Television, for all its silliness, remains a potentially powerful medium. It comes alive inside people's homes, where it can, if tasked to do so, plant the seeds of important ideas. I challenged David with never having nailed his colours to this mast. I felt he could use his world-wide fame much more effectively to tackle some of the problems that loomed large to me then, like deforestation, over-fishing and the massive illegal trade in animal parts. He said his low-profile stance was deliberate. He had decided long ago that in preaching lay the graveyard of reputation and that by becoming embroiled in controversies you lost half your audience. His role, he said, was to inspire people with the beauty of nature, surprise them with its intricacy and keep them interested in its stories. It was for others to fight the battles. His job was to maintain an audience of potential allies. I found myself thinking more and more about this over the coming years. David's manifesto made perfect sense and may well explain the longevity of the wildlife strand in television. But while I agree that most nature films should concentrate on inspiring and informing, some should definitely go further. And I worry that by perennially parading a myth of nature's pristine state – a myth we maintain by rarely showing the thirty jeeps surrounding a panting cheetah in the Masai Mara, or the clamouring masses trying to spot a tiger in Kanha – we accidentally reassure our audience that all is well in the natural world. But it isn't. Nature is hanging by a thread. It seems to me that as wildlife filmmakers we face an increasingly uncomfortable dilemma. If we show the grisly facts of nature's demise, our stories lose the lustre of romance and we risk losing our audience. If, however, we don't show those facts and continue to grandstand a fabricated Eden that no longer exists, we risk losing our subject.

It's interesting that when David Attenborough did finally put his head above the parapet, at the very end of his career, in the first place with a film about plastics, he galvanised the world into action. It's not

David's fault that, between his plastics film and our conversation during the floods in Chitwan, the BBC had been peddling 20 years of natural-history clichés. The truth is that the wilderness days are mostly over and we must learn to love and care for the scrappy fragments at our door. I was pleased to see that the latest series of Planet Earth, Planet Earth 3, released in 2023, finally recognised this.

13

WINNERS AND LOSERS AND THE ABOMINABLE TOURIST

D espite the lengthy rain delay, the shoot in Nepal was very efficiently wrapped up and everything we filmed appeared in due course in The Private Life of Plants. Meanwhile, three months later, I was in Gujarat, in Western India, filming Indian lions. One BBC producer who was never afraid of tackling conservation issues was Richard Brock. He had phoned me with an intriguing proposal. When I was a boy, ten or eleven, I had been mesmerised by a series of films shown on the BBC by a German cameraman called Eugen Schuhmacher. He had travelled the world in the late 1950s and early 1960s filming animals and birds that he feared might go extinct. The BBC had broadcast the results in black and white, with a thoughtful commentary by Peter Scott and entitled The Rare Ones. Richard had discovered that the films had not actually been shot in black and white. They had been filmed in top quality 35 millimetre colour. Furthermore, the BBC had rights to the lot. Richard's idea was to revisit the stories that Schuhmacher had told to find out how the subjects had fared during the thirty tumultuous years that had followed. Richard wanted me to write a two-part series, round the theme of Winners and Losers. A team of camera people, including me, would do the update filming and David Attenborough agreed to narrate my commentary. This gave me the opportunity to show how conservation strategies had evolved, from the simple command "do not kill", followed by "and also do not destroy the habitat" to the emerging realisation that, for sustainable results, you had to involve local people. Winners tended to be fluffy or engaging enough to attract funds, and had the best chance of surviving now in the very countries that had got rich by destroying them. Losers tended to have pernickety requirements and inhabit idiosyncratic ecological niches. The texture of the two films was very unusual. I kept relevant parts of Peter Scott's delightfully old-fashioned commentary, interweaved with David's measured, authoritative tones to cover the updated film and provide the modern context. When Richard left the BBC, he took this idea with him and established a stream of eighty Winners and Losers films. As part of The Brock Initiative, these can all be downloaded for free from the internet.

The Asiatic lion, which I was filming to update Schuhmacher's story, was the lion of the bible, the lion that Daniel had to appease, the lion that Hercules clobbered with his club. Originally, it had extended from North Africa, up through Turkey, into Northern Greece, across the Middle East all the way to Northern India. Now, it was only found in a single forest in Gujarat. During the 186,000 years since it had separated from its genetic source, in central Africa, it had evolved some minor characteristics of its own, mainly to do with the morphology of the skull. Otherwise, to all intents and purposes, it was a slightly smaller version of an African lion, with a less impressive mane. The Asiatic lion was both a loser and a winner. It was clearly a loser because it had lost all its friends and relations. But it was a winner because it had, ultimately, survived. In 1901 the British Viceroy of India, Lord Curzon, was invited to hunt lions in Junagadh but when he learned that they were the only lions left in Asia he suggested that the Nawab might like to stop hunting them and conserve them instead. The Nawab must have thought this was a jolly good idea because he set up what was probably the first real conservation initiative in India. He saved the lions and preserved the Gir forest and by the time Schuhmacher filmed them, numbers had recovered from around 30 to more than 200. During my first visit in 1994, I was told there were over 300. The fourteenth Asiatic Lion Census of 2015 found 523 animals and the latest, 2020 estimate, puts the population at 674.

The lions in the forest of Gir have one other advantage. They have an important ally in the Maldhari people. The Maldharis are buffalo herders. Like the Masai of East Africa and their cows, the Maldhari don't eat their buffaloes. They use their dung for fuel and flooring, their muscle to move things and every day they churn the buffalo milk into a thick, sour yoghurt which is their staple diet. During the day the Maldhari men accompany their buffaloes as they graze through the forest. At night they bring them all safely inside the naas, the homestead which is surrounded by a high wall of thorns. The Maldhari champion the lions because they know that while the lions are there, their beloved forest will be protected. And the lions respect the Maldhari because they know if they scoff a buffalo they'll get whacked by a stick. Wherever they go, the Maldhari carry a stout, hardwood staff to which the lions are curiously subservient. This unique symbiosis of man and lion makes the story very attractive.

When Patricia and I arrived in Gir that December, we discovered that one of its many charms was that it was mostly safe to film on foot. One day we heard roaring, long and loud. We stopped the jeep and I crouched down with the camera on a low tripod by the left front bumper and Patricia squatted with the microphone on the right. Then two big male lions came running, with their manes swinging, down the sandy track towards us. They didn't miss a beat. They came straight at us, one brushing the camera as he galloped past me, the other knocking the microphone as he passed Patricia. Another day someone came running to say we must come quickly because lions were mating. We rushed to the place, up a little bare scrubby hill with just a bush and no lions. We stood breathlessly by the bush while I called out jokingly "where are the lions then?" At which point a huge lion head poked itself out of the bush beside me and let off a humungous roar. The sound waves were so powerful that I felt the cavity of my chest collapse and swell again. When I looked at Patricia, who was a pretty brave person, her whole body was shaking like a Martini. I think it was the funniest thing I'd ever seen.

I loved our early mornings in Gir. We would drive in just before dawn and on several mornings, we were accompanied by a huge male leopard, silvery in the half-light, keeping pace with us in the undergrowth. Gir, with its dry, deciduous woodland and its many herds of spotted deer, is brilliant for leopards. Our lodge was a very comfortable, stone villa, owned by a successful young businessman from Ahmedabad. When our host discovered we had been recording the roars of the lions he wanted to show off his brand-new stereo system. One night, he wired the tape-recorder into his amplifier and pointing the huge speakers at the forest he sent our roars out to the lions in the night. The result was astonishing. The invisible jungle came to life, reverberating for half an hour with the answering roars of puzzled lions and the anxious piping of all the animals that fear them. I felt a little guilty and we probably shouldn't have done it. I can only imagine the gossip we may have sparked among the lions themselves: what was Mrs X doing outside the forest at that time of night?

In the fiery heat of the day, we took to resting under a large banyan tree not far from a well-ordered naas. We used to watch the handsome Maldhari girls swaying up the slope from the river, with vast stacks of fresh cut grass balanced effortlessly on their heads. At first, they were very shy, particularly of the microphone, or rather the big grey, hairy cover that shielded it from the wind. I hate to think what they thought it was, especially as it was usually Patricia who was holding it. After a couple of days, however, they relaxed and I asked them, by sign language, if I could film them carrying their loads up to the naas. Yes, I certainly could. Lots of smiles and laughs. But then I had to let them film me doing the same. Many more laughs at that idea. So, I filmed some beautiful scenes of those graceful girls and then it was my turn to heft the load. When I bent down to lift one of the stacks, I couldn't believe how heavy it was. I had to bend my knees and strain like Charles Atlas to get it up onto my head and then its unwieldy shape required all my strength to keep it there. I staggered up to the naas, counting every step, trying to look as nonchalant as I could, while the girls watched me through the camera. There was no way I was really going to let them film this, but they were laughing too much to do that anyway. They knew I was being drilled into the ground like a tent peg by their standard grocery delivery. I was reminded of this a few years later, when I was filming on Mount Everest. I had a small team of Sherpa ladies carrying my gear for me. The cameras and tripods and film boxes, magazines and lenses, were all piled into wicker baskets which they hung on their backs, supported by straps passed round their foreheads. They walked fast, straight up the mountain, chattering like schoolgirls – and they said they were actually impressed with me because I could keep up with them. But I was empty-handed and they each had fifty pounds of equipment on their backs. My guide warned me to peg the door of my tent tightly closed at night. He said they were naughty girls and covered in lice. Who knows, but I thought they were brilliant.

Because we came every day, we grew friendly with the people of the naas in Gir. The old lady, who seemed to be the matriarch, would carry down a charpai, a string bed, for us each afternoon and offer us tea. I say old. She was probably my age, but she looked seventy. She asked for a photograph of me. I returned some years later and she still had it on her wall.

One big worry for the Asiatic lion is that the entire population is in a single unit. A disease like canine distemper, that wiped out a third of the Serengeti's lions in 1994, could decimate such a vulnerable group. Zoos, especially in America, realised that they could play a role in preserving the genetic purity of the race as a backstop against some catastrophe occurring in the wild. A studbook, recording the whereabouts of purebred captive Asiatic lions had been established in 1977, by the Fauna Preservation Society and Jersey Wildlife Trust and in the early 1990s three European zoos had eventually acquired breeding pairs. Two of these went to London Zoo and, while we were filming Winners and Losers, they had cubs. This was clearly part of our story. It meant a trip to Regent's Park where I filmed a gorgeous, robust two-month-old bundle of fur dismantling

Patricia's sweater with its claws and stripping the hairs off my arm with its sandpaper tongue.

After Winners and Losers, we spent the first three months of 1995 in Nepal, making a short film for UNDP, the United Nations Development Programme. Our task was to record the first buds of a new type of eco-tourism that was predicted in Nepal and to show the nationwide efforts to prepare for it. The gap between hope and reality was enormous and the work involved us in some strange experiences.

After a couple of days in Kathmandu we drove through the night to a remote village in upper Langtang. The small wooden houses were tucked into a cold cleft in the mountains that the sun never reached before 11 o'clock. So far, no tourist had ever set foot here. On our first morning, after a breakfast of minute, shrivelled potatoes that were the only vegetable that would grow in the frozen ground, we were told that our host had hanged himself during the night. The villagers then lined up for us to film them learning how to wipe their noses. Suicide was rare in Nepal but leprosy, spread by people wiping their mucus on door frames and handles, was rife and not at all eco-friendly. Next, tables were brought out and the more ambitious youngsters of the village were given chef's hats and taught how to dismember imported chickens. While we were filming their attempts at butchery the police arrived. They cut down the unfortunate corpse that we now discovered had still been swinging in the house behind us and carried it out to our tables. There they proceeded to open up the clothes with their koukris to make sure there were no hidden injuries and that it really was a suicide. It was very hard to concentrate on the chickens, especially when we were told that one of the boys doing the chopping for us was the son of the dead man. To add to the surreal tragedy, he was apparently the cousin of Nepal's prime minister yet no-one would move the body because it was a suicide. I had to hire porters to carry him away. Even then they weren't allowed to carry him through the village as that would bring bad luck. Instead, they had to take the steep route round, with the poor man slung from a pole like a dead leopard.

Back in Kathmandu, one night we set off through the old part of town in search of a Newari folk group that had kindly agreed to let us record them playing their music, music almost unknown in the West. The Newari are the original ethnic group of the Kathmandu Valley and their ancestors built many of the famous cultural monuments there. Now, however, they represent only about five percent of Nepal's population, many of them tucked away in the near-impenetrable labyrinths of the old city. We were on foot, carrying our recording equipment. It was pitch black, only candle light seeping from the cracks in the mud walls of the houses. The winding paths got narrower and narrower, the sewage trenches increasingly pungent. It was a Friday night and with our torches we began to pick out dead bodies. There were several, placed at right angles from the houses, wrapped in shrouds, as if awaiting a municipal collection. When we found the house with the musicians, they were all inside, waiting for us, with lights and tea and smiling faces, all eager to begin. But somewhere out in the maze of mud houses I could hear the hissy crackle of a half-tuned radio. Such a shame to have that in the background. No problem. Someone ran off to silence the obviously good-natured neighbour and then the pandemonium of the music let rip. It was drums and wailing, nasal flutes and a two-string violin belting out through that eerie mausoleum and for several hours I think we lost ourselves.

We spent a week hiking the tiered mountain trails of Pokhara in the Annapurnas, West of Kathmandu filming the stony lives of the villagers there. We were to be picked up by helicopter from a small shelf, a thousand feet above a deep gorge. As I stood waiting near the edge, a huge lammergeir, the bearded vulture that drops bones on stones to crack them for their marrow, suddenly appeared right beside me. It must have ridden a thermal straight up the sheer side of the gorge below me, invisible until we were face to face. It hung there for a minute on its eight-foot wing span and I saw that its eyes were like burning gold, rimmed with red fire.

When our little helicopter arrived, it contained an unscheduled passenger. I was always pleased to see the smiling, friendly face of Dr Chandra Gurung, WWF's representative in Nepal. I'd met him when

I was filming Man-Eater and he always seemed to be a cheerful man. Now, however, we had a problem. The pilot didn't seem to have allowed for the hundred and fifty kilos of extra weight that our equipment amounted to. Chandra was quite a big chap and with four of us and the gear we would be way over the stated capacity for the chopper. The pilot was adamant it was safe but I was worried. Safe on the ground, I said, but not over the Himalayas if the weather changed. I insisted that we would have to do two runs and Chandra would wait for the second. The pilot was furious. Perhaps I was wrong, but Chandra's love of helicopter rides was to prove fatal. Tragically, he and most of his WWF team were killed ten years later in a helicopter crash. They were not an infrequent event.

We were off to film a women's project in Janakpur in the Terai, where the Hindu deities, Sita and Ram were supposed to have married. As the Himalayas peeled away a few hundred feet beneath our shaking capsule, we began to look forward to a little well-earned luxury. The past week had been tough walking, tough filming and tough sleeping – on hard mats. Now we were booked into The International Hotel and were dreaming of a hot shower. The helicopter, with its monosyllabic pilot, finally touched down in the middle of a flat field. It left immediately and we were completely alone. Apart from a mildly reassuring weather balloon flapping in the breeze and a rather less reassuring hut, this didn't look good. There was nothing to do but wait and see what happened. After twenty minutes we saw two bobbing heads on the horizon. As they approached, we saw they were the guiding intelligence atop two cycle rickshaws. This didn't look good either. When they finally squeaked and squelched their way up to us over the grassy field, the riders were sweating profusely. They piled in the heavy metal cases and tripods and us and then began, painfully, foot by aching foot, to heave us towards town. It was soon clear we would never get there, so, at the risk of massive loss of face, we dismounted and pushed.

The hotel, when we staggered up to its grimy door, was a typical edifice of the period: single-storey and concrete. Our bedroom was decorated in traditional rustic style with the spattered blood of generations of squashed mosquitoes and someone had conspicuously used the toilet wall as loo-paper. We washed as best we could and that evening, as we sat in the uncultivated garden someone very quietly brought us a meal. It was extremely simple: rice, sauce, a few vegetables lightly cooked, all garnished with fresh coriander, cumin and a whisp of lemongrass. It was absolutely delicious.

Those were strange months. We filmed the beautiful ancient temples in the Pashupati area of the Kathmandu Valley, where I lost my lovely Zeiss wide-angle lens. I must have put it down on a wall as I changed lenses and forgotten it, the sort of stupidity I thought I had weeded out of my repertoire. I needn't have worried, however. A young local who had probably been watching us, rescued it and brought it to me with a gentle smile. We filmed a gracious and kindly interview with the Rinpoche of Tengboche, perhaps the second most sacred Buddhist Lama in the world after the Dalai Lama. I still have the white cloth he blessed and gave to me. High up on the slopes of Everest, we also filmed his monks, in the Tengboche Monastery singing a special service of good luck for our project. In the deep snows just below Base Camp, we filmed rare musk deer picking their way through the forest and garish, blue and purple impayan pheasants.

The finished film was, in its way, stunning, slightly haunted and fatally candid. We called it "The Abominable Tourist". It nearly didn't make it through the labs. I was salmon fishing with my father in Scotland, for the last time as it turned out, when a call came through from Ted Shorthouse at Colour Film Services in Perivale. I'd worked with Ted for 15 years by then and I knew the special tone he used for bad news. In this case, the bad news was that the negative, which had been reported as perfect after initial development, now seemed to have all sorts of weird marks on it and these had produced an unusable print. The negative was the original film from the camera. It was conformed to the cutting copy after editing was complete by aligning tiny unique numbers on the edge. This was a delicate and specialised job for people without marmalade on their hands. If the negative had been perfect after the initial development, the cameraperson could not be at fault. Labs and negative-cutters, however, always blamed each other when a problem arose further into the project. This meant you had to claim on insurance. But film insurance policies were geared to studio work. They required you to have your film developed every few days during a shoot, a condition that could rarely be met by film-makers like us, operating in remote locations. I asked Ted to tell me exactly what might have happened in the lab and then I asked him to wash the negative. This was a risky process but it was my only chance. I remember the wait for the next phone call very acutely because my anxiety was overshadowed by the circumstances surrounding one of the other guests at the hotel. Hugh Heptonstall, was a few years younger than me. I'd known him since I was twelve. He was one of the owners of the river where my father always fished and had grown into an Adonis of a man, tall, witty and a brilliant fisherman. But now he was on his last visit to Scotland, nailed into a chair near the phone, dying inexplicably of a brain tumour. His predicament put mine into perspective.

The next day, when Ted's call came through on the hotel phone, his voice was gleeful. The washing had worked. It had been a fault in the drying process. Now, the film looked perfect. We managed to secure an international distribution agreement with Jane Balfour, one of the top independent distributors in the UK. This was a feat almost unheard of for a short, one-off documentary of this type. Sadly, it was to no avail. Several members of the government committee that had overseen the project, some of whom had slept during the interminable meetings that had hammered out the very precise terms of engagement and disengagement, found the film insufficiently glossy. They had wanted a chrome-plated promo not an art work and they vetoed it. Consequently, the film was never broadcast. In fact, we were very nearly not paid for it, and since we had been working at cost, this would have left us seriously out of pocket. For the only time in my professional career, I hired a lawyer, a contract specialist at Schilling and Lom in London. I also contacted a respected colleague and friend, Norman Myers, who knew the head of UNDP and he agreed to have a word on our behalf. To my enormous relief, the money came through quite quickly. When I phoned the lawyer to thank him, because I knew he had charged a very modest fee, he said he liked these cases because, however small they were, he always learned something new. I asked him what he had learned this time. "Well, "he said, "it seems that United Nations agencies can't actually be sued."

14

LAND OF THE TIGER

A round the time that The Abominable Tourist was simmering, Mike Birkhead, who had produced Tiger Crisis, took me out to lunch. Nothing posh. We went to the pub in Stanton St John, the next-door village to mine. It was early summer and we sat in the rose garden while he outlined his new project. It was a major, six-part BBC series on the wildlife of India. He wanted me to be one of the first-team cameramen. Twelve years earlier, I'd tinkered with an idea like this myself. I'd teamed up with my CalArts friend, BR Ramkumar, who had a film studio in Chennai but Indian TV, which had been our target, had had neither the interest nor the resources. I'd realised then that the rich world of Indian nature, beyond tigers, was scarcely known. Film-makers had focused, understandably, on Africa where the animals were, on America, where the money was and on the Poles where nothing was. India, with its steaming jungles, its lofty mountains, its deserts, its floodplains and its ocean, had been mysteriously neglected. Mike explained that the series would be narrated, onscreen, by Valmik Thapar whom we had featured in Tiger Crisis and who was now recognised as one of India's most outspoken conservationists. The thought of being involved in such an in-depth, conservation-minded series about India was extremely inspiring. I pondered Mike's offer for at least two nano-seconds before accepting.

My first assignment was to film the courtship and mating display of the beautiful barasingha, the rare and endemic swamp deer. This show had been written about in various ancient tomes but never filmed before in its entirety. The barasingha is a large deer, the size of a red deer. Its breeding coat takes on a glorious orange hue in late summer and the antlers of the males are like a spectacular set of brackets, jutting forwards. In Hindi, bara-singha means twelve-pointed and few mature stags disappoint. Barasinghas were once quite common in the lowlands bordering the Himalayas but now there were probably fewer than five thousand left, mostly in isolated pockets. According to the BBC researchers, one of these pockets, indeed one of the most important, was in Dudhwa, in Uttar Pradesh, near where my hero Frederick Champion had photographed his tigers sixty years earlier.

On 12th October 1995, we set up camp, on the edge of the forest in the heart of Dudhwa National Park. "We" meant I had help. My old friends from Tiger Mountain, the company who ran Tiger Tops, had sent down two delightful young sherpas to be my cooks and washers of bottles while my driver was Druv. Druv Singh was not really a driver. He was a close relative of the Maharaja of Rewa and his mother was a Nepali Princess. He'd grown up around Bandhavgarh, a wonderful tiger reserve in Madhya Pradesh. He knew a lot about the jungle and, though he was only 21, he had the chutzpah to galvanise the locals into action when needed. Usable vehicles were very hard to find in Dudhwa but Druv came with his own Maruti Gypsy Jeep, hence "driver". He was the best possible companion and helper. The reserve was closed to visitors for the season so we were able to commandeer the empty rangers' huts in the forest compound. This was surrounded by a chain-link fence to keep the tigers out. The whole place was deserted. We had it to ourselves. It was perfect. All we had to do was to film the barasinghas.

The problem became clear quite quickly. The deer were there. We could hear their breathy rutting calls all over the place. But we couldn't see them. The ground was flat, the elephant grass was tall, there were no small hills, no watch towers, no clearings. The whole drama was designed for radio but not television. What to do? The answer was, phone Toby. Toby Sinclair worked for Cox and Kings in Delhi and was the "fixer" for the series. He was well-connected, well-informed and what Toby couldn't fix probably couldn't be fixed. He certainly helped to iron out all the creases in the locations where I was to film. Toby drove all the way from Delhi, saw our predicament and we put our heads together to look for an alternative. We came up with a likely-looking marshland near the lovely, little-known forest of Kishanpur, about an hour and a half's drive away. From the woods above the marsh, you could look out across miles of reeds and there in the heart of them was a beautiful, short-grass clearing, edged with little knolls and packed with randy swamp deer. The only difficulty was how to get out to the clearing. At this point, we had no boat, so we cut a large dry oil drum in half, piled my hide, my camera equipment and my trousers into it and then I pushed it through the waste-high water to the edge of the clearing, three quarters of a kilometre from the bank. This bit of water sports took me more than an hour and when I arrived it was not a complete success. The deer, of course, ran away while I sloshed around putting up the hide and, though the lure of love eventually brought them out again, there was no dry spot for me, so the hide, the tripod and I all had to stand with our feet in the water.

By the end of the second day, it was clear that I needed to change my modus operandi. I don't particularly mind leeches. They hurt when they bite your stomach or when they slide up your body and fasten onto your neck, but my real enemies were the waterweeds. Their submerged fronds inflicted a thousand invisible cuts to my legs which itched ferociously all through the night. A new plan was called for. I asked Toby to source some sort of a boat while Druv and I went to the local village to commission an edifice, two in fact. I wanted two simple square-topped metal platforms, one for deep water, one for the shallows, that would sit just above water-level, their feet planted firmly on the mud below. On the mud, not in it, so the feet needed large metal plates to sit on. The tops would be rimmed inside so that a metre-square plank could sit firmly on them. The plank needed four holes for the poles of my hides and I would then be able to sit in comfort, invisible, above the water, on one of the nice straw stools I'd just bought for 25 rupees. These were the sort of contraptions that any self-respecting iron-monger in the UK would be able to knock up for you in a month or two. The lads in the village, instructed by Druv, took twelve hours, with everything built to perfection.

The next morning, a forest tractor bellowed its way through the jungle bringing us a beautiful boat. It was wooden, flat, had oars and, most important of all, a punting pole. The four of us, Druv, the cook-boys and I, celebrated with the inaugural official Kishanpur hide-dressing ceremony. We balanced our new platforms on the boat, loaded the hides and straw seats and ourselves and poled our way out to the rutting arena. I'd already settled on what I thought were the two best locations for light, coverage and concealment and when we'd manoeuvred the platforms into position and erected the hides on them, we cut grass and tied it all round them so that their contours were hidden. From now on I would be filming from what, to the barasingha, would appear to be two piles of old reeds.

For the next two weeks, we followed a regular though somewhat idiosyncratic regime. Each morning the boys would wake me up at 1.30 am with a cup of tea and a biscuit. I'd always hated getting up early. When I was a boy, my father, who was unbearably bouncy and tiggerish around dawn, would shout upstairs "it's half past seven and I don't know what you're going to do." It seemed an odd thing to say and I was always stumped by such an existential question so early in the day. I often stayed in bed pondering it for hours. Now, However, I had people working for me. They never once complained. They were always smiling. I had to pretend to feel the same. The funny thing is, after that trip, I never ever had a problem getting up in the small hours again.

By 2.00 am Druv and I were in the open jeep, rattling down the long empty road from Dudhwa to Kishanpur. It was always a slightly hair-raising journey. Not far out of Dudhwa the route crossed the wide, deep trench of the Sarda River. This was spanned by a huge railway bridge and for nearly two kilometres, road users had to drive up onto the tracks and bump along them to cross the river. During the day, each end was policed by a railway-wallah who was supposed to know when a train was coming and ensure that cars and chuff-chuffs didn't mix. At 2.00 am, however, the ends of the bridge were deserted. Every morning, before mounting the tracks, we pressed our ears to the rails like scouts in a western, to check there were no rattling wheels on the way. Then we'd drive along the endless bridge as fast as we could, with our hearts in our mouths. The metal walls were high and the rails sat snugly within them. If a train were to come, the only escape would be to abandon the jeep and jump far down into the river. The relief when we lolloped back onto the road on the far side was always immense. Perhaps we needn't have worried. There were probably no trains at that hour. A train did nearly get us in the end though. One afternoon we took time off and decided to explore the forests of Dudhwa itself. We forgot that the railway passes right through the reserve. Chatting and bent on spotting wildlife we didn't hear the train as we crossed the line. We got a hell of a shock when the train missed us by about two feet. For hours after, every time we looked at each other we had to laugh.

Each day, well before daybreak, Druv and I would have reached Kishanpur and boated out to the hide. I would be installed and he would have long gone, with a pick-up time arranged. I aimed to sit in the darkness before sunrise for at least an hour, to ensure that each filming day began with the minimum of disturbance. What I witnessed and tried to film over the following weeks was very interesting. Twenty or thirty hinds would walk out cautiously from the reeds into the wide marshy clearing in front of me. There they would nibble the grass and watch the males. The younger males chased each other and jousted, their antlers rattling in the morning air. Then a couple of big males would arrive. They ignored the youngsters. They would stand apart for a while and then head for one of the saucers of mud scooped into the marsh. Soon their handsome orange coats, that I had thought were very chic and in season, would be covered with black mud. After a long wallow, the stags would stand again and dig at the turf with their antlers, building a nice wad of gunge and shattered grass stems which stuck out from their prongs like hay on a fork. Then, when they were fully armed, they would take turns to walk very slowly to "the hill". "The hill" was the highest knoll which rose at one end of the arena. Finally, with great dignity, the lone stag would climb to the top where he would stand, in splendid silhouette, the black mud and the straw in his antlers accentuating his size and magnificence. After a while, a hind would saunter to the foot of the hill and raise her tail. The stag would descend, flehmening furiously, his lips drawn back as he tasted the air around her and then she would walk and he would follow, and she would walk and he would follow, in the dance of love with which all honest men are familiar, until finally she might stop just long enough for him to mount her. Or she might not. Either way, the rocket would only last a few seconds after launching.

Nature is efficient. Why fight when a coat of mud can speak for you? A breeding male needs his energies to service the females and still have enough in the tank to zip away from a hungry tiger. Fighting other dominant males is risky. The jostling youths sort out the hierarchies in those semi-serious bouts long before they reach full maturity, when fighting could be lethal. The truth is fights are rare in nature. They do occur and they can be deadly but fights to the death serve no purpose. Instead, breeding is mostly governed by female choice not male prowess. The image of the mighty male, beating every other male to a pulp and rounding up his harem of quivering, terrified females, what I call "The Monarch of the Glen Syndrome" is mostly nonsense. It is a construct of poor observation, patriarchal misinterpretation and, often, of inaccurate film-making. Or of good studies carried out in unnatural circumstances that skew the results. Tim Clutton-Brock's scrupulous, seminal research on red deer on the Scottish island of Rum, is a good example. His male deer did sometimes fight to the death. But they exist in a glorified zoo-world without natural predators. A deer that has to keep an eye out for tigers, wild dog, wolves, lynxes and bears is going to be somewhat circumspect about exhausting itself tussling with love rivals. The barasinghas of Kishanpur, at any rate, seemed to have worked this out. I never saw the hint of a fight between two males who'd been up "the hill" and none of the youngsters ever tried to mount it.

The dominance-plan didn't always work, though. One morning there was great excitement among the hinds. They began to stamp their feet and bark their high-pitched alarm calls. I'd seen a tiger watching from the reeds, far away, the previous day. Now all the hinds were staring at one point in the long grass and I focused on it, waiting for the cat to emerge. What came out, however, was a walking haystack. One of the stags had overdone it with the grass on the antlers stunt. He had such a huge pile of reeds on his head that he couldn't see where he was going and the hinds couldn't see what he was. They all ran away and he staggered around alone in blind disappointment.

Long days in the hide meant that I needed to deal with calls of nature in the dark before getting into the boat. Every morning, I would walk from the lake edge back into the pitch-black forest, cross a deer path which I would inspect for tracks with my torch and then I would dig a hole at the base of a tree about 15 metres into the jungle. The most dangerous thing you can do is squat. While to a tiger we may be enigmatic monsters with no back when we are standing, we look very different and much more edible when we squat. Suddenly we have an obvious rump and become just the size of a juicy wild boar. This is why I always like to have a tree at my back if I have to use the jungle as a toilet. I also rely to some extent on my sixth sense. Whenever I spend longish periods in the field, I develop a strong feeling about the things that are around me that I can't see and a peculiar ability to predict what will happen. I've had this all my life and I think it's quite normal among people who do the sort of work I do. But one morning it clearly wasn't functioning. I'd finished my ablutions and walked the few steps in the pitch darkness to the path and there I saw in the torchlight huge fresh prints of a tigress pressed into the soft mud. They had certainly not been there three minutes earlier. A nine-foot cat had just padded silently past me as I squatted and I'd had no warning at all of her presence. I've written about this experience in my tiger book. Had her radar also been switched off? Was she not hungry? Or was she simply at peace with the world? In the late afternoon, after filming, we decided to track her. Further up the trail we discovered she had attacked a huge python and eaten great chunks of its tail and back. So, not peaceful and not replete.

I loved Kishanpur. We had another extraordinary tiger experience a few evenings later. We'd just set off home in the dark through the forest. In the first glimmerings of the moon, we saw a shadow slip into the jungle from the track ahead. Druv was sure it had been a tiger so when we reached the spot, he switched off the engine and I tried my rabbit squeal call. Picture us there in his tiny jeep. We've taken the doors off so I can film unobstructed. The invisible jungle is a few feet from where I'm sitting and the sandy track, pale in the moonlight, stretches away in front of us. I can see nothing but after a minute Druv whispers "it's coming". Then, about seventy metres ahead a young male tiger steps out onto the path. He looks at us and then turns back into the bushes. I call again and again Druv whispers "I can see him, he's still coming." This time he appears on the track not twenty metres away. He stands looking at us and then vanishes again. I try once more, sucking hard on my hand, peering into the darkening forest. And then I feel a ghost of warm air on my arm and he is there, right beside me, staring into the jeep... I stopped sucking. I felt a bit foolish. I'd meant to call him up to us not onto us. I don't think either of us drew a breath. We just watched him from the corners of our eyes. Then he seemed to relax. Perhaps he decided we were not significant intruders. He walked round to the front of the jeep, scent-marked into the bushes and then allowed us to watch him for nearly an hour as he led us slowly on our way through the forest towards the main road and home.

We had fun in our camp during those weeks. It was Divali, the Hindu Festival of Light, and one evening I came home to find Druv had arranged for hundreds of candles to be lit all along the path to our huts. We were adopted by a pretty young spotted deer that used to come on our balcony and ask for food. I had company, too, inside my hut. It was a rat that used to emerge from the toilet pipe to forage after dark. One night I woke to find it running over my face. I didn't specially mind being walked on by a rat but the thought that it had come up out of the toilet without wiping its feet was most unappealing. The boys did their best to cook for us, hampered only by the fact that someone had packed all the stores in the same container as the paraffin for the stove. Paraffin-flavoured Kit Kats and paraffin-flavoured biscuits were all the rage that Divali. Our cooks were mountain boys. They'd never been in the jungle before, so of course we had to tease them. One night we crept outside their hut and began to roar, very like tigers we thought. Apparently, they thought so too. Their scared faces appeared at the window, as they pointed shaky torches in our direction. Later that night a real tiger roared. Very close. It didn't sound like us at all. It seemed to fill the jungle with a bellow of steam. We shone our own shaky torches into the darkness and there we saw our compound had filled with anxious jackals – dozens of them – and beyond, pressed against the chain-link fence, looking in, were the glinting terrified eyes of fifty spotted deer.

For the next five years, when I wasn't filming in Ireland, I was to spend most of my filming days in India. Druv Singh joined me on my next posting for Land of the Tiger, which took us to Gujarat in Western India, first to the Little Rann of Kutch, to film the Indian wild ass. The Little Rann is not very little. It's not very hospitable either. It is basically a five thousand square kilometre salt marsh, a dry, dusty excrescence of the vast Thar Desert. We arrived at the beginning of February. There was still a little monsoon water swilling in the seasonal depressions and these were crowded with elegant demoiselle cranes, thousands of them, gathering for the long trek to their Siberian breeding grounds. Small flocks of sandgrouse were coming to the water too and, because we were still at the early stages of filming for the series, I was given carte blanche to film a bit of whatever I wanted. I love cranes and sandgrouse so I spent some very happy days in my hide. My main focus, however, was the wild ass. There are seven species of wild equines – horse-type animals – left in the world. These include Africa's three species of zebra, Mongolia's

Przewalski's horse, which is nearly extinct, the African wild ass, the Tibetan kiang and the onegars. It's a good rule of thumb that the stranger the name, the rarer the animal. The plains zebra is plainly very common. The Przewalski's horse is deservedly nearly extinct because no-one can remember how to spell it. The Indian wild ass is one of four subspecies of onegar, five if you count the Syrian onegar which has already died out. An onegar is a wild ass by any other name but the Indian onegar saddled itself with a double whammy by insisting it was called a khur. As such, it too came close to extinction. In 1960 there were just three hundred and sixty left. In 1973, however, it seems to have settled for being called the Indian wild ass, a smart move as this enabled the authorities to create India's largest wildlife sanctuary in its name, covering the whole Little Rann. By the time I was there to film them, numbers had recovered and there were reckoned to be a couple of thousand. Since then, they have expanded well beyond the confines of the reserve. A survey in March 2020 put the current population at over six thousand.

The Indian ass, as it is now proud to be called, is a handsome animal. It stands about a metre high at the shoulder. If you draw a straight line along its flanks and through its face you create a nice two-tone look, the top half being orange-faun and the bottom, bright white. There's a nice black stiff little "wild-horse" type bristle-mane which dwindles to a smart black line all along the spine. In keeping with this sporty look, the ass is extremely nippy and can speed-gallop at eighty kilometres per hour. When it does go for a run, it sends up clouds of dust which, if backlit, with the ass between your camera and the sun, leaves a trail of millions of glittering particles which look splendid on film. I did manage to get a few sparkles but, contrary to popular opinion, asses are no fools. Temperatures in the Rann can easily top forty degrees and more, so the asses' default mode is standing still and cooling itself with its tail.

I already knew a bit about the private life of the zebra. This had been brilliantly studied by Hans Klingel and others in the Ngorongoro Crater and the Serengeti in Tanzania. Zebras form extended family groups, led by a dominant stallion. Even in a vast throng, there's no such thing as a herd of zebras, only groups of family groups. The bonds between family members can be very strong, especially, apparently between father and son. On one occasion in the Crater a son tragically died after being sedated for a radio-collar. His father, the dominant stallion, didn't know what had happened or why his son had suddenly disappeared. He detached himself from the group and searched round and round the crater for nearly a year before he gave up and returned to lead the family once more. From what I could understand, the wild asses formed into four conspicuous social classes: family groups of mainly related females and females with calves, dominant stallions, expelled dominant stallions and bachelor groups of young males. Dominant stallions tried to monopolise the better feeding and drinking areas. This they did in time-honoured fashion by biting and kicking their rivals. Family groups and especially females with breeding potential could then enjoy the fruits of these battles free from harassment by uncommitted males and with the added bonus of a little hanky-panky with a dominant male if they so wished and if they happened to be in oestrus. Bachelor herds and ousted stallions tended to keep away. It was fun trying to film some of this story under the white desert sun.

Far out on the infinite salt marshes, wild asses have few enemies. The main threat is disease. The wipe-out in the late 1950s was caused by Surra, a wasting disease caused by a tiny, worm-like Trypanosoma parasite, spread by flies. In 2009 there was an outbreak of equine flu amongst domestic horses in Gujarat, prompting concerns that so many asses in one location were vulnerable. Natural predators are few. The lions that must once have hunted asses have long since retreated to Gir, three hundred kilometres away. There are still a few wolves, however, and they occasionally kill asses. At the time I was filming, the wolves were being studied by Yadvendra Jhala, who was later to lead the national tiger census with such distinction. We spent a couple of wonderful days together looking for carnivores. The landscape was utterly bare. There were rocks and gullies and stony hills and endless hot, empty plains but no trees and almost no clear landmarks. I, who have a good sense of direction, was lost in an hour.

Jhala, however, took me unfailingly to the earth of an Indian fox, where I managed to film a roly-poly of adorable cubs. How did he do that? Well, he had a magic box called a GPS. I'd never seen one before. I was analogue man, still firmly rooted in the cumbersome world of compasses, trigonometry and map-readings – all of which usually sent me astray. Jhala, however, simply pointed his magic box at the sky, took a timed reading from an invisible passing satellite and could forever more retrace his steps to within a couple of metres. We also found wolves. We were able to creep quite close to their layer among the rocks and I filmed them too, when they stood up and strutted quite nonchalantly away. These were my first Indian wolves and I was struck by their appearance. All wolves have very long legs. But these animals, adapted to a hot climate with their short fur, looked much more stilt-like in comparison to the heavy-coated wolves of the North that I knew much better. And they were not grey. They were almost red: red, rangy desert wolves.

From Kutch, Druv and I drove four hundred kilometres south to the Palace of Utelia, which would be our home for the next ten days while I filmed the courtship of the blackbuck in Velavadar. Utelia, the original palace of the aristocratic family which once ruled a swathe of central India all the way to Rewa in Madhya Pradesh, is now recognised as a heritage hotel. But in that spring of 1996, I had the feeling I might have been their first paying guest. You needed a GPS to find your way around my bedroom. I'm not sure anyone had been in the room for fifty years other than to put sheets on my bed. The splendid Rajput furnishings were fascinatingly dusty, the great four poster bed made even my six-foot plus frame feel puny and the crumbling colonnades and stone staircases, turrets and battlements put me quite at my ease. Our host, who was probably one of Druv's relatives, was extremely gentle. He was the grandson of the current ruler of Utelia. This was an elderly little man whom most days I could barely see as he sat at the far end of a long marble corridor, seemingly besieged by an eternal queue of local petitioners. I have often wondered if the British Raj wasn't a sort of scum that formed on the surface of India. The British thought they were ruling but underneath, the old life of India continued, almost unaffected and often unseen. This patient line of petitioners was part of that old life. Our host explained that, though his grandfather had no legal position, the people still looked to him to solve their more intractable disputes. They had a choice. They could go to law where cases might linger unattended for eternity. Or they could come to his grandfather, who, like Solomon, would listen and adjudicate promptly and without prejudice. Most people chose this expedite but completely illegal form of justice. What happened, I asked, if people didn't like the outcome and ignored his grandfather's decision. This very rarely happened, said our host. Having brought the case to the grandfather in the first place, to then oppose his finding would be deemed a grave discourtesy. I got the impression that a grave discourtesy was a very bad thing, indeed that it might trigger a visit from Frank the Arm-Breaker.

The nearby National Park of Velavadar is, to me, one of the most beautiful places I have ever filmed. In mid-February it is yellow. Not just yellow yellow, but every possible shade of yellow, from green, through ochre, to brown. But, like Monet's dining-room in Giverny, all with the yellow tinge of sunshine. These multifarious monotones recall something of the beauty of the nature reserve at the tip of the Cape of Good Hope, where the prodigious variety of proteas are every tone of green. And of course, it is a bit like a little slice of the Serengeti set in India. For essentially, Velavadar is a dry grassland, flat, edged with thorny forest, dotted with low acacias. This was the best place to film the lekking of the blackbuck, a courtship that was more or less unknown to television audiences at the time. For all sorts of reasons blackbuck are very special. For one thing they are the only extant species in their genus, the genus Antilope. They are found nowhere else in the world outside India and Nepal. Blackbucks are kept very busy in Hindu mythology, drawing the chariot of Lord Krishna while, in their spare time they offer regular rides to the Moon God, Chandra and to Vayu the Wind God, and also carry the divine nectar, Soma. The Bishnoi, a Hindu sect of the Thar Desert, revere, protect and feed them and Hindus generally regard them as sacred. Nevertheless, the Maharaja of Bhavnagar was still hunting them with his pet cheetahs in Velavadar up to the outbreak of the Second World War. From my point of view, as a film-maker, however, the blackbuck's most important attribute is its beauty and the most important thing it does is the annual lek.

The blackbuck is a medium-sized antelope, larger than an African Thomson's gazelle, closer to a springbok, and like springboks, it has a penchant for pronking – bouncing up in the air like a rubber ball – when excited or frightened. The male is a handsome devil. He has long, tightly spiralled, sharp-tipped horns. He has a beautiful black back, a black face and black lines down the outside of his legs. He has bright white spectacles and a white line behind them and his underside is also pure white. Females (no horns) and young males (shorter horns) have the same patterning but the black coat is replaced by a less flashy tone of pale brown. In the early spring the blackbucks of Velavadar gather on the lekking grounds for their annual mating exhibition. It was on one of these, that I set up my hide for the next ten days.

The breeding males scatter across the wide, short-grass mating arena where they each mark out a small display circle for themselves. Here they stand for hours every morning, like Amsterdam ladies in their red-light shop windows, hoping to attract the attention of the opposite sex. The arena can become quite crowded with males so they often have to defend the boundaries of their little show-case. Whenever an intrusive male gets too close to their window, they perform an elaborate sort of shadow-boxing. They dip their heads menacingly and they strut up and down their boundary on straightened legs, their bodies hunched into attack pose. If the opposing male happens to be the neighbour, he will defend his shop too, and the pair will mirror each other in a ridiculous sort of slow-motion dance. Only it's not ridiculous. It saves a lot of trouble. It says "here is my fence. If you cross it, I will have to poke you with my horns. They are long enough to go right through you. This will be the end of you and will also probably break my horns which won't grow again because I am an antelope not a deer and then I will no longer look beautiful. So, for both our sakes stay the right side of the line." This message had to be spelt out continuously, but it appeared to be well understood. I never actually saw a serious fight.

All this prancing up and down gets really tiring and as the sun gets higher and the morning turns to noon, the males mooch off one by one to grab some lunch in the nearby woodland. Towards the late afternoon, the exhibitors ooze back to their stands. At this point I noticed that there seemed to be an amnesty allowing free passage of males between their shops and the wood. As long as they didn't stand around nosily on other people's patches, they could leave and enter the arena without being challenged. After lunch you need a poo. Don't do this in the forest, it's a waste. Instead, you have your poo right in the middle of your display circle. You do this every day. Consequently, the size of your dung pile shows how long you've been able to stick it out, displaying in the sun and doing the dance of death with the chaps next door. The females, meanwhile, are doing what females do the world over. They are having a good time. They are chatting and they are eating. Mostly eating. This they have to do because pretty soon they are probably going to have a baby to nurse.

Eventually, out of the characteristic kindness of her heart, one of the females will wander over to the males. They will all stand stiff to attention but she ignores them. She strolls across the arena checking the dung piles: a sniff here, a sniff there. What is she looking for? Well, I suspect that each dung pile gives her a useful readout of the properties of its owner, not just his stamina, measured by the height of the poop, but also his general condition, presence or absence of parasites and probably the names of his parents and grandparents. When she strikes gold, she lifts her tail and lures the male from his shop. He in his turn will prance and display and flemen, sifting her odours, and then, usually beyond the perimeters of the arena, they circle each other. She stops, he jumps up on his hind legs and makes a blind thrust and Bob's your uncle. That last, all-important effort usually lasts just a few seconds.

Tucked into my hide, watching this comic ritual, I was ecstatically happy. But as the days progressed, I noticed another little drama unfolding. During the winter, the wide-open grasslands of Velavadar provide night-time roosting for thousands of harriers, large, long-winged hawks. In 1997, the year after I was there, the December peak was estimated at three thousand birds. Even in February, there were hundreds of these handsome raptors, mostly Montague's and pallid harriers, but with some marsh and pied harriers as well, cruising around hunting insects lifting from the grass in the afternoon sun. Their favourite food there seems to be large locusts but they also hunt small birds. The dung piles of the blackbucks were probably full of seeds and certainly buzzing with little flies. Both seemed to attract constant visits from little flocks of short-toed larks that were also wintering on the grasslands before heading up to Mongolia for their own nuptials. The blackbuck made the dung, the dung attracted insects, the insects brought the larks and the larks drew the harriers, sweeping over the arena, amongst the antelopes, trying to grab a bird for supper. It was a fascinating little cycle of life. I'm not sure I did it justice with my filming but I certainly had fun trying.

One of the cleverest ideas in structuring "Land of the Tiger" was to begin the whole series with a sequence about lions. There's nothing like a surprise to grab the viewer's attention. As I already had experience filming the lions of Gir, I was asked to shoot this opening section. As usual, I was dispatched a few weeks ahead of the main crew, to film the bulk of the wildlife scenes. I arrived in Gir in early spring 1997, where I was looked after by the Taj Hotel, who provided my driver and vehicle. My stay at the Taj was memorable for several reasons. Firstly, it was a brand-new venture for the Taj company. Gir was only just beginning to open up for tourism and for most of my stay I was their only guest. I liked being the only guest. Being looked after like a king after fourteen hours in the field is very cosy. Even more cosy was the fact that the manager turned out to be the brother of a friendly connection of mine from Madhya Pradesh, so I got to know his wife and small child. And finally, there was the miracle of the comet. The Hale-Bopp comet had just re-emerged from the dazzle of the sun and during the first months of 1997 it blazed a visible trail across the night sky. Every evening, after dark, it would

hang its tail high over the hotel and as I drove home after filming, out
of the forest towards a village dimly lit by candles and hurricane
lights, the long orange flare marking my destination seemed to
impart an extra meaning to my mission. Apparently, other people
were similarly exalted. A few weeks later, in March 1997, 39 members
of the Heaven's Gate Cult from San Diego committed suicide together. They believed that their spirits would hitch a lift on the blazing
tail, which they thought was an extraterrestrial spacecraft tracking
the comet. It must have been important to them not to miss the
opportunity. Hale-Bopp won't return again to the inner solar system
until around the year 4385.

My guide in the forest was a young Maldhari. He was very
different from the old man who had accompanied me before and
who had derived most of his information from interminable conversations during frequent tea-breaks. This young man was fit and keen.
He was attuned to nature and he knew exactly where the lions were.
One morning he led me on a long walk deep into the forest. We
shared the gear and he ranged in long, quiet strides, across streams,
under cloistering bamboo, through thorn and thicket until we arrived
at an acacia bower beside a trickle of water. There, he showed me a
lioness with three very young cubs, maybe two and a half months old.
We sat down about 30 metres away. She watched us alertly for a few
minutes and then relaxed. Very slowly, we moved a little closer. The
cubs began to play, clambouring among the roots of the bushes and
grabbing at each other's tails. We moved closer still. Eventually we
were maybe five or at most six metres from her. My companion had
his stick but she didn't seem to feel at all threatened and I was able to
film a beautiful sequence of family life as the cubs squabbled and
suckled and scampered around. After a couple of hours, we slipped
away, leaving our new stars unperturbed. If we could somehow get
this relaxed and photogenic little family to meet our presenter,
Valmik Thapar, the series could begin on a high note.

Valmik Thapar was a big man with a big beard and a big ego. He
was very clever and he didn't suffer fools gladly. Unfortunately, he
thought nearly everyone was a fool, including me I suspect, and this

sometimes made him hard to like. He was, however, an inspired choice as presenter – authentic, original and authoritative – and he never fluffed his lines. Absolutely key to our efforts was to shoot a scene where Valmik is on one knee in front of a group of lions and they must be close enough and stay long enough for him to speak the opening lines of the series. These would be something like this: "I am here with this family of lions. But this is not Africa. This is INDIA. We are in the forest of Gir in Western India, the only place in the whole world outside Africa where you can still find wild lions." One morning my guide came to say that our lioness had moved. She was in an open glade quite close to a track. We all headed straight to the spot, trying to control the enthusiasm of our drivers who if told to hurry would inevitably arrive with racing engines, screeching brakes and a ten-minute dust-storm. The location was perfect, open, easy to access, softly lit – beautiful. And there at the back of the glade was our mother and her bundle of cubs. We all knew that this was a clincher. Valmik had his microphone pinned on, the sound check was clear, the camera was in position and then, just as Valmik was about to creep to the lions something funny happened. A striped hyena came walking across the scrub straight towards us. Hyenas in India are shy, solitary and very rarely seen. In all my years of working in India, this is the only one I've seen in broad daylight. Valmik, being a genuine enthusiast, was very excited and insistent that we film it. But we were all set up for one of the most important sequences in the whole series, with lion cubs that we just might not see again. To film the hyena in any meaningful way would mean a change of lens and it would eat into our magazine of film, which might then need to be changed. Would the lion family give us that extra five minutes? Mike Birkhead, with characteristic clarity of mind, vetoed the hyena. This was an excellent decision. Film-making is about telling a story. We focused on the lions, Valmik spoke his piece and we secured a memorable opening to Land of the Tiger. We never saw the striped hyena again and to this day, I have never filmed one.

Before we finished shooting in Gir, I had something of a near-death experience. We had found an old lioness with two nearly full-grown cubs. The cubs were play fighting in short, yellow dead grass. I was accompanied by Mike and my guide but, so as not to draw attention to ourselves, I asked them to hide under a nearby tree while I moved to a better filming position. I didn't try to get too close. I was probably fifty metres away. I knelt down to get a nice low filming angle and waited for the mother to get out of my picture. Her face was etched with old wounds, her ears were moth-eaten and she was so scarred and ugly that she could never be cut into a story without some explanation. It is easy when you're filming, to get absorbed into the magical world inside your viewfinder. Filming the exuberant cubs, I forgot about the mother. But she didn't forget about me. After twenty minutes or so I suddenly snapped out of my reverie with a distinct feeling of dread, stood up and turned. The ugly old lioness was crouched right behind me. While I had been filming, squatting and vulnerable, she had been circling back through the bushes to stalk me from behind. Paintings of hunting lions usually show ears stretched back and a vast snarlful of teeth. They are wrong. When a lion is about to kill you, it puts its ears forward, closes its mouth and focuses its eyes not on you but through you. No roaring. Just a silent, hideous unity of purpose. In the split-second that I turned, her ears were forward, her mouth tight shut and her eyes were glazed horribly. She sprang and so, with a yell did I, straight at her. Her spring became a somersault, Mike and the guard were running at me, the lioness was gone. We just looked at each other and shook our heads. I was later told that a few months earlier she had killed a little boy. He had asked if it was safe to get out of the car to squat in the bushes. Apparently, it wasn't.

I don't know whether it had anything to do with Hale-Bopp's comet or any subconscious wish to attach my spirit to its tail, but this was only the first of several close shaves I had during 1997. From Gujarat, in the far West of India, I now flew right across the country, to Assam in the far North-East, near India's border with Burma. This was to be my last assignment for Land of The Tiger and the first session of filming for a new project, called Rhino Journey. Kaziranga National Park, where I was to spend a total of nine months over the next two and a half two years, lies in the flood plain of the great Brahmaputra River. It covers a total of four hundred and thirty square kilometres of grassland, flood-formed lakes, sandbars and subtropical moist broadleaf forest and it is the most important refuge on earth for the greater one-horned rhinoceros, the Indian rhino. Like the Gir lions, the initiative to conserve the rhinos seems to have originated with the Curzons. Baroness Curzon, the Viceroy's wife, apparently visited Kaziranga to see the famous "unicorns" in 1904. She didn't spot any and when it was implied that there might only be eleven left, the reserve was established the following year. Despite falling to such a low number, research has shown that the rhinos enjoy a high level of genetic diversity. This is probably due to the very old age of the genus. Some estimates put that at nearly sixty million years. The rarity of the species was not due to any congenital failure but entirely the result of hunting. For many centuries, rhino horn, like tiger bone, has been highly valued by practitioners of Traditional Chinese Medicine. Ground to a paste and mixed with water and other ingredients, the horn, which is made mainly of keratin, like our own hair and nails, is taken as a remedy for fever, gout, arthritis, high blood pressure, typhoid and snakebite among other things. Their proximity to the oriental medical market spelt near ruin for the rhinos but in the last fifty years they have been vigorously protected in Kaziranga by armed guards and numbers have recovered dramatically. When I was filming there, I often began at dawn, driving though the Western range of the reserve. If I encountered no distractions, I would arrive at a quiet watch-tower overlooking miles of prime grassland. There I could see vast pastures of bright green, short-grass meadows, surrounding small lakes, or beels as they are called, and rimmed themselves by even larger expanses of yellowish-grey elephant grass. Every morning, for an hour or so, the rhinos would emerge, one by one, from the safe invisibility of the long grass to graze on the fresh shoots in the green meadows and I would count them. This would give me a clue as to the best place to try filming that day. One morning, with a single slow sweep of the binoculars, I counted 82 rhinos. When Alan Root, the famous veteran of African film-making visited, he said wistfully that it reminded him of East Africa in the early 1950s, before black rhinos were decimated there. A full census in March 2018 put the total population in Kaziranga at two thousand four hundred and thirteen individuals, about 65 percent of the world's one-horned rhinos.

The Indian rhino is a big animal, the biggest of the world's five rhino species. A full-grown male stands some six feet at the shoulder and weighs around two thousand two hundred kilos. It's also the most aggressive. For the first few weeks of filming, I was attacked every day. A German TV team had been there just before me and I was told that they had been goading the animals. Whether or not that was true, the rhinos did settle down after a while but I could never entirely relax. Every now and then one would lower its head, start snorting and puffing and then charge full-tilt at the vehicle. We had two lines of defence. We could accelerate away in a cloud of dust and, if that didn't work our guard had his gun. This was an ancient .303 rifle with a standard issue of three bullets. Often a charge could be averted simply by rocking the bullet in and out of the breech. The mere sound of the lock seemed to dissuade the attacker from further action. In an extreme case, however, the guard could fire near the animal's feet. Every bullet had, of course to be accounted for, so he would be rightly loath to do this. Sometimes one bullet wasn't enough. He had to fire two. That was a two-bullet attack. Very occasionally he fired all three; a three-bullet attack. Pretty serious because the next level was smash, a mighty wallop into the side of the vehicle which left a hell of a dent and, if you were very unlucky, could turn you over. I counted every attack as a failure. I didn't want to be part of the story. I was trying to film the natural life cycle of the animal, which did not include me and my jeep.

The most dangerous incidents occurred when I was on foot. I didn't want to do all my filming from the vehicle. Sometimes I needed a change of angle, to film from lower down. Sometimes I needed to walk into a site or work from a hide. The first foot attack played out a bit like a Buster Keaton comedy. I was creeping through the long grass on the edge of a wallow. I thought I had checked it out but there was a rhino there that I hadn't spotted. Boy did it move fast. Although rhinos are not famed for their athleticism, they accelerate from nought to fifty faster than a Porsche. By the time this one had sprinted forty metres I had only managed to heave up my camera and whack my knee against the point of my tripod. Fortunately, it was a young rhino and it had run in the opposite direction, but I was unnerved by its astonishing speed and by the fact that my guard, who had fired his gun to make it officially a one-bullet attack, had put a neat hole straight through the jeep at exactly the point in the back where I usually sat. Two holes actually. The bullet had gone through one wing of the jeep and out the other.

The second foot attack was my second near-death experience of the year. It was my fault really because I was being a bit lazy. When they are not trying to kill you, rhinos don't do very much. They graze, they wallow and mostly they hide. So any bit of action is a bonus. On this particular afternoon I'd decided to try to film near a wallow where I thought the rhinos would pass close by after their daily bath. It wasn't worth taking the time to put up the hide so I left the vehicle, checked the breeze, settled onto my sturdy metal camera case and threw a camouflage net over myself. It was a technique I often used when I needed quick concealment. Sure enough, after half an hour, a rhino came trudging past and I filmed some nice close ups as its feet crunched into the grass. When the next one came, however, I knew I was in trouble. It was a small calf. Unlike African rhino calves, Indian calves are full of curiosity and like to lead the way. Right behind it, of course, came the mother. That was dangerous already. But this wasn't just any mother. I knew this female by now. She was so aggressive that she would throw other rhinos out of the wallow when she wanted a bath for her baby. She didn't usually use this spot but there was no mistaking her. I called her Long-Horn for conspicuous reasons. What should I do? If I broke cover and tried to leg it back to the safety of the jeep, she would almost certainly catch me. If I kept still, they couldn't smell me and they might not see me at all. On the other hand, every step brought them closer and made any chance of escape impossible. I stayed put, the light was beautiful and

I started to film. Mother and baby. Beautiful shots. Just what I needed.

I nearly got away with it. They had almost passed me when the calf probably caught a glint of silver from my case. "That's interesting" it thought, and turned at right angles straight towards me. Long-Horn realised her calf had deviated towards an alien object and she charged me. I had no time to move. She slammed straight into the camera case, knocking it out from under me. She must have locked onto the same glint that the calf saw. Then she swung her great head for the terrible bite. She could swing right and bite me through the knees, or left and bite the big canvas fishing bag where I kept my spare magazines and other precious equipment. She swung left. I've no idea why. She delivered the killer bite to the bag. The strap caught on her horn and she rushed on, deep into the long grass where she tossed the heavy bag back high into the air over her shoulder.

Sometimes, I seem to be a bit of an idiot, especially in retrospect... Instead of scrambling back towards my jeep, I ran after her. I think I had the daft idea that I could catch the bag before it smashed back onto the ground. If so, I didn't succeed. By the time I reached it, crunched in the earth, Long-Horn and her calf were long gone. I looked anxiously inside, expecting to find twenty thousand dollars-worth of magazines and film in pieces, but they seemed surprisingly chipper, mint even, and never gave me any trouble. Arriflex, stout stuff.

I returned to Assam in July to film the monsoon. When I landed at the little airport in the capital, Guwahati , I noticed that the new airport building, which they'd been working on for as long as I could remember, was finally complete. It was white and marbled and very smart. Kaziranga looked and smelt different. Huge, dense towers of dark bulging clouds would build up and up each day, germinating from tight balls into heaven-filling rain tubs. The atmosphere would grow hotter and hotter and closer and closer until, with an enormous explosion, half the world's water would come crashing down all at once, as if it had fallen through a vast crack in the sky. The thunder and lightning shows were spectacular. I love thunder storms and these were the most thunderous and stormy I'd ever experienced. When I'd filmed enough rain and clouds, I enjoyed watching the storms from the bamboo balcony of the lodge where I was staying. I liked to see the lightning fork its way right down to the garden and the pond at the back. But one day there was an eye-splitting flash and a bolt came straight at me. My friend Richard Kemp was struck by lightning when he was filming in the Pyrenees. Richard always said he could be a little obtuse and he was carrying a set of metal pylons for a bird hide up the side of a mountain when his storm was brewing. One minute he was staggering up the hill, the next he felt an almighty whack and he woke up lying on his back several yards away with the soles of his boots belching smoke. This is not at all what happened to me. Instead, I saw a blinding white flash and the whole right side of my face went hot. I guess that the lattice work of the balcony somehow deflected the full force of the strike and I was probably protected by my rubber boots. It sobered me up a little. I didn't stop watching the storms but I was a bit more careful to stand under cover.

The purpose of coming back in the monsoon was to film how the change of season alters the way the animals behave and how the forest guards try to protect them. As the storms mount, day after day, week after drenching week, the flood plains of the Brahmaputra become floods and the plains disappear, mile after mile, under water. The quicker-thinking rhinos, along with the deer and the tigers, head up into the surrounding forests where they can disperse. Stragglers congregate on small islands that the park authorities have thrown up as high-water refuges. Here they are at great risk from poachers so the guards patrol constantly by boat. After each spell of rain the skies clear and a glorious relief of fresh, cooled air and stunning, clean, pin-sharp light follows. This lasts for several days until the clouds start to simmer again. Some of the most beautiful sequences I shot were of the rangers, slowly paddling their heavy wooden punts, their old .303 rifles stacked in the gunnels, under the vast arch of a perfect rainbow. And all day and most of the night, the Indian cuckoos whistled out their tuneful, four-note calls.

It was always a long drive back to the airport, many many hours on bad bad roads. My drivers always used to stop for a break at a forest lodge in a little woodland clearing about half way. When we stopped on the way home after the monsoon shoot, I sat on a wooden chair in the clearing drinking cha while the driver and the foresters sat inside. I noticed a flea-ridden dog scratching away beside me and suddenly I thought he'd struck up against my chair, because it began to shake furiously. At that moment, my companions rushed out of the hut shouting and gesticulating. I stood up and found the earth beneath me had turned to jelly. It was rolling and pitching. All the firmness that you take for granted when you take a step had melted. I felt like I was a boat in a rough sea. I'd been in lots of earthquakes before, but I'd never felt anything quite as odd and whoosy as that. We were told later that it had been a massive quake, around 7.8 on the Richter Scale, centred in Tibet. When we arrived at the airport, we found the proud brand-new marble walls were all split and spoiled. It seemed that, notwithstanding the murderous lioness, the angry rhino, the lightning and the quake, I had not been nature's intended target after all.

15

RHINO JOURNEY AND BEYOND

L and of the Tiger was a great success. It made Valmik Thapar a minor celebrity in England and even me a very minor one in India. The fact that I had worked on such a ground-breaking series earned me respect there. For while the series was very well received worldwide, in India it was a game-changer, a true water-shed. It did what television should do. It altered perceptions and made Indian city dwellers realise what an extraordinary natural heritage they had on their doorstep. When I first went to India, it was hard to find anyone in the national parks who actually knew anything. The guides who took up obligatory space in your vehicle rarely had either interest or knowledge about anything with wings or more than two legs. Now a younger generation of excellent amateur naturalists is growing up all over India. They are discovering new species, particularly of small reptiles, amphibians and insects, becoming nature guides and making their own films. Land of the Tiger, well-produced by Mike Birkhead and his team, definitely contributed to this burgeoning of awareness and concern.

Our film Rhino Journey was also supposed to change perceptions. No-one had ever made a programme about the Indian one-horned rhinoceros showing its whole life cycle, and its spectacular mating display had never been filmed in full. When a female rhino comes into oestrus her scent attracts competing males and she chooses her preferred mate by making them chase her. She hurtles at break-neck speed round and round the dense meadows of elephant grass squealing stentoriously with anticipatory lust and the sweating males have to maintain very hot pursuit. These chases can last half an hour or more and this serves to weed out the laggards with low stamina. The final consummation is an eye-watering affair. A mating pair looks a bit like a train-wreck in the middle of the grasslands, one huge coach piled on another. Male rhinos are notoriously well endowed and once the mighty organ has found its repose it can stay locked in position for hours. No doubt this has contributed to the rhino's mythical prowess. Rhino parts, horn, even urine, have been imbued with all sorts of magical properties and these have, as is now well-known, led to the species near extinction at the hands of people eager to partake.

Indian rhinos are not particularly empathetic. They live a mostly solitary, somewhat grumpy life, becoming tetchy, even downright dangerous if another rhino, or indeed anything, comes too close. A rhino's zone of comfort is quite large, roughly the size of a football field. They would definitely not enjoy a ride on the Clapham omnibus, shoulder to shoulder with their fellows. Up to a point, I sympathized and felt there was something there worth championing. There are only three areas of their lives where they are required to let down their guard and I felt these were aspects worth concentrating on. The first, of course, is when they mate. The elongated intimacy required must be very embarrassing for them, so the hormonal impetus must be extremely strong. The second is when they congregate in the wallows. I loved filming the wallows. Every day sometime between their mid-morning coffee break and lunch time, depending on the heat of the season, every rhino in Kaziranga, all two thousand of them, head to one of the shallow, muddy ponds that are punched into the grassy floodplains to cool off. One by one, they stop what they are doing, which is usually nothing, or eating grass, and plod purposefully for the nearest lido. When they arrive, they may find other rhinos are already soaking, just their great prehistoric heads sticking out of the water like the prows of sunken ships. In that case, the newcomer patiently follows the bank until it finds a suitably unoccupied space, turns lugubriously round and ever so gingerly lowers its bulk down backwards into the water. Funnily enough, tigers do the same, albeit more gracefully. Rhinos at the wallows were almost always polite to each other. Indeed, it became obvious to me after observing for some weeks, that individuals had not only preferred wallows and favoured locations in the wallow, but that they had friendships. Some adults, particularly females, would tuck themselves quite cosily next to a companion, yet I rarely saw them together out on the open grasslands. Perhaps they were cousins, or long-separated mothers and daughters. I would have loved to have marked them and stayed to find out. On just one occasion I did see four females walking nose-to-tail across a wide meadow. Since rhinos only have one calf at a time these cannot have been sisters with full-grown calves. And yet... who knows. I filmed a pair of equal-age youngsters who played incessantly as if they were twins and I only ever saw one parent.

The wallows etiquette seemed to be very specific and rigorously adhered to. With one exception. Long-Horn, the mother rhino who had smashed into my camera case and was inches from killing me, was a law unto herself. No pussyfooting round the wallows for her. She hit the scene like an angry express train, puffing and snorting and charging at the other occupants, often clearing an entire pond for herself and Little Lord Fontelroy, her calf. She was a film-maker's dream. As long as she was at least fifty metres away. I have to admit, I adored her.

In fact, Long-Horn, in her endearing way, was a good example of the third and by far the most significant area of a rhino's life which called for intimacy: the mother-calf relationship. This bond, which can last up to five years before the calf matures and is ready for the gloom of solitude, is intense, sometimes heartbreakingly so. We witnessed such a heartbreak early one morning, far out in the Western Range. Rhinos are not particularly chatty. For special occasions they have the mating squeal. For all other purposes, mostly involving curt dismissal, the threat to deploy biting and trampling gear or the actual deployment thereof, they snort. Snort is not a good description. The sound is more like a massive, shuddering letting off of steam. It's very hard to imitate, unless you have a head the size of an armchair. My friend Dan Bahadur, who was a genius, is the only person I met to come close to making the sound. During the course of my filming day, I was snorted at frequently, but always with the sound of the jeep in the foreground. The snort was a vital component of any natural soundtrack, but how to obtain a virgin one, with no engine accompaniment? This particular morning I'd had an idea. Out in the Western Range I'd noticed an old friendly male. He was fading and, tired of being whacked and threatened, he had taken up residence in a patch of grass a few hundred yards from a guard post, a location too exposed and disturbed to appeal to his fitter colleagues. In the early mornings I'd noticed he was nearly always in the same place, standing with just his rear end protruding from the elephant grass. I reckoned that if we drove as quietly as possible across the bumpy grassland and stopped stealthily just behind him, we could turn off the engine and attract his attention. He would turn round, get a mild shock and give us a nice pure snort, maybe even several. I gambled that he was too slow to attack, that if he did, we would have time to reverse away, and anyway, he would never press home his charge.

Everything went to plan. We arrived in perfect light at the guard-post and there, just as I had predicted, was the rhino bottom sticking out of the long grass. We managed to bump across to him with very few rattles and my driver, Gour, switched off the engine a few yards behind him. I gave him my best snort as a prompt. Only I'd made a mistake. It wasn't the old friendly male. Not a friendly anything. It was an incandescently furious female. She swivelled on a sixpence and came straight at us like a ballistic missile. Somehow, Gour in the very action of starting the engine, managed to throw the little tinny Gypsy jeep into reverse and we hurtled madly backwards. My guard fired a quick warning shot which provided just enough respite for Gour to turn the wheel and find a forward gear. I remember I was holding his arm and saying "don't turn us over, don't turn us over." I thought we might weather the rhino's attack, but if the jeep tipped, we might well be killed. We bucked and kicked sickeningly across the tussocky meadow but the rhino was right on our tail, topping fifty kilometres an hour. A second and a final, third shot, made no difference at all and then to my amazement I saw the rhino's head was actually inside the open bed at the back of the jeep, her huge teeth gnashing closer and closer towards Patricia's unprotected feet, while she did her best to cradle the unused tape recorder. The guard, out of bullets, started with a sort of gallows' concentration, to poke his empty rifle up the rhino's nose.

There was a small hillock nearby, hardly ten foot high. "Head for the hill" I said to Gour. He did and it was just enough to break the rhino's impetus. We stopped precariously at the top and she ground to a halt below us and we all waited. After a few minutes, she turned and ran straight back where she'd come from.

Once it was clear we were safe, Gour let the jeep slide back onto level ground. Then as one, he and the guard fell out of the car, one on either side. They both lay on the hard earth, the guard in fits of laughter, Gour, who had probably saved our lives, in uncontrollable shivers of shock. Neither of them was a day over 21. They'd acquitted themselves pretty well. We wrapped Gour in the blankets we always carried to ward off the early morning chill and we plied him with hot tea. Meanwhile, I was wondering what could have made that rhino so blisteringly angry. She'd chased us far further than necessary or normal and had really meant to pulverise us. This was no threat display, this was an act of war. I had to find out what was in the patch of grass, though I already thought I knew.

We sat watching patiently for several hours until finally we saw her great angry bulk mooching off towards the wallows. Perhaps surprisingly, everyone was willing to go back, so that I could check out the spot where the attack had started. There, Gour kept the engine running just in case I'd made another mistake, and with some trepidation I climbed down and pushed my way into the elephant grass. After about ten metres I reached a little clearing. In the middle lay a very young rhino calf, hardly two months old, still with the tell-tale tinge of pink that they are born with and which soon fades. It was stone dead. On its head were the two clean puncture marks of a tiger's canine teeth.

This was something I had to film; a mother dealing with the loss of her baby. But here in the middle of the high grass I would be unable to see what happened. I started to drag the dead calf away from the clearing, back through the high, dense-packed elephant grass towards open ground. I had to leave it as close to where I'd found it as possible, but somewhere where I would be able to observe and film from a safe distance. The calf was surprisingly heavy. It must have weighed at least a hundred lbs and I was shaking with fear. I was very worried that the female might come back and catch me molesting her baby and blame me for its demise. I really didn't think I would survive that encounter but I had to rely on my companions to shout a warning if by any chance she cut short her wallow. As soon as I could settle on a spot, I let go of the calf and retreated, stooping as I went to pull up the threads of grass and weeds that might obscure my filming view. Then I hurried back to the jeep so Gour could drop me and my equipment at a spot about seventy metres away, downwind from the calf, where I could lie and film the female's reactions, while the jeep stayed in the distance but close enough to mount a rescue if needed.

After a couple of hours, the mother returned. She knew immediately that her calf had moved. She must have smelt it. She paced around it, perhaps puzzled by its apparent choice of a more exposed position, sniffing it and sniffing the ground. Then she took up position and stood guard. I suspect she had chased the tiger away the night before and still thought her calf might have survived the attack. That would explain her furious protectiveness. She stayed almost motionless for hours and I slipped away. I was back the next morning and so was she. She guarded her baby until the heat of the day called her to wallow. On the fourth day the vultures arrived. They hunched on the ground watching the rhino while she watched the calf. When she left, they moved in, when she returned, she charged them and chased them all away. Day by day her baby disintegrated. Soon it didn't smell right anymore and she was confused. She knew this diminishing tangle of skin and tendons was no longer her darling but she was also convinced that it hadn't gone anywhere else. It was and was not there. Every day she came back to the disappearing little corpse at around 10.30 in the morning. Every day she would chase away the vultures and search the ground. She kept returning for two weeks, by which time there was nothing left of her baby except the four hard little hooves. On the fifteenth day she came no more. We are trained not to anthropomorphise, not to look for human emotions in our animal subjects. Yet, for me, there is only one word for what I witnessed. The word is "grief".

In Rhino Journey we had decided to tell the story of a fictionalised female rhino from just after her birth until the moment when she would leave her mother and find a mate of her own. It was an ambitious project and we had teamed up with another, experienced production company, Cicada Films, to help raise the necessary funds. National Geographic had initially shown interest but we didn't have the patience to deal with them. Everything had to be decided by committees, nothing from them went down on paper and we were constantly being asked to supply more and more information and material. It felt like we were being pumped. I had heard similar worries from other freelancers so we disengaged and were relieved when, instead, Discovery came on board along with NHK Japan. I must say we never had any difficulties with either of them. But things did not all go to plan. When I arrived in Assam to start filming, I thought I detected an odd atmosphere. I was surprised to find very little encouragement from the staff at Kaziranga National Park, even though we were paying them high filming fees. And at Wildgrass, the lodge where I was to stay, on and off for nine months over a two-and-a-half-year period, the service was minimal. The resident naturalist was never once allowed to come out with me and the owner never once spoke to me during my entire stay. There was an Indian filmmaker in residence who was trying to cobble together a rhino film for Survival Anglia. Perhaps he saw me as unwelcome competition, even though he should have realised I was working for an entirely different, global market. I was told that someone had tried to get a new law passed to stop more than one film team operating in a park at the same time. Failing that, whoever it was seems to have lobbied the Kaziranga authorities and various friends and contacts at Wildgrass. Whatever the truth, the result appeared to be that, while my colleague was given free run of the whole park, I was restricted to a tiny area and had to ask for specific permission to visit any other regions, which I needed to do for coverage of the story.

Funnily enough, these shackles turned out to be a blessing in disguise. My little patch was full of rhinos and having nowhere else to go, I focused on it. I got up at 4.30 every morning, was in the park every single day from dawn to darkness and bit by bit I got my key sequences. In the evenings I loaded my magazines, cleaned my gear, charged my batteries and made sure I was ready for all eventualities. And I had my driver, Gour, who became passionately loyal and flourished as my occasional sound recordist and full-time assistant cameraman. He was clever. He soon learned to handle the big professional Nagra tape recorder and quickly got to know every lens, magazine or piece of equipment I might ask him for. We had a lot of fun together. In the summer we'd take a midday break and he would shin up the bare trunks of the tall mango trees to pluck me fresh fruit. The mangos were beyond delicious. Mind you, every single one we opened contained, at its very heart, in the kernel, a kind of shield bug that must have grown there as a larva and awaited this unreliable moment of release to open its new wings and fly away. I worked sixteen hours a day, non-stop, often for two to three months at a time.

At the start of each filming period, I had to pay the district forester my camera fees. He was a shifty man who never lifted a finger for me but always eyed my brief case with a disconcerting hyena look. The park director, to whom I also needed to pay my regular respects, was a different character altogether. At every meeting we would go through a charade as I listed my key sequences and asked for advice on how to get them. He found my Item Number One, the mating sequence, particularly amusing, being convinced I would never get it. Despite the fact that he couldn't be very helpful, we liked each other and Item Number One became quite a joke between us. I think he was very impressed when I achieved it, as was I. Years later I was honoured to be invited to give the annual Kailash Sankhala Memorial Lecture in Delhi. It was quite a grand event and I was a little nervous until I saw, sitting in the middle of the very front row, beaming encouragement at me from his fine, open face, the Kaziranga park director. He'd come all the way from Assam to hear me speak.

I can't believe it was my Indian colleague, himself, who had been trying to block me. He was a member of the IAWF and as Chairman, I had been instrumental in ensuring that he was paid for a contract that a producer was threatening to renege on. It was an Italian producer, new in the business, who had employed this man and two other, very significant cameramen and for some reason had withheld all their pay. Of course, I wasn't paid to be Chairman, it was simply an interesting position and my experience had been that members helped each other. They had certainly helped me in the past. I had phoned the Italian producer and explained that if he didn't pay my members, no-one in our field would ever work for him again. This, I hastened to add, was not because I had any undue influence but because all the leading wildlife film-makers in the world at that time knew each other, most of us were friends and news of his default would spread like wildfire. I was entirely sincere and he found the missing money.

The odd stalemate over access in Kaziranga had, apart from helping me to focus, another benefit for me. Sadly, my anxious Indian colleague ventured forth less and less frequently and Survival decided to send reinforcements. The first to arrive was Tony Bomford, one of my best friends among film-makers. Unfortunately, he had hurt is hip just before coming and was walking with a stick. While he was around, we hugely enjoyed each other's company but one evening I returned to the lodge to find him gone. He'd had another fall, had been taken to the local hospital where an X-Ray had revealed something so disturbing, he was transferred to Delhi.

Within a couple of years, the bone cancer they had spotted in Assam had killed him. Needless to say, Survival sent another of my good friends to replace Tony. This was Richard Kemp, he of the Pyrenean lightning strike. I always found Richard to be very kind. He came with an enormous trunk full of European delicacies and he bribed me shamelessly with McVities chocolate biscuits. In return, on one of my home breaks, I carried, along with my own material, all the footage that Survival had shot so far back to England for processing. Despite having a huge film industry, India had no labs that could be trusted to develop film in a consistent and high-quality way and if left around for too long in the heat, exposed film will deteriorate, so a courier is essential. But it has to be a courier who will defend with his life the footage from X-Ray machines at the airports. I would have done it for free, but Survival kindly paid me a fee for this little act of friendship.

I grew to love Kaziranga. Gour and I would enter the park at dawn, pick up our guard and drive slowly down the long west trail. Most mornings we would find something to film. Sometimes we'd find a gang of otters, thirty strong in the river. They'd crowd round us, the males standing high out of the water, whickering suspiciously. Then they'd swim away across the river, oozing out over the bank in a long, undulating line, to nose around in the short grass or feed on a big dead catfish. One day we found a pangolin for me to film, another day a big orange-and-black-striped snake, a crate - very poisonous Gour warned me, as I manoeuvred round it with my camera.

During the early spring, the rangers set fires in the dried, year-old grass. This could lead to scary conflagrations, often hardly held in check by windbreaks and barefoot staff wielding broomsticks. The fires could be spectacular and had an interesting effect on the wildlife. The black drongos, like small black magpies, were experts at diving into the flames to catch the dragon flies that were stirred up from the grass and when the fires had burned down, the rhinos would tiptoe through the cooling embers to lick the ash from the charred grass stems. They would hold the blackened grass gently in their lips and delicately turn their heads to gather in the vital potash.

One day a guard came rushing to find us. Rhinos were mating he said. We drove with him fast to his ranger station where there was a wide lake with an island in the middle. "Rhinos other side" he said. I had to take his word for it. The flames were leaping up in the distance and the fire was spreading fast towards us. He had a hollowed-out tree trunk, which was the latest in Kaziranga boat design. Into this I piled my priceless camera, tripod, lenses and spare magazines, with no clear idea what I was going to see, and we teetered across to the island. As I crawled up the bank, I came almost face to face with two huge mating beasts in the water on the opposite side. The ranger was terrified of them. "One minute" he kept saying. I think he assumed I'd take a quick snap and depart. But this was a chance of a lifetime. When he realized I intended to stay for hours he panicked, jumped back into his treetrunk and fled. What I filmed was, possibly the best sequence I've ever achieved. As I started filming the mating pair, another rhino appeared, attacked them and chased off the incumbent male. He then followed the female out onto dryland on the far side, still just twenty or so metres from me where he mounted her and I filmed all the bits of mating tackle in full deployment. What made the sequence sensational was the fact that the flames of passion were literally leaping up in great orange tongues right behind them, because by now the big grass fire had arrived at the lake's edge. This was clearly going to be the climax of our film, when our baby rhino has finally grown up and found a mate of her own. The sequence was also put to another use by our agents. It was used as an advert by a well-known manufacturer of condoms. They paid several thousand pounds for two seconds.

It is true that at the beginning of my filming stint in Assam, I was attacked by rhinos nearly every day. We would drive along my restricted route and sooner or later a rhino would object and start into an aggressive canter. Sometimes a few bangs with the flat of the hand on reverberant sides of the vehicle would deter them. Often if the guard merely rattled the lock of his gun in the chamber, they would veer away but sometimes only a shot at their feet would stop them. As the weeks, wore on, however, these indiscriminate attacks tailed off and the rhinos settled back into a calmer regime. In fact, I suspect that the most dangerous part of my work was actually the daily drive from Wildgrass to the reserve and back. This took me along the main Assam-Burma highway, a potholed road with barely space for two cars to pass. All day heavy lorries and overloaded buses ground their way up and down this unlikely motorway, frequently forgetting to dodge each other. The smash-ups were monumental and the carcasses of past mishaps lay where they'd fallen. Half way between the lodge and the Western Range of the reserve the road made a distinct turn. This was obviously a danger point so the religious authorities had built a little shrine there, a place of prayer, occupied by a holy man or two. This had massively increased the peril because every single driver felt obliged to offer a prayer to the shrine as they passed. The hands would come off the steering wheel, a quick puja would be offered, an earnest prayer for safety on the road, while the vehicle careered briefly out of control. One morning we drove out to find a big lorry had embedded itself in a tree, presumably during this invocatory process. I felt this was extremely ominous. On the way home in the evening the police were slowing the traffic and directing it round some sort of catastrophe. The driver of a bus, crammed with villagers, had been so mesmerized by the shrine and the treed lorry that he'd missed the bend and gone straight into the small ravine the bend was there to avoid. The following morning, we found another lorry had ploughed into the remains of the first one which had still not been cleared from the road. Into thy hands oh Lord...

In order to concentrate on the filming, I had ceded the writing of the narration of Rhino Journey to Patricia. It was a bit of a fairy tale and, as such, I had to admit it did require music. I had built up quite a rich sound track of natural sounds but the key characters, the rhinos themselves, were never very vocal and music was needed to point up the emotional sensitivities of what were, at first obvious glance, pretty thick-skinned protagonists. In the event, setting the rhinos to music turned out to be a real pleasure. We found our way to the studios of the composer, Nick Hooper. He had a sound-proof cabin in his garden from where he was developing an interesting career in film music. He wrote a whole medley of melodies – a symphony to the rhinoceros – full of pathos, fun and otherness, which was very effective. Ten years later, he would be busy writing much of the music for the Harry Potter films.

One of the reasons we had wanted to produce our own "blue-chip" special, rather than trying to do it direct with the BBC, was financing. There was a growing problem in the way wildlife camera people were treated by the BBC. This was partly rooted in the origins of the Natural History Unit which had evolved from amateur enthusiasts which had kept it on a path rather separate from the rest of the organization. In many ways this was a strength. We were still all enthusiasts, albeit no longer amateur. We all loved what we did and no-one I met worked primarily for money. The problem lay in the cost of equipment. Most of us came on location with a full range of cameras, long lenses, macro lenses, tripods and various specialist gismos. On average each package was worth a minimum of a hundred thousand pounds. Just to hire this on the open market, per day, without an operator, would have cost the BBC more than they were paying most of us for person plus equipment. Indeed, jobbing news camera people in London were charging nearly three times our daily rates. We all knew that the Unit couldn't function on that basis. Wildlife filming involves remote locations and massive uncertainties. To have so much equipment on standby, maybe for months on end, would have bankrupted the Unit. It was clear that the cameramen and women were subsidizing the BBC's output to a considerable degree. I regarded trying to rectify this situation as a major challenge of my Chairmanship of IAWF. The committee included my friend Tony Bomford, who was more radical than I, and other outstanding figures in the industry like Sean Morris, of Oxford Scientific Films and Doug Allen and Alistair McEwen, both very fine cameramen. All were in agreement that a sensible solution would be for the BBC and other TV commissioning agents who could not meet the real costs of our services should offer us a royalty instead. This seemed particularly obvious as BBC World apparently regarded their natural history portfolio as their most saleable item. Surely sharing some of these profits in the form of royalties, which already applied in the case of writers and producers, was the best way to go. This seemed particularly apt because many of us worked alone, designing shoots and solving problems on location without the input of any other director or producer – all criteria that might justify royalties. This was flatly refused. A vehement opponent of the idea appeared to be the Unit's new head, Alastair Fothergill. Alastair proved himself to be a stalwart producer. When he was in charge of The Blue Planet, one of the programmes had only managed five minutes of finished film a few months before airing time but Alastair never panicked and never leant unfairly on the people working on that strand. In the end it was a huge success. On the other hand, he stood much too close when he spoke to you and he didn't see sense over the royalty plan. The result was that I took the IAWF membership into BECTU, the TV Trade's Union. There are now fewer, better paid camera people and many fewer programmes being made. Meanwhile, I am told that Alastair, having left the BBC now runs his own production company and may have changed his view of royalties.

After the successful completion of Rhino Journey I returned one more time to film in Kaziranga. Martin Hughes-Games, who had been a producer on Land of The Tiger, had devised what seemed to me to be a worthwhile BBC series highlighting the work of the foot-soldiers of conservation. He had chosen the poorly armed but fiercely protective squad of rhino guards in Kaziranga to be the stars of one of his films and he asked me to join the team and film the background wildlife material. The project involved reconstructing real incidents that had occurred in recent years: the moment a tiger smashed through the mud wall of one of the guard huts when the occupants were sleeping and the time an elephant lifted up one of the jeeps. We would film the daily infestations of leeches, inching through the eyeholes of the guards' boots as they sloshed through the swamps. And, of course, we needed to show the perennial risk of being attacked by the rhinos themselves. In normal circumstances I wouldn't have wanted deliberately to annoy a rhino, but this might be a justified context in which to do so. We had a willing senior forester, Mr Partha Das, who was already something of a friend of mine. Could I, asked Martin, find a convenient rhino who would oblige us all by chasing him?

We agreed that it would only be this once and yes, indeed, I knew exactly the rhino for the job. The next day we set off, with Mr Das sitting in the tail of the jeep, to find Long-Horn. We cruised the Western Range for an hour or so and then, alongside a narrow strip of water, bordered with tall grass I spotted her. She had a new small calf so I was confident she would react. I explained to the driver that he needed to drive slowly past her, very close, with the idea that she would stick to us like a magnet as we passed. I told him not to stop and make the pass look as natural as possible. I would be perching on the crossrail at the front to film the whole scene if she did as I hoped. The driver managed a perfect manoeuvre but Long-Horn took us by surprise. She came straight at us at full tilt. And she didn't stop. She pounded after us, half a metre from the back of the jeep, across the grass, onto the track and on and on, further and further away from her calf. What could we do? I filmed her in super close-up, I filmed her crunching hooves, I filmed two-shots of her and Mr Das, wide-angles, slow motion, still she came thrashing on until, as before with the mother of the dead calf, the road hit a steep incline. At this point two things happened. Firstly, mercifully she stopped. Secondly, I saw a tiger, away behind us in the distance crossing the meadow where she'd left her calf.

I wanted to drive straight back to protect the calf, but we couldn't. The steaming mother rhino was blocking our path and she would not move. We waited and waited and I grew more and more anxious. At last, after nearly half an hour, she moved off into the long grass and we went back to where I'd seen the tiger. There was no sign of it now but I had a hunch it was tucked into the strip of grass by the lake. It had been heading for the huge reed bed that lined the far side of our track. To reach it now, it would have to cross the grassland in front of us and I felt, at least, that it might not look for the calf while we were there. We settled in for a long wait, to give Long-Horn time to work her way back. Meanwhile, I pointed my camera at the densest stretch of grass where I guessed the tiger might be. After about twenty minutes, his head appeared right in the middle of my frame. A bit of a lucky hit. And he did walk across the meadow towards us and he didn't eat Long-Horn's baby. Phew!

Over the next ten years, I began to change my way of life. In 1993, my friend Roz Kidman-Cox at BBC Wildlife had asked me to lead a specialist wildlife tour to Nepal for some of the magazine's readers. A small high-end travel company called Spencer Scott was going to arrange all the logistics and they wanted someone known to the readers to lead the trip. I had said no. I was too busy and I did not want to become a phony great white hunter leading a pack of acolytes round the jungle. Definitely not for me. But Roz asked several times until, reluctantly, I had to agree. I loved it. So, as I began to reduce my filming schedule, stepping away bit by bit from the pressures of pitching projects and trying to raise funds, I signed up to lead more tours. I took people to the Galapagos, to Svalbard, often to the Serengeti, to Kenya and the Masai Mara and every year to India. In 2004 my tiger book was published by the BBC. I wrote it partly because I couldn't find a book that said what I wanted to say to my clients. There were several things I enjoyed about leading trips. It turned out, embarrassingly, that I did quite like being the big white hunter. I liked being in the field with only a pair of binoculars and not being encumbered by cameras and the predatory urges they promote. I liked being away from home for shorter periods but best of all I liked sharing that profound moment when an interested amateur sees their first polar bear, their first blue whale and above all, their first tiger. Many of them are deeply moved by these experiences and to be partly responsible for that is spiritually uplifting. I went into films because I wanted to influence an audience. I discovered that the people who come on my trips are that audience personified. And so, if the future allows, I will continue...

This evolution towards a more personal relationship with an audience had, in an odd, inexplicable way, to do with the deaths of my parents. On the 31st August 1996 my father phoned me and told me it was time to come home. A year earlier he'd been diagnosed with advanced and terminal lung cancer and I had promised to nurse him through his last weeks. This was our code to signify that the end was close. I was filming in Ireland but I caught the next plane home. My parents had been married for 53 years. My mother was devoted to him but, somehow, I'd come to understand that she couldn't face her rock crumbling, her super-hero withering away. Indeed, during the final days she hardly entered the room. When he picked me up in Oxford from the airport bus in his shiny, brand-new turbo-charged Volvo, he didn't look like a man on the edge. That afternoon the family doctor, David Stern came to check on him and me. He was an empathetic man and we were all fond of him. As I walked him back to his car, I asked him how long dad had: two months? three months? He screwed up his face and said "two weeks at the outside". The next day I saw a barn owl. In all the forty years the family had lived at Suntrap, we'd never had a barn owl on the property and dad wanted to see it. But already he couldn't walk so I put him in the car and drove half way down the long drive to the little field where I'd spotted it. The barn owl flew up out of the long grass and landed on a fence post quite close to us. That was the last time my father left the house. The following evening, I had to carry him upstairs to the master bedroom. All that fierce muscle had dwindled to dusty sinews and he was as light as a child. Two days later we put up a bed for him in the grand sitting room he had created, with its elegant colours and wide plate-glass windows looking out over the valley to Shotover. In his later years dad had become a recognised authority on old English water colours. I remember a beautiful little picture by Brabazon hanging over his new bed, a sober William Callow and a David Roberts – the original frontispiece for his famous Scenes from the Holyland which I inherited and still treasure. Perhaps his tiring eye wandered over these. I don't know. He died on the 11th September. I took it as a bad omen that he didn't shave that day. I never knew him not to shave. Even through the hardships of his desert war he'd carried his cut-throat razor, which he sharpened on a strap. Not to shave made him feel dirty he said. In what was to be his very last moment he suddenly sat up and pointed at the ceiling. The expression on his face was not one of fear. It showed no pain or anguish. It was one of pure surprise. And in that moment of extreme mystery, I was left holding in my arms nothing of him at all.

Two days later, I took my fly rod and a single fly made by Luke Davies, the son of his last good friend Hywel and I drove to the River Test in Hampshire to fish the beat we had been planning for weeks to fish together. We had assumed it would be our last outing. The fly was a top-heavy, golden nymph. Nymphing is a form of fly fishing which requires special skills, manoeuvring the fly under the water, and I'm not very good at it. That day, with that one fly, I caught three huge trout, all well over eight lbs, all far bigger than any trout I've caught before or since.

My mother stayed on alone in the big house. She was full of optimism. Whenever I was home from filming, I would stroll up to see her of an evening from the house where I lived at the bottom of the drive. Sometimes I would find her asleep, her face resting against the kitchen window from where she'd been waiting hopefully for my approach. But she always said she'd been watching the sunset, which may also have been true. In her 81st year she was still youthful and supple but she had a fatal aneurism. On the day the pain hit, I was entertaining a good friend, Michael Greenall, a well-known Oxfordshire surgeon. We hurried up the hill to help her but as soon as he saw her Michael knew it was all over. The pain wasn't from the aneurism but from the onset of sepsis. In effect, she was already dead. We rushed her to the hospital but there was little they could do but settle her with morphine. As she fell asleep, she said, full of happiness, that she was looking forward to the morning because her eldest grandson Julien would visit and his father David would be home from Greece. But I knew there would be no morning, only the tolling of bells.

Again, it was two days later that the little miracle occurred. My brother Terry and I were sitting sadly out on our parents' wide front lawn, discussing the funeral and looking up into the empty sky. And then far, far up, as far as my eye could focus, I saw a strange bird. It was a white stork. Terry saw it too. It was impossible. In those days there were no white storks in England. We'd seen lots abroad but in all our years birdwatching at home we'd never seen such a thing: a white stork, symbol of birth and rebirth and, in Hindu mythology, of immortality.

EPILOGUE: A STATE OF GRACE

The human condition is all about loss. Never again will I watch my father carve the wide arc of a Scottish salmon river into perfect slices, every cast hawkeye straight, uncoiling from the rod as if the tip of the line could defy gravity as it rolled apparently effortlessly towards the distant bank. Never again will I sit under the manzanita trees in Green Valley, aromatic in the warm dark, arguing with Jim Hoag about Nixon's presidency or see him staggering through the surprising snow with his huge wonderful grin and a large paper bag of the best Santa Maria Tip steak to relieve us from penury. Never again will the childhood me sit with my hilarious companions the two Mikes and Giles in our study at school listening endlessly to Bob Dylan and saying he was a poet and should win the Nobel Prize. And I won't again have the chance to be inspired by my college friend John MacAuslan, perhaps the cleverest person I've ever known. Gone is my childhood home at Suntrap, bristling with brothers. Gone are the silly games on the cork floor at Church Cottages with little Turlough and Katie, me pretending to be a car and telling them to switch on its radio which always, mysteriously, had an interview with the famous naturalist Stephen Mills. The loved ones and friends who have died, all uniquely irreplaceable, the career ended, the houses sold, the beloved landscapes destroyed or built upon, all are gone forever. And yet I have come to understand that I have lived my life in a state of grace.

My Godfather Grahame Baker ended his career as Dean of Ontario, a respected and much-loved priest. He was full of fun but he was also sharp and profound. A brilliant musician, he had subjugated his talent entirely to his belief in God. He was disappointed that he couldn't share this with me but he did try to explain it. Faith, he said, is not an intellectual statement. It does not primarily partake of reason. It is more of a sensation, a sense of the meaningfulness of life, a state of grace. As conservationists, I and my wildlife friends scattered round the world and the wider circle of passionate defenders of the quiet places on earth, people whom I don't have the privilege of knowing – we all have, necessarily been focusing on rational arguments for why nature should be preserved. But there is a deeper truth that has nothing to do with reason. When I go out on a winter evening on the Dutch polders where I live now and hear the excitable whistling of the wigeon cutting through the cold starlight air, I feel it. When in spring I kneel to hold the warming soil in my hands and listen to the two-toned godwits, suddenly back from Senegal, reeling out their mating displays high above me, I feel it. And when, as an eight-year-old boy, out over the new-mown night-time hay fields I called foxes to my feet, I felt it then: a sense of the connectedness of everything, of fox and boy, field and folk, into which we are not finally lost but simply subsumed. It is an overarching love of life, not God-given but a gift of nature: a state of grace.

ACKNOWLEDGMENTS

Firstly, I should like to thank everyone mentioned in this book, friends, family, colleagues and acquaintances, for contributing to my story and helping me follow the thread. I feel a special debt of gratitude to Chris and Wendy Mills, Lisa Miller and Julie Beecher who gave support when it was most needed. Thank you also to Sarah Speller and to Karen Macauslan, Simon Pettit, Jeffrey Rijpkema, Roz Kidman-Cox, Suzan Brenninkmeijer and Wendy Mills for reading my first draft and encouraging its completion. Finally, I am grateful to Stuart Leasor for liking the book enough to publish it.

ABOUT THE AUTHOR

Stephen Mills has made over 40 films for television and is a former Chairman of the International Association of Wildlife Filmmakers.

He wrote the award-winning BBC films Tiger Crisis and Wolf Saga, wrote and filmed the BBC tiger film Man-Eater: To Be or Not To Be and filmed for major BBC series including The Private Life of Plants, Land of the Tiger and Winners and Losers. He has published over 500 papers and articles, writing extensively for New Scientist, The Times Literary Supplement and BBC Wildlife Magazine.

He is the author of Nature In its Place (Bodley Head) and Tiger (BBC), is a graduate of Oxford University and California Institute of the Arts and a Churchill Fellow.

Milton Keynes UK
Ingram Content Group UK Ltd.
UKHW011811110224
437584UK00003B/38/J

9 781916 556300